The Dark Side

THE DARK SIDE

CRITICAL CASES ON THE DOWNSIDE OF BUSINESS

Edited by Emmanuel Raufflet and Albert J. Mills

© 2009 Greenleaf Publishing Limited
Copyright for each case is held by the author of the case, except where otherwise stated

Published by Greenleaf Publishing Limited
Aizlewood's Mill
Nursery Street
Sheffield S3 8GG
UK
www.greenleaf-publishing.com

Printed in Great Britain on acid-free paper by CPI Antony Rowe, Chippenham, Wiltshire

FSC
Mixed Sources
Product group from well-managed
forests and other controlled sources
Cert no. SGS-COC-2953
www.fsc.org
© 1996 Forest Stewardship Council

Cover by LaliAbril.com

British Library Cataloguing in Publication Data:
   The dark side : critical cases on the downside of business.
      1. Social responsibility of business. 2. Corporations--
      Corrupt practices.
      I. Raufflet, Emmanuel, 1967- II. Mills, Albert J., 1945-
      658.4'08-dc22

   ISBN-13: 9781906093204

Contents

The critical need for critical cases: the dark side of business

Emmanuel Raufflet and Albert J. Mills

Introduction: the end of history?

In his landmark book *The End of History and the Last Man* (Fukuyama 1992), Francis Fukuyama argued that the end of the Cold War and the fall of the Berlin Wall in 1989 represented the end of the evolution of human history as a struggle between ideologies. Fukuyama predicted the global triumph of political and economic liberalism and the end of history, i.e. the universalization of Western liberal democracy as the final form of human government and the market economy, as defined in the USA in the beginning of the 1980s, as the dominant economic system. With "the end of history" came a certain vision of capitalism based on deregulation, low taxes, and the mantra of less government. These conditions would create the conditions for business to flourish and prosperity for the whole society.

Sixteen years later, this optimistic panorama has changed. The turn of the millennium brought its share of global threatening economic, social and ecological challenges. Recent events, including September 11, 2001, corporate scandals and the increasing questioning of business and corporate practices, the rise of China and India, the resurgence of Russia as a global power, the climate crisis, increasing inequalities between the rich and the poor in and between societies, and, more recently, the financial and economic crisis since 2008 suggest that we are witnessing what Fukuyama (2008) coined "the Fall of America Inc." This "Fall of America Inc." represents an overall discredit of a certain brand of capitalism, dominated by short-term thinking (Waddock 2005) and a systematic neglect of the social, regulatory, and economic conditions in which business ought to operate. What we have learnt is that we are entering a time of trouble and questions. What we know is that we are near an era of economic, social, and ecological turbulence.

Hence the critical need to examine, explore, and understand these different multifaceted, complex phenomena of our late capitalist era. Hence the critical need as business educators and trainers to expose students, course participants, and managers to these issues. Hence our responsibility as business educators and management scholars to foster a climate for business managers to reflect, feel, and think differently both ethically and cognitively.

Beyond ethical muteness in business: training responsible managers

Bird and Waters (1989) proposed the idea that managers in business organizations tend to be morally mute, as they avoid moral references in their work-related activities. They mention ethics only when things go wrong, in situations such as price-fixing, bribery, or scandals. As such, they tend to avoid "moral talk," as such moral talk is perceived at odds with an image of individual and organizational effectiveness based on diligence, efficiency, competence, and competitiveness.

Bird and Waters highlighted the fact that one of the consequences of this moral muteness is to create and to reinforce moral amnesia, or "a caricature of management as an amoral activity, and a very narrow definition of morality" (Bird and Waters 1989: 79). In a later book, Bird proposed the need for "good" conversations, or conversations that would help managers be more aware of the moral dimensions of their decisions and actions (Bird 1996). According to Bird, the role and responsibility of managers is to foster good conversations in business settings—be they teams, business units, business organizations, or projects. Such good conversations will allow organization members to become aware of the ethical dimensions of their own activities and to surface their dilemmas and doubts. It will equip them with tools and lexicon to express and share around ethics in business life.

Beyond instrumental short-term thinking: training cognitively equipped managers

Westley *et al.* (2006) introduce the differences between simple, complicated, and complex problems. **Simple** problems—like building a chair—can be addressed using patterns and behaviors established by routine craft or commonly held knowledge; while **complicated** problems—like building a plane—require a high level of technical sophistication and precision, and tight coordination through rigid protocols. Success in a complicated problem will result from sticking to these rigid protocols and strict application of pre-established rules and roles. Laxness or negligence likely leads to catastrophic results in addressing a complicated problem.

By contrast, a **complex** problem—like raising a child—requires sensitivity to the uniqueness of the situation at hand, and recognition that approaches used to address simple or complicated problems may not work or may be counterproductive in such a context. Complexity involves thinking about the problem in a different way, both in terms of being aware of and sensitive to the connections that need to be made as well as in terms of the knowledge needed to address it. Using critical and complex teaching cases in the classroom helps make students aware of the limitations of the methods used to solve problems that are only simple or complicated.

Our business courses have their shares of simple recipes and complicated formulas (Ghoshal 2005). What may be needed is to train students and business managers to think about problems and issues using insights from complexity.

To train managers to think and be aware, we believe that the case studies in this book have the potential to contribute to addressing these ethical and cognitive challenges. Both the content and the format of these cases are innovative. First, these cases are innovative in terms of contents. Whereas most teaching cases focus on managers in situations and tend to be oblivious of other groups or logics, these cases acknowledge the diversity of actors and interests in and around organizations. These cases have different levels of analysis and propose different points of view and logics. They recognize that decisions, seemingly good at a given moment of time, may actually contain the seeds of their later demise.

Second, these cases are innovative in terms of format. Whereas most cases are formatted along decision and decision-making lines, these cases are more diverse and open-ended. This diversity and open-endedness allows for the formation of judgment among managers. Judgment is defined is as the capacity to synthesize, integrate, balance short-term and long-term effects, appreciate effects on different groups, learn to listen, and evaluate. Whereas decision-making is key for complicated issues, matters and situations, judgment-making relies on experience and may be better suited for complex, murky, and gray areas.

This set of outstanding cases aims to achieve this. These 16 cases were selected as finalists or winners of the seven first years (2002–2008) of the Dark Side of Business Case Competition—a joint event of the Critical Management Studies and the Management Education sections of the Academy of Management (AoM).

2001: a dark side odyssey—the case of the Darkside Case Competition

In the late summer of 2001, Paul Adler and other members of the Critical Management Studies Interest Group (CMSIG) found themselves at yet another annual meeting of the Academy of Management—this time in Washington, DC. Among the many informal conversations that Adler found himself in, one turned to the issue of case studies and the absence of those that dealt with the darker side of business. It occurred to Adler, Professor of Management and Organization at the Marshall School of Business at the University of South California (UCS), that:

> [business] case libraries are almost exclusively devoted to "best prac-
> tice" cases or difficult decisions by basically well-managed firms. When
> we want to talk to our students about the more typical cases, let alone
> the really scandalous practices of the worst firms, the cupboard is
> almost entirely bare. It's almost impossible to even find a reasonably
> rich case on a labor/management conflict.[1]

Following the AoM meeting, Adler—a founding member of CMSIG and part of its executive group—undertook to develop his idea further. In an exchange of emails with leading CMSIG members, Adler argued that the CMS Interest Group should "organize an award for the best case-study on worst business practice."[2] Outlining an argument for such an award, Adler made four main points.

First, that the Harvard Business School:

> . . . folks justify [the] bias to best practice saying there's 100 ways to go
> wrong for every 1 way to go right: we challenge that premise, arguing
> that the patterns we observe among the wrong ways tell us a lot about
> the nature of the broader system of business, and that our students
> need to be given the chance to think through the scope of feasible
> and appropriate action if they happen to find themselves working for a
> poorly managed firm or for a bunch of scumbags.

Second, "our union friends are particularly eager to see more cases available that raise issues about union organizing rights and more generally about the difficulties workers encounter in expressing voice at work."

Third, "we seem to have abandoned the heritage of 'muck-raking'—the best of this tradition seems to be in the *Wall Street Journal* of all places!"

Fourth, he referenced the practice of US Senator Proxmire who:

---

1 This account is based on an email exchange with Paul Adler. Adler recalls that the idea of a
   dark side case competition was likely his but that "such recollections are unreliable" (email
   to Albert J. Mills, November 13, 2008).
2 Undated email from Paul Adler to "CMS Steering Committee."

... gave out an annual "Golden Fleece" award for the military contractor who demonstrated the worst price-gauging practices. It served very effectively to provoke some real debate.[3]

For Adler, if such an award was to be developed by the CMS Interest Group, the competition needed to encourage a focus not on:

... individual bastards, but on cases that tell us something about the broader system and how it permits, encourages, even forces firms to do terrible things.[4]

In other words, Adler continued:

... the "damage" we're looking to document would presumably be to employees, but perhaps also to local community, environment, [etc].[5]

Following a further exchange of emails among group members, Paul Adler developed a proposal based on responses from Marta Calas (University of Massachusetts, Amherst), Bill Kaghan (University of Washington), John Jermier (University of Southern Florida) and Linda Smircich (University of Massachusetts, Amherst). The focus of the developing case competition would be on teaching cases (rather than research papers based on case studies)—the goal here was "the development of good classroom materials."[6] The award was to:

... go to the best case study—not to the worst corporate offender ... The goal would therefore be to encourage the development of teaching cases that revealed the "dark side" of corporate America.[7]

The new competition was agreed by the CMSIG Executive in time to be launched at the 2002 annual meeting of the AoM in Denver, Colorado. The competition was co-sponsored by the Management Education Division and was called *The Darkside Case-Writing Competition.*

The call for cases was accompanied by the following explanation:

This competition ... aims to encourage the development of cases that provoke reflection and debate on the "dark side" of contemporary capitalism. Some might argue that we are promoting "muckraking." They are correct: we feel that if there's so much "muck" out there, it behoves us to look at it squarely and decide what should be done about it. For both teaching and research purposes, it is critical that we have well documented worst-practices cases on the table, so that we have the

---

3 Ibid.
4 Ibid.
5 Ibid.
6 Email from Paul Adler to CMS-SG, September 24. 2008.
7 Ibid.

opportunity to understand how such organizations come in being, how they function, and how they might be challenged and changed.

We especially want cases that lead discussion to the broader social-political-economic structure and help students critically think about the consequences of this structure. In particular, we encourage submissions focused on labor relations—instructors in this area are especially eager to see cases that raise issues about the difficulties workers encounter in organizing unions and otherwise expressing voice at work. We also encourage submissions focused on environmentally harmful practices—we need to understand better the factors that entice firms to pollute, and how these conditions might be changed. Other foci are also welcome.

From the beginning, the Darkside Competition aimed at encouraging the writing of cases that would integrate socio-political issues with organizational dynamics, thus contextualizing organizational and management problems within the broader system of capitalism.

The Darkside Competition in the shadow of 9/11

In the period between discussions around the idea of a dark side case competition and its eventual implementation, terrorists attacked the World Trade Center and the Pentagon in September 2001. The impact of this momentous event did not dissuade the CMSIG from launching the competition, but perhaps surprisingly in the face of evidence of organizational politicking and incompetence on the part of those charged with the security of the U.S.A., no cases came forward examining the background to the 9/11 attacks.[8]

The announcement of the competition attracted a number of entries from the U.K. (work victimization), U.S.A. (including cases on business ethics, attacks on public education, unionization), Australia (the impact of corporate culture), New Zealand (workplace distress), and Canada (power and politics at work). The international sweep of these cases put the competition judges on notice that the focus was not simply on "corporate America" but global capitalism. However, the winning case—by Paul M. Swiercz of George Washington University—met one of the original aims of the competition: to deal with issues of labor relations.

In "Food Lion vs. the UFCW: time for a change?" Swiercz presents an account of the operations of a Belgian-owned supermarket chain in the U.S.A. and its struggle against unionization by the United Food and Commercial Workers (UFCW).

---

8 The organizational dark side of U.S. security organizations are, however, examined in a vignette in Mills *et al.* 2006: 14-17.

The case follows the various strategies adopted by the company and the union as they struggle over unionization at Food Lion. This case appears in Part 2 of this book on the interactions between business and local communities.

As the winner of the case competition, Paul M. Swiercz was awarded a certificate of merit and the dubious honor of organizing the second year of the competition.

The 2003 competition was won by Caroline O'Connell and Albert J. Mills of Saint Mary's University in Canada's eastern province of Nova Scotia. Their case, "The Westray mine explosion," maintained the trade union focus of the previous year but was centered on events leading up to the deaths of 26 miners in the 1996 mine explosion in Nova Scotia's Pictou County. The case appears in the third part of this book and takes students through a range of structural and behavioral problems to make sense of how various factors led to the deaths of so many employees.

Like Paul Swiercz before them, O'Connell and Mills were awarded a certificate and the honor of running the third Darkside Case Competition. This led to some changes, with the third year of competition seeing the selection of the top five finalists in the competition being asked to present their cases at the annual meeting of the AoM. Furthermore, thanks to the sponsorship of Saint Mary's Sobey PhD in Management, the winner was awarded a check for $500.

Darkside III

The third year of competition in 2004 saw finalists drawn from:

- U.S.A.—Paul Swiercz was back with a case on union struggle in the newspaper industry

- New Zealand—Kate Kearins, Keith Hooper, and Belinda Luke presented a case of entrepreneurship, state sponsorship, and marginalized groups[9]

- Canada—Gina Grandy's case focussed on careers in the U.K. exotic dancing industry,[10] Jean Helms Mills examined the impact of change programs on employees[11] and Rosemary McGowan looked at the problem of work and eldercare

The eventual winner was Rosemary McGowan, with her case "John Hamilton's work and eldercare dilemma. Break the silence? Sustain the silence?" This case is included in the first part of this book.

---

9   This case appears in Mills *et al.* 2006.
10   This case can be found in Mills *et al.* 2005: 291-304.
11   This case appears in Jones *et al.* 2006 and Mills *et al.* 2006.

Darkside IV

The fourth year of the competition took place in Honolulu and saw a winning case that focused on the impact of a multinational company on a small rural community in India. Competition was strong, with cases on:

- "Bhopal Gas" by Sanjib Dutta

- "Manipulation, placation, partnership or delegated power: can community and business really work together when surface mining comes to town?" by Sherry Finney

- "Nestlé's social irresponsibility in developing countries" by Shirisha Regani and Sanjib Dutta

- "Poison gas in a northern copper mine" by Tupper Cawsey and Gene Deszca

The Finney case appears in the second part of this book.

In the winning case, "The dark side of water," Latha Poonamallee and Anita Howard (both of Case Western Reserve University) look at the appalling irony of how a multinational water bottling company depleted the water supply of a local community. This case appears in our fourth part on business and the global economy.

Darkside V

In 2006 the AoM moved to Atlanta in Georgia and the Darkside Case Competition was held for the fifth year. The strong competition generated three of the cases that are published in this book. Two finalist cases bookend the collection: Francine K. Schlosser's "Leading the team out of the hazing blues yonder" deals with the problem of hazing and is the opening case of this book, while an examination of "Genocide in Rwanda: leadership, ethics, and organizational 'failure' in a post-colonial context," by Brad Long, James D. Grant, Albert J. Mills, Ellen Rudderham-Gaudet, and Amy Warren is the final case in the book. The 2006 winning case by Monique Le Chêne and Emmanuel Raufflet, "The smell of power: Yves Rocher in La Gacilly, France," describes the challenges of a dominant company on a local community and appears in the book's second part.

Darkside VI

Philadelphia was the location of the AoM annual meeting for 2007 and the sixth year of the Darkside Competition. This year's competition also provided three cases for our collection.

In "The story behind the water in Walkerton, Ontario," Elizabeth McLeod and Jean Helms Mills detail the management failures that led to the deaths of several people from tainted water in a small Canadian community. This case appears in Part 3.

In "Who takes responsibility for the informal settlements? Mining companies in South Africa and the challenge of local collaboration," Ralph Hamman examines corporate responsibility for events in local communities. This case is included in the second part of the book.

And, in the winning cases, Anne Lawrence examines human rights and corporate global citizenship in "Google, Inc: figuring out how to deal with China," and Kevin McKague and Oana Branzei in "City Water Tanzania" highlight innovative forms of providing water in Dar es Salaam. Lawrence's case forms part of the book's fourth part.

From Darkside VII to the Dark Side Case Book

The seventh Darkside Competition provided no less than four of our featured cases. In 2008, at the AoM meeting at Anaheim, California, the CMS Interest Group was promoted to a full division and participants of the Darkside Competition heard cases about:

- A chlorine spill and stakeholder responsibility ("Dark territory: the Graniteville chlorine spill" by Jill Brown and Ann K. Buchholtz—see Part 3)

- Global corporate relations and the production of hazardous materials for toys ("Mattel Inc.: lead-tainted toys" by Adenekan Dedeke and Martin Calkins—see Part 4)

- Dubious marketing strategies ("Antiquorum Auctioneers: building brands on ignorance?" by Benoit Leleux—see Part 1)

- A business model based on employee degradation (winning case "Hugh Connerty and Hooters: what is successful entrepreneurship?" by Mary Godwyn—see Part 1)

As the 2008 AoM conference loomed, the Darkside Case-Writing Competition was entering its seventh year and had generated dozens of cases, including 25 finalist cases—a veritable wealth of teaching material. Yet, paradoxically, with one notable exception,[12] the wealth of critical cases had not been published in a collective sense nor were they easily accessible. It was at this point that we, as former competition winners and organizers, decided to seek a publisher for a selected collection of cases. To that end, we began with competition winners, supplemented by other finalist cases that would round out each of the four sections of the book. This collection is the result of what we hope will become a series of critical case study books in the field of management and organization.

These cases form a diverse and rich set from several countries, continents, and issues pertaining to interactions in business organizations as well as between business organizations and groups and societies. The book is divided into four parts. The first sheds light on gray areas in the behavior of businesses. The second concerns the interactions between business and local communities in diverse countries. The third part concerns crises, and specifically how companies may create or manage crises. The fourth and last part concerns gray areas in business behavior in the global context.

References

Bird, F.B. (1996) *The Muted Conscience: Moral Silence and the Practice of Ethics in Business* (Westport, CT: Quorum Books).

—— and J.A. Waters (1989) "The Moral Muteness of Managers," *California Management Review* 32.1: 173-88.

Fukuyama, F. (1992) *The End of History and the Last Man* (New York: Free Press).

—— (2008) "The Fall of America Inc.," *Newsweek*, October 2008.

Ghoshal, S. (2005) "Bad Management Theories are Destroying Good Management Practices," *Academy of Management Learning and Education* 4.1: 75-91.

Hamschmidt, J. (ed.) *Case Studies in Sustainability Management and Strategy: The oikos collection* (Sheffield, UK: Greenleaf Publishing).

Jones, G.R., A.J. Mills, T.G. Weatherbee and J. Helms Mills (2006) *Organizational Theory, Design, and Change* (Toronto: Pearson, Canadian edn).

Mills, A.J., T. Simmons and J. Helms Mills (2005) *Reading Organization Theory: A Critical Approach to the Study of Organizational Behaviour and Structure* (Toronto: Garamond Press, 3rd edn).

——, J. Helms Mills, J. Bratton and C. Foreshaw (2006) *Organizational Behaviour in a Global Context* (Peterborough, ON: Broadview Press).

Waddock, S. (2005) "Corporate Citizen: Stepping in to the Breach of Society's Broken Contracts", *Journal of Corporate Citizenship* 19.3: 20-24.

Westley, F., B. Zimmerman and M.Q. Patton (2006) *Getting to Maybe: How the World is Changed* (Toronto: Random House of Canada).

12 McKague and Banzei's case was published in Hamschmidt 2007.

Acknowledgments

The editors would like to thank Direction de la Recherche, HEC Montréal, for their financial support as well as David Paton for his much-appreciated assistance and support in this project. We would also like to thank our many friends throughout the critical management studies communities who encouraged this project.

Part 1
Gray areas in the behavior of businesses

1.1

Leading the team out of the hazing blues yonder
The case of the Windsor Spitfire hockey team[1]

Francine K. Schlosser

This case deals with moral issues surrounding initiation rites (hazing) in organized hockey. The author profiles the attitudes and actions of several stakeholders including the players, the coaches, the team owner, the public and the Ontario Hockey League (OHL). Hazing made headlines when the Ontario Hockey League's Windsor Spitfires let it happen among their players. A string of hazing-related incidents created conflict between experienced and rookie players, fragmented the Spitfire team, and resulted in the loss of two key players and the head coach.

Hazing has long been a tradition in organized sports and was justified by proponents as a means for players to bond with each other. Officially, the OHL prohibits teams from participating in hazing activities. The hockey community is divided on it—some stakeholders view it as a part of developmental hockey, while others feel it has no place in organized hockey at any level. This case questions the need for hazing and how big of a negative impact it has on the players and the teams. It draws attention to the dark side of sports management in the business of profit-generating sports attractions. The author also challenges the readers of this case to make strong recommendations to the new coach regarding leadership, change management, and team-building strategies.

This case would be suitable for in-class discussion in both undergraduate and graduate level business and sports management courses. It is particularly suitable to courses

1 I'd like to recognize the research contribution of Odette MBA students Justin Goggins, Syed Junaid ul Hasan, Andrew Stansell, and Xun Daniel Sun.

that cover ethical decision-making, social identity, leadership and change management. The case encourages discussion of mainstream ethical issues and will help students to deal with large social issues by identifying how they can shape the moral development and citizenship behaviors of their followers.

Leadership and group initiation

Initiation rites have played a traditional role in stimulating membership in close-knit teams. They may be formal orientation events sanctioned and organized by team management. Alternatively, they may be informal events organized by dominant players or employees. Events that are designed around the goals of the team have the potential to introduce and align new players with the team. For example, universities commonly have a type of "frosh" week, where new students are involved in many activities. Some of these activities are purely social, but others may involve community fundraising and academic challenges. However, in recent years negative initiation activities have been increasingly profiled in the media, especially with respect to team initiation on sports teams and in the military.

This case profiles the story of hazing in a Canadian junior hockey team and its implications for the players, coaches and managers of the team. It profiles the pressures of sports as a business and challenges for leaders of professional sports teams. In examining this situation, we need to ask whether the hazing was symptomatic of a lack of team leadership. It also challenges the readers of this case to make strong recommendations to the new coach regarding leadership, change management, and team building strategies.

The issue of hazing

Hazing can be defined as:

> Any willful act . . . by a member or associate member, directed against another member or associate member, which . . . is likely to: cause bodily harm or danger, offensive punishment, or disturbing pain, compromise the person's dignity; cause embarrassment or shame in public; cause the person to be the object of malicious amusement or ridicule;

cause psychological harm or substantial emotional strain; and impair academic efforts.[2]

Hazing occurs in academic institutions, sports clubs, armed forces, police forces, and in the workplace. There is no legitimate reason for hazing. However, proponents of hazing rationalize that the commitment of the newcomers to the team escalates when performing some unwanted and uncomfortable small tasks. Hazing may include spanking, assigning tedious cleaning jobs, servitude, wearing unusual or shameful clothing, wearing of symbols, being tied together, excessive or unwanted eating.

Considering that an Alfred University survey found that 80 per cent of college athletes had undergone a hazing initiation rite, the vast majority of hazing incidents on the high school, college and pro levels go unreported. Nonetheless, incidents that eventually gain the attention of the news media have increased steadily since 1980, when the abuse of athletes by athletes first began to receive public attention.[3]

At the National Hockey League (NHL) level, hazing usually takes the form of a dinner in which rookie players pay for the entire team. "They even got out of hand, as far as people trying to run up the bill on these kids," Maple Leafs head coach Pat Quinn said.

> I guess hazing has been around since Plato's time, probably. I don't have the particular answer to it . . . It doesn't seem to have anything to do with team building, as far as I'm concerned. I did not personally [get hazed] because I was tougher than most of the guys.[4]

Some NHL players regard hazing as a rite of passage. Toronto Maple Leafs forward Darcy Tucker described an initiation prank as:

> . . . amusing . . . It just happens—it's part of being a rookie. It [initiation] was kind of a laugh for all of us, it kind of brought us closer together . . . if you take it as an embarrassment, it'll follow you for the rest of your career.[5]

Mark Shaller, a psychology professor at the University of British Colombia, suggested that:

> Researchers have shown that people who suffered in order to attain a goal or in order to be a part of a group have ended up accepting the ritual and even appreciating this group that much more.[6]

2 depts.washington.edu/ovpsl/greek/terminology.html, accessed June 29, 2009.
3 espn.go.com/otl/hazing/list.html.
4 www.cbc.ca/sports/story/2005/10/19/tucker051019.html, accessed June 15, 2009.
5 Ibid.
6 www.cbc.ca/sports/story/2005/10/19/tucker051019.html, accessed June 15, 2009.

Everyone does not share the view that hazing is acceptable. For example, Wayne Gretzky, the NHL's all-time scoring leader and now rookie head coach of the Phoenix Coyotes, asserted:

> There's no room for it . . . It's the most ridiculous thing in sports. It's hard enough for a young guy to go into a locker room. We never had an initiation with the [Edmonton] Oilers . . . Lee Fogolin was our captain, he didn't believe in it and, when I became captain, I kept that going. It's just wrong. It's hard enough for a 16-year-old. As a captain, as a hockey team, I didn't like it and didn't allow it. There's no room for it.[7]

The Windsor Spitfires: a promising hockey team

The Windsor Spitfires are one of 16 Junior A teams playing in the Ontario Hockey League (OHL). The OHL is comprised of two conferences (Eastern and Western), with eight teams in each. The teams are further placed into two divisions in each of the conferences (eastern conference: east and central divisions; western conference: midwest and west divisions). The Spitfires have produced many great players and coaches who continued with hockey careers in the National Hockey League (NHL). NHL players who grew up with the Spitfires include such skilled National Hockey League stars as Jason Spezza, Ed Jovanovski, Adam Graves, Cory Stillman, and Joel Quenneville.

A successful local businessman owned the Spitfires for more than a decade. The team experienced a number of different head coaches in the past 15 years, and, in this case, head coach Mantha was less than one year in the position. His two assistant coaches were ex-NHL players and had a longer coaching history with the Spitfires.

In recent years, the Spitfires provided lackluster showings in the league standings. However, the 2005 playoffs saw them lead the Western Division and challenge the Western Conference title. This improved performance signaled great potential for the 2005/6 season. Two of the top 20 scorers in the league for 2004/5 were on the Spitfires.

Moe Mantha, the new head coach of the Windsor Spitfires was extremely excited coming into the 2005/6 Ontario Hockey League season. After all, there was a strong team, including three-year veteran Steve Downie, a first-round draft pick of the National Hockey League's Philadelphia Flyers, and stand-out player Akim Aliu, a 16-year-old rookie. However, what occurred September 28, 2005, during a routine practice would cause their season to come to a halt and bring negative national attention to the Ontario Hockey Association and the City of Windsor. Events created a call for action and increased public concern regarding

7   Ibid.

hazing in sports activities throughout Canada. An effective solution demanded strong and ethical team leadership.

The players at the centre of the controversy

The key players in the Fall 2005 controversy were players Steve Downie and Akim Aliu, and coach Mantha. Steve Downie was a seasoned veteran of the team ready to move up to play in the National Hockey League whereas Akim Aliu was a rookie, hired only a few months earlier. Although both had exceptional hockey ability, they came from very different backgrounds.

Steve Downie, at 5'10" and 191 pounds, had played the last few seasons with the Windsor Spitfires. The previous season saw him score 21 goals, 52 assists, and 179 penalty minutes in 61 games.[8] Downie, an 18-year-old native of Queensville, Ontario, and his brother were raised by their mother.[9] When Steve was only ten, an automobile accident killed his father, John, as the two were on their way to a morning hockey practice during some stormy weather.[10] Steve described his hockey playing as:

> I put everything out there, I think when I grow older I'll learn when not to do something. But that's just how I play now. I put everything I have into it.[11]

Downie was drafted in the first round with Philadelphia first NHL pick. Bob Clarke of the Philadelphia Flyers was quoted as saying:

> The way he plays is the way he is. He's an aggressive, hard-nosed player and he's tough. What I like about him is he's humble; there's no ego. He's the kind of kid you want in your locker room.[12]

Steve planned to try out for the Canadian World Junior Hockey Team in the Fall 2005.[13]

In contrast, Akim Aliu, a 6'3" and 209-pound right-winger, had recently arrived from Toronto where he played for the Toronto Marlboros.[14] At 16, Aliu had been playing hockey since the age of nine. He was born in Okene, Nigeria, before mov-

---

8   www.ontariohockeyleague.com/stats/player.php?id=3007.
9   Ibid.
10 www.canada.com/sports/hockey/nhldraft2005/story.html?id=10c41e46-4d79-4be8-a831-539168ebe1c4, accessed November 1, 2005.
11 Ibid.
12 Ibid.
13 www.ysehockey.com.
14 www.windsorspitfires.com.

ing to Russia when he was one year old.[15] In 2005 he was the Windsor Spit-fires' first-round pick. By September 2005, he had played 18 games, scoring three goals, four assists, and 25 penalty minutes.[16] Akim Aliu was viewed as an imposing physical specimen with good skills. He could skate, handle the puck, and shoot. Akim felt his parents were the most important people in his hockey career. He was quoted as saying:

> For sure my parents, no doubt about it. They've been through so much
> just to let me play the game and have worked just as hard as me to get
> to where I am now. They deserve the credit.[17]

Moe Mantha

Maurice "Moe" Mantha, a 44-year-old native of Sturgeon Falls, lived in Ann Arbor, Michigan, with his wife Kathy and their three children, Ashley, Devin, and Brody.[18] He began coaching in 1992 and since then has served as head coach in the American Hockey League, East Coast Hockey League, and Ontario Hockey League, as well as two seasons as head coach of the United States under-17 hockey program.[19] In May 2005, he was named the Spitfires new head coach and general manager.[20] Steve Riolo, Spitfire owner, said this about hiring Mantha:

> I believe that we have the right person to build a very competitive
> program for our organization and the Spitfires fans. He offers a wealth
> of experience from all different levels of hockey.[21]

In the late seventies, Mantha played two years of junior hockey in Toronto. In 1980, he was drafted in the second round by Winnipeg in the NHL. He played over 650 games in his NHL career that spanned more than a decade.[22]

A series of unfortunate events

Blowout on the ice

On September 28, 2005, hockey practice was proceeding as normal. The fight started after a drill that Aliu was not completing properly. Downie and Aliu

15 Ibid.
16 ibid.
17 www.windsorspitfires.com.
18 www.timestoppers.ca/moemantha.html, accessed November 1, 2005.
19 Ibid.
20 Ibid.
21 Ibid.
22 Ibid.

exchanged words, and Downie came off the bench. In the ensuing fight, Downie crosschecked Aliu in the mouth and damaged two teeth. After the fight, Aliu went to the locker-room and Mantha allowed the practice to continue. A short time later, Aliu came back out and fought Downie at centre ice, while Spitfire players and coaches watched. Although Aliu was physically larger, Downie was older and held his own. The local news media was present and recorded the entire fight. In only a few hours, this fight made headlines all over the national news, radio, and television. Citing concerns for his son's safety, Aliu's father intervened by removing Aliu from team play until the incident was investigated. After all, how could a coach let this happen, especially in the public eye? Rumors began to spread that coach Mantha's philosophy was for players to deal with their problems on the ice and use their fists to figure things out. It took days for coach Mantha and the Windsor Spitfires to figure out what went wrong.

The organization and its leaders were definitely under pressure when more rumors surfaced, this time about the implications of an earlier hazing incident. Subsequently, the Ontario Hockey League launched an investigation to find out whether hazing had occurred. Not unexpectedly, the turmoil within the ranks did not improve the team's season, with the Spits experiencing mounting game losses.

A tiny bathroom, a large predicament

Aliu and Downie had clashed prior to the fight at practice on September 28, 2005. An earlier incident occurred on September 9, 2005, during the bus trip back from a pre-season game in London. On the bus, rookie Spitfire players went through an initiation that involved seasoned players ordering rookie players to strip and stand in the washroom at the back of the bus. This type of hazing reputedly had a long history with junior teams and earned the nickname "the hot box."[23] Five players were supposedly involved in the Spitfire incident, but only four were crammed into the washroom. Aliu was the sole rookie who was not crammed in. He refused to cram his large six-foot frame into the tiny room with the other four large players. Mantha and the Spitfires owner were on the bus at the time of the incident, but were either unaware that it was happening or chose to ignore it.

The Ontario Hockey League's decision

The OHL investigated the incidents to determine whether they were considered hazing. The League wanted to portray itself as being a safe environment for junior players. Therefore, the League enforced their official zero tolerance stance on hazing and punished Mantha and the Windsor Spitfires organization.

23   Keller, T. (2005) "No Greater Love," *Maclean's*, October 31, 2005: 38-39.

The OHL found that the team had indeed engaged in a hazing incident and that the coach should have intervened to stop it. Mantha was suspended for 40 games as coach and the team was also fined a total of $35,000. The League also suspended him from the position of general manager for the rest of the regular season and the playoffs. Mantha's suspension as coach was 25 games for the hazing and another 15 games for the fight. Mantha, as head coach and leader of the team, was held responsible for the safety of the players and their development. The OHL intended to send a message to the rest of the teams in the league that hazing was unacceptable. The Windsor Spitfires were also held responsible and were fined the league maximum of $25,000 for the hazing and $10,000 for the fight.

The Spitfires imposed a five-game suspension on Downie including mandatory participation in a personal counseling program. Aliu, Windsor's first-round pick in 2005, received a one-game suspension and was also instructed to attend counseling sessions.

Team Canada director of player personnel Blair Mackasey described the situation in Windsor as "very uneasy . . . not just for him [Downie] but for a lot of kids." Mackasey noted that Downie:

> . . . was made out to be a bit of a villain. I'm not saying he's an angel, but he is a kid and I don't think he deserved some of the criticism that came his way.[24]

Later developments: the loss of key people

Downie left the Spitfires and the City of Windsor and returned home. He was later traded to the top-ranked team in the OHL, the Peterborough Petes. Ironically, the Windsor Star ran an article December 14, 2005, noting Downie's attempts to battle the "bad boy image" and better develop his own leadership abilities on his new team.[25]

Fifteen games into Mantha's suspension, the Windsor Spitfires terminated his contract as head coach and general manager and agreed to a financial settlement.

Forced to play with a team many believed he was responsible for fracturing, Akim found the situation untenable. Only three months after joining the Windsor Spitfires in September 2005, Akim Aliu quit and returned home, preferring to wait for a trade to another team.

---

24 Ewen, S. (2005) "Ex-Spit Downie battles bad boy image," *The Windsor Star*, December 14, 2005: D1 (Canwest News Service, Vancouver).

25 Ibid.

The team owner refused to respond to public calls that he sell the Spitfires and give them a new start. Instead, he recruited a new coach, a former hockey scout from a neighboring city.

The challenges facing the new coach

The new coach knew that the OHL had no choice but to enforce its zero-tolerance regulations regarding hazing. Like the National Hockey League, the OHL is a money-making organization. The OHL's objective was to attract the best teenage hockey players in Ontario and the U.S. This strategy created short-term profits accruing from game attendance, and established the OHL's long-term credibility as an NHL feeder organization. Many players count on signing lucrative contracts with the NHL.

It had come as no surprise to the new coach when Ontario Hockey League Commissioner David Branch released this statement on what the league felt caused this incident and how they feel about hazing:

> I conclude that the lack of leadership and what transpired were dishonorable and prejudicial to the well-being of the league and its players. The OHL has a zero tolerance policy against hazing, our member teams know that, and that is why it is imperative that the league make a strong statement against it.[26]

The new coach was skeptical about these public statements. Who would enforce these lofty ideals? After all, what could he really do to change a tradition so strongly ensconced in the sports psyche?

As the new coach reflected on the hazing controversy, he thought to himself:

> Maybe hazing wasn't such a big issue because research suggested that many cases of hazing were not even reported—so it couldn't be that bad and, to a certain extent, new players probably even expect to be hazed. Of course, it wasn't like Windsor was the only team to run into a spate of bad publicity, every year someone seemed to be written up and publicly flogged . . .

A recent incident at McGill University in Montreal involved rookie football players being stripped and prodded anally with a broomstick. In response, McGill University took a strong stand against hazing, and voluntarily forfeited the entire Fall 2005 football season. The Spitfires situation was a bit different because a forfeited OHL season would force a loss of profit. Unlike the Spitfires, McGill's players were all above 18 years of age and, as a not-for-profit institution, the university team did not face monetary loss, just a wounded reputation.[27]

---

26 www.tsn.ca/story/?id=140174, accessed June 15, 2009.
27 www.tsn.ca/story/?id=140211, accessed June 15, 2009.

In spite of these reservations, the new coach was aware of how hazing might lead to serious or fatal injuries. The negative publicity associated with the Spitfire hazing incident wasn't helping ticket sales or player recruitment either. The new coach knew that the culture would need to change. He needed some advice. To what extent was change needed, and how could he best proceed with the change?

He thought about his options. He could take a very directive approach, supported by strong disciplinary actions for cases that were discovered or reported, the implementation of behavioral standards, and use of law enforcement in preventing hazing incidents. Or maybe a softer team-building approach to culture change would be warranted? And he did acknowledge that maybe he could just make sure that the team was clear that hazing did not happen "on the job" but that hazing outside of this time was really not the coach's concern anyway. What route should he take, and how could he make sure that it would succeed?

Discussion questions

1. When are initiation rites acceptable?

2. Why was Moe Mantha suspended? Was it because his inaction "on duty" implied official support for hazing? Or because he was not smart enough to keep the hazing underground? Or because he did not set and enforce ethical standards? Explain.

3. What could Mantha have done to prevent this hazing incident from occurring? Compare and contrast positive and negative strategies for team-building in a sports and business context.

4. How did the use/misuse of power contribute to negative group norms such as hazing?

5. How can the new coach turn around the culture? What type of leadership style and change management tools should he use?

6. Businesses have frequently used sports leadership models for building teams in the workplace. How can we translate this issue of hazing and sports leadership to non-sports business organizations?

Teaching notes for this case are available from Greenleaf Publishing. These are free of charge and available only to teaching staff. They can be requested by going to:
www.greenleaf-publishing.com/darkside_notes

1.2

John Hamilton's work and eldercare dilemma
Break the silence? Sustain the silence?[1]

Rosemary A. McGowan

The case describes the experiences and perspectives of two individuals at Alpha Software in confronting the issue of work and eldercare. The case describes the first-hand experiences of employee John Hamilton, a 46-year-old software project head, who becomes increasingly stressed by his attempts to balance full-time work responsibilities with care for his aging mother. The case also describes the concerns of Barbara Verdun, the human resources manager at Alpha Software. Barbara has heard rumours that some employees are struggling to balance their work commitments with care for aging relatives, yet are unwilling or unable to talk about their situation. The case describes the use of silence by employees as a strategy for managing the day-to-day demands, and the challenges that the strategy presents to employees and managers, and to human resource policy development.

The case has two primary objectives.

First, to provide students with a case that describes the demands and challenges of a particular form of work and family balance, namely work and eldercare—an issue facing a growing number of Canadian employees. The case also provides statistics on the work and eldercare situation facing organizations.

1 Case Study Number: 140040-W. Copyright © 2004 Wilfrid Laurier University.

No part of this publication may be reproduced, stored in a retrieval system, or transmitted in any form or by any means—electronic, mechanical, photocopy, recorded or otherwise—without the permission of The School of Business & Economics, Wilfrid Laurier University, Waterloo, Ontario, N2L 3C5. This material is not covered under authorization from CanCopy or any other reproduction rights organization. To order copies or request permission to reproduce materials, please contact The School of Business & Economics at 519-884-0710 ext. 6999, or visit the website at www.wlu.ca/sbe/cases.

Second, the case considers strategies of voice and silence within organizations. The case provides users with an opportunity to discuss the personal and organizational motivations for, and outcomes of, strategies of silence. The case affords instructors the opportunity to identify and discuss the factors that contribute to employees' willingness to give voice (or not) to personal issues of concern.

It was Tuesday evening at 7.45 pm and John Hamilton, senior project head, and his assistant Taylor Roberts were meeting late to review the software revisions prior to Wednesday's 9 am project launch. John's phone rang. It was a call from his mother's Lifeline[2] system. His mother had fallen and needed assistance; John knew that he would have to leave immediately. When he put the receiver down, John looked at Taylor who sensed that there was some kind of problem. John told Taylor that his home alarm system had been triggered and, since his wife was out of town, he had to go home immediately to reset the system. He told Taylor that he would be back in about 45 minutes and asked if Taylor could stay at the office until his return. He hadn't told anyone at work about his mother's increasing care needs, and more importantly his role as her primary caregiver and he wasn't about to start now with the project launch date so close. As he quickly prepared to leave his office, he wondered how much longer he could manage the balance of work and eldercare and, more importantly, how much longer he could sustain his strategy of silence.

John Hamilton's work: Alpha Software

John Hamilton, 46, had been with Alpha Software for almost 25 years. He joined the firm immediately after graduating with a degree in computer science. In his fourth year at the University of Waterloo, one of his professors told John that he was developing a software start-up company and he felt that John's specialized skills would be an excellent fit for the organization. John had been with Alpha Software since graduation. The last ten years of the computer company were

---

2 Lifeline Systems Canada Incorporated provides a 24-hour personal response service. Subscribers are linked to Lifeline through a two-way communication system connected to their personal telephone line. Subscribers wear a small personal communicator fashioned either as a pendant or as a wristband. In case of an emergency, a subscriber presses the emergency button on the communicator. Depressing the button triggers a signal to the Lifeline system. Lifeline then calls back to the subscriber to determine the nature of the emergency. If the subscriber does not answer, or if the subscriber needs immediate assistance, Lifeline calls the emergency contacts on the subscriber's Lifeline contact list. If no one on the contact list is available, 911 is dispatched to the subscriber's home. Additional information on Lifeline Systems Canada Inc. is available through its website (www.lifelinecanada.com).

marked by exponential growth in product demand and employee numbers. John had no trouble remembering the firm's early days when "everyone knew everyone" and Christmas parties for the original 20 employees and their partners were held at his boss's home.

Four years ago the firm underwent two major expansions. First, they bought out another local software firm and then 18 months later Alpha was acquired by a large U.S. software house. The U.S. parent decided to retain the Alpha name for its Canadian operations. The U.S. parent was determined to grow the size of the Canadian operations. In the space of those two hectic years, Alpha went from 65 employees to over 300 employees. Alpha had by and large escaped the high-tech meltdown faced by many in the computing industry—in fact, its growth in sales and employees had continued on a positive note. John no longer knew even a small fraction of the employees and, when he looked around the cafeteria, everyone looked so young. In a recent in-house human resource newsletter, Alpha offered a demographic profile of the employees. Almost 80% of the employees were under 40. One article titled "Thirty under Thirty" profiled the 30 most recent hires—all, as the title of the article suggested—were in their twenties.

While John really enjoyed working with these young computer graduates, he also felt that their lives were in a very different place. Lunch conversations usually focused on the latest "toys" they purchased—plasma screen televisions, sporty cars, high-end mountain bikes, snowboards, and snowboard gear. In recent months, he was becoming envious of their ability to work long hours without substantial personal commitments or responsibilities.

John's schedule was pretty typical of those in the software industry—long days (8 am to often 8 pm or later), Saturdays and/or Sundays in the office, as well as out-of-town, out-of-province, and out-of-country meetings with clients. After dinner, John often retreated to his home office to find 30 or 40 email messages in his inbox, most of which needed immediate reply. After almost a quarter-century in the industry, John was more than accustomed to the intense work demands. John also knew that in his company if you weren't able, willing, or interested in keeping up with the demands, there was always an abundant supply of up-and-coming software specialists ready to make the commitment. Early in their marriage, John and his wife Eileen decided that they wanted to commit themselves to their careers and to travel in their spare time. The decision not to have children had worked out well for them. They had both achieved a fair degree of professional success and had just returned from a trip to New Zealand; the airfare had been managed through their frequent-flier points. The busy professional life had been good.

John Hamilton's Mom

Eighteen months ago, however, life started to change for John, not because of the dramatic changes in the software industry or his own company's rapid growth, but because his mother's health had started to falter. In the late fall of 2002, John noticed some changes to his Mom's memory. She would repeat herself, forget phone numbers, and misplace her bills and the keys to her house. At first, John didn't pay too much attention to some of these episodes. After all, John's own tendency to misplace his key had become a running joke between himself and Eileen. But then he noticed that even simple, routine activities that his Mom had previously had no problem with were presenting new challenges. For example, grocery shopping was becoming increasingly difficult. His Mom could not remember where items were in the store, a store where she had shopped for almost a decade on a weekly basis. In one of their last shopping trips together, John found his Mom passing her wallet over to the cashier to count out the money owing on the grocery bill. She seemed to have a momentary loss in her ability to calculate change. John felt alarmed and uncomfortable with his Mom's increasing difficulties.

Approximately three months after John had started to notice changes in his Mom's demeanour. John's Mom experienced a fairly dramatic health event that signaled a real change to her, and ultimately to John's, situation. John had gone over to his Mom's home on one of his regular Friday after work visits. His Mom seemed particularly disoriented. She was trying to prepare dinner for herself but could not remember what she was doing, where the various ingredients were or what she had to do next in the recipe she was trying to make. Worse yet, she gave nonsensical answers to very simple questions. Thinking that perhaps she was just tired, he suggested that he would finish dinner while she went to rest. An hour later, when his Mom arose from her nap, she was still confused and disoriented. John took her to the emergency department of a local hospital. The emergency room physicians diagnosed her as having suffered a minor heart attack and suffering from mild dehydration. His Mom was put on an intravenous drip and kept in hospital for a few days of monitoring and stabilization. That weekend, John spent many hours in the hospital visiting his Mom and helping her with her meals and generally keeping her company. Government cutbacks to nursing services meant that there was minimal assistance available for patients who needed help with eating, getting an additional drink or help getting to the washroom.

When his Mom was in emergency and through her stay in the hospital, John realized that perhaps his neatly segmented life was evolving into something that was new, unfamiliar and somewhat unsettling. Prior to his Mom's discharge from hospital, John and Eileen met with the discharge planning nurse. Through the Community Care Access Centre (CCAC) they arranged for daily visits from the Red Cross homemaking staff. They also arranged for visits from the occupational and physical therapists. The discharge planning nurse suggested that John, or

Eileen, should be present for the first visit by the homecare supervisor and the occupational and physical therapists, so that he could provide information and verify any information given by his Mom. Sheepishly, John asked whether or not those healthcare professionals made evening or weekend appointments. Not surprised by the answer of "unfortunately, no," John knew he had to figure out a strategy for being at work and being available for those visits. To get to the hospital for the meeting with the discharge nurse, he just told his assistant that he had a meeting with a client and he left a message on his voicemail that he would be out of the office for the morning meeting with clients and that he would return in the afternoon. For almost all of his working life, John had been able to go to work largely unencumbered by personal or family caregiving concerns. For John, work was more likely to spill over into personal time, than vice versa. Now, however, John felt like he was slipping into a situation where the boundaries between work and family during work hours were no longer going to be "neat."

Over the next few months, John found himself spending much more time during the workday assisting his mother than he had ever anticipated. His mother's spotty memory meant that he had to accompany her to every doctor's appointment. Her capacity to manage her bills was diminishing, so John was managing all her financial affairs. John soon realized two things. First, that his mother would not be able to cope on her own much longer and, second, that he would not be able to manage his mother's increasing needs. John contacted the CCAC to find out about nursing home placements. He and Eileen visited a few nursing homes in the area to view the facilities and to meet with the personnel. He was impressed with the facilities, particularly those built within the last couple of years. They seemed much less institutional than his grandmother's nursing home that he had visited when he was a teenager.

At the start of April, 2003, he registered his mother's name with a local nursing home. He was told that the wait list for a ward[3] room would be approximately six months to a year. During the spring and summer, his Mom's situation was fairly stable. The homecare worker, who visited twice daily, offloaded much of the day-to-day responsibility and care for John and Eileen. By late fall, however, his mother was starting to confabulate. She would tell him that there were people wanting to come and live at her home and that people were stealing her things. Of course, none of this was true but it was difficult for his Mom and frustrating to listen to nonetheless. In November, she twice let a pot burn dry on the stove. Shortly thereafter the stove was disconnected and all food was prepared in the microwave by the home maker. His mother could no longer remember how to sequence the buttons on the microwave.

In January, 2004, he called the CCAC again to see where his mother was on the waiting list. John was told that there was no movement on the list—there

---

3   Ward rooms were defined as two beds per room with two rooms sharing an adjoining washroom. Semi-private rooms had two beds per room with one washroom for the room. Private rooms accommodated a single resident and had their own washroom.

were still two individuals ahead of his mother on the waiting list. Those two individuals had been on the waiting list since 2002. John was concerned because initially he was told that the wait would be approximately six months to a year, and now after being on the waiting list for nine months, his mother was no closer to placement than she had been in April of the previous year. At that point he learned that the waiting lists for ward rooms were the longest of the waiting lists. Apparently some people registered for private or semi-private rooms and then, once they were residents, they put their names on an internal waiting list to move to a ward room.

Mulling over options

Throughout all of this, John had not mentioned his situation to anyone at work. Part of the reason for the silence while he was at work was that he liked to keep his work and his personal affairs separate. Part of his motivation for silence was that he did not want to seem less than fully committed to work. And who could he talk to? How could a 23-year-old software/snowboard whiz relate to John's current situation? He had chatted about his situation with a few close friends outside of Alpha Software and the advice on raising the issue of his eldercare with work colleagues or superiors was contradictory. He played their comments back in his mind.

Anne, a friend since university and an IT manager at a competitor, had told him:

> There were times where I was, um, not deceptive but I'd have to sneak it in. I didn't always want to own to my employer that I was taking time off to get my Mom to the doctor. The written policy at XXX was that you could take time off in lieu. The cultural policy was that that was not done. So, I would say something like, "Oh, I'm going off, um, I'm going to be at XXXX and then I've got some other running around to do." So, I would make a point of making sure that I went to one of my work-related places. It might just be to drop off an envelope but at least it gave me a legitimate work-related reason to be out of the office.

Karen, another longtime friend suggested to John that:

> The prime piece of advice would probably be, for the sake of your peace of mind, would be for you to figure out how much you could reasonably handle and not try to go beyond that.

Joan, a neighbour and manager at a local financial institution, had herself been a caregiver for her own Mom for the last ten years. Based on her experience, she suggested to John that, regardless of what you're coping with, with respect to aging parents, or other personal issues:

> You have to maintain a façade, an image of stability, a strength. You can't show people that maybe you're suffering as well.

Vic, a friend who managed an IT department in another local firm, suggested to John that as a manager:

> It is part of your job to sort of shoulder all of the things that are happening in the organization and in turn not pass on any of your own angsts. Talking about any of your concerns about your mom, well, I would consider it unprofessional. Anyone who is a manager should somehow be able to compartmentalize their life. That's what I do when I'm at work. That's my image of how managers should manage competing personal and private demands.

Terry, who had been John's mentor for the past 15 years, told him simply that:

> It's none of their (employee's or employers') business. I don't talk to anyone at work about any of the personal stuff. I believe that managers should be strong, should show strength and should be slightly less human than their subordinates. There is an element of me that expects that if you are a manager, at some level you should swallow a lot of things that are going on and keep going.

Only Francis, a mutual friend of both John and Eileen, offered different advice. She suggested to John that:

> I think you should be frank with your boss. Do we really live back in some pre-enlightened era? I don't think that you have to live the kind of lie that I did when I had small children and they were sick. You know calling into the office with the "Oh, I can't come in today because I'm sick," when the reality was that the children were not well and I needed to stay home with them. Please don't tell me that we're now lying about personal responsibilities for our aging parents!!

The advice that John received had almost unanimously leaned in the direction of continuing to soldier on in silence. It was only his wife Eileen who suggested that he talk with the Human Resources (HR) department at Alpha to see what type of programs or policies might be available. John had to admit that contacting the HR department wasn't something that was top of the mind for him. He had little contact with HR, except for the quarterly in-house publications that crossed his desk, or monthly statements of earnings or updates to the company's benefits packages. Reviewing the index to the Employee Benefits Package, he noticed a fairly short set of listings for personal leave options such as maternity and paternity benefits and flexible workplace programs for those balancing work and childcare. He knew that an updated Employee Benefits Package was in preparation but did not know if there would be anything relevant to his particular situation. In the meantime, he had just become too busy with current software projects to really follow up with the HR department. It just seemed simpler to take care of things for his Mom first thing in the morning and then come in late for work and make up the missed time by working late, or just weaving his caregiving commitments into his day and masking those commitments by the messages he left with his co-workers on his voicemail.

The Human Resources department at Alpha Software

The HR department at Alpha was less than five years old. For the first few years of Alpha's operations, the company's focus was on software development. A couple of senior managers served double duty overseeing accounting and human resource issues. However, with the growth and organizational changes that occurred over the past four years, Alpha needed an HR department, if only a fairly small one.

Barbara Verdun joined Alpha as the manager of Human Resources five years ago in 1999. At first, the workload was overwhelming. Human resources programs and policies were needed. Yet it was an exciting and invigorating challenge for someone who had been a senior HR manager at a large, well-established insurance company. She moved to Alpha because she wanted to work in a less bureaucratic environment and for a company that she perceived to be dynamic and fast-paced. She had looked forward to developing leading-edge programs and policies in order to retain employees in a high-velocity environment known as much for its volatile stock prices as its employee turnover.

Under her leadership, Alpha formalized its human resource policies and practices. They also brought in a work/family policy. Initially, her senior colleagues questioned the need for work and family policies. After all, they had never had one and there did not seem to be a need. These discussions initially frustrated Barbara. How could an organization where 80% of the staff was under 40 not need work/family policies? She had heard rumours that some of the female software engineers, driven by the demands, competitiveness and rapidly changing nature of the software industry, took less than two weeks off work after giving birth before coming back to work.

Recently, Barbara became increasingly interested in developing programs for the other end of the work/family spectrum—work and eldercare. It was actually the introduction of the Compassionate Care Leave program instituted by the Canadian Federal Government on January 2, 2004, that was her catalyst for thinking more about the needs of those managing work with care for aging parents. She recalled a conversation with a friend in healthcare who said that the Compassionate Care Leave program was overdue but, in her friend's mind, still inadequate. As a professional in healthcare, she had seen many individuals burn out trying to balance work and caregiving for aging parents or spouses.

Although, 80% of the employees at Alpha were under 40, there were still 20% who could be potential caregivers for aging parents. Barbara also realized that just because someone was 37, for instance, did not mean that they did not have caregiving responsibilities.

In reviewing government reports, items in popular business press and health research reports, Barbara had developed a summary of issues relevant to work and eldercare in Canada. Many of the points supported her initial gut feeling about the eldercare issue, but some of the research findings took her by surprise. So far her list included the following:

- **Informal family caregiving of the elderly**
  - Family and friends are frequently the providers of care to aging relatives and friends. Over 2 million (2.1 million) Canadians, or nearly 11% of the population 15 years of age and older, provide informal care to one or more seniors with long-term health problems. More than two-thirds of informal caregivers were between the ages of 30 and 59, with the average age of 46 years for women and 44 years for men (Frederick and Fast 1999)
  - Women tend to be the predominant providers of informal care to aging relatives. The 1996 General Social Survey (GSS) found that 1.3 million women provided eldercare; the 1.3 million represents 61% of those providing eldercare. The GSS survey also found that women employed full-time provided just slightly fewer hours of care per week than did those who worked part-time (4.2 hours versus 4.6 hours). These hours translate to approximately one-half day per week of informal caregiving. By contrast, men who worked full-time reported, provided on average, 2.6 hours of care per week; men who worked part-time reported providing, on average, 2.3 hours of care per week (Frederick and Fast 1999)
  - Eighteen per cent of men and women expect to provide care within the next five years. Recognizing men in their role as "working sons," not just "working fathers" would factor significantly in the balancing work–family equation in the next decade (Levine 1997)

- **Work and caregiving interface**
  - A 1999 Conference Board survey of 1,500 Canadian workers found that a sizable proportion of individuals across all age groups surveyed provided care. While 30% of workers 55 and older provided eldercare assistance, 30% in the 45–54 group also provided care, 20% of men and women aged 34 and younger, and a similar percentage in the 35–44 age group also reported that they provided eldercare assistance
  - Findings of a regional Canadian study of over 5,000 employees in Southern Ontario reported that 34% of respondents were involved in general eldercare while 12% were involved in providing assist-

ance with personal eldercare. On average, those providing general eldercare were involved in three hours of caregiving per week, while those providing personal eldercare were involved in an average of nine hours of care per week. Twenty-six per cent of CARNET's sample reported providing both child care and eldercare (CARNET 1993)

- A large US national study of caregivers indicated that 31% of all caregivers surveyed were also employed (whether the employment was full-time or part-time was not indicated) (Stone *et al.* 1987)
- A survey of over 3,600 employees of a major Southern California employer reported that approximately 23% of respondents provided some level of eldercare (Scharlach and Boyd 1989)
- One study found that approximately 25% of caregiving employees categorized themselves as management-level employees. On median, those caregiving employees had been with their current employer for eight years. The same study found that younger employees were also involved in eldercare. In fact, as many as 23% of employees in their thirties and 11% of employees in their twenties were providing some kind of assistance to an elderly relative (Scharlach and Boyd 1989)
- Employees are more likely to provide eldercare as their tenure with an organization increases. Hence, eldercare is an activity that tends to present itself later in someone's employment cycle and eldercare co-exists with employment for a substantial period of time (Gibeau and Anastas 1989)

- **The caregiving experience**
  - Employees seriously underestimate the duration of their involvement with eldercare. Matthews and Rosenthal (1993) reported that 38% of caregivers had been providing care for five to ten years, while 13% had provided care for more than ten years. Wagner *et al.* (1989) reported that, on average, employees are involved in providing eldercare for five years. As Matthews and Rosenthal (1993) and Wagner *et al.* (1989) point out, caregiving can potentially affect a significant portion of an employee's working life

Barbara's concern about the work and eldercare situation facing employers was starting to materialize at her door. In mid-January, one of the department managers came to talk to Barbara about one of his direct reports. The employee had missed a number of days of work since November, 2003, and when she was at work, she frequently returned late to the office from lunch breaks and was on the phone with what, to the manager, did not seem to be work-related calls. Through the company grapevine, he had heard that the employee was trying to manage care for her mother following her mother's hip replacement surgery. The manager was very concerned, yet frustrated. He was genuinely concerned about the health and well-being of his employee but whenever he asked how things were, he always got the same answer, "Fine. No problem. Everything's great." He did not know how to help an employee who seemed so reluctant to talk about her situation. After reviewing the work/family policies, the manager realized that existing policies were not worded in such a way to make it clear that they could apply to an eldercare situation. This was not the first time that Barbara had heard rumours about employees silencing eldercare responsibilities. She was not sure why this was happening but was concerned.

John's decision

Wheeling back into the company parking lot from helping his mother after her fall in her own home, John felt exhausted—exhausted from trying to balance the competing demands for the past few months, exhausted from feeling that he being deceitful with his boss, his co-workers, his team, and with his company. By his own estimation he was spending anywhere from five to 12 hours a week doing things for his Mom, and, with the current nursing home situation, there was no end in sight. He had recently read a study suggesting that approximately 35% of employees in the U.S. and Canada are providing some level of care for an aging parent. More startling was the fact that such care usually lasted from five to 15 years. He wasn't sure if the silence strategy was going to be sustainable much longer.

References

CARNET (Canadian Aging Research Network) (1993) *Work and Family: The Survey* (Guelph, ON: Canadian Aging Research Network).

Frederick, J.A., and J.E. Fast (1999) *Eldercare in Canada: Who Does How Much?* (Report No. 11-008; Ottawa: Statistics Canada).

Gibeau, J.L., and J.W. Anastas (1989) "Breadwinners and Caregivers: Interviews with Working Women," *Journal of Gerontological Social Work* 14: 19-40.

Levine, J.A. (1997) *Working Fathers: New Strategies for Balancing Work and Family* (New York: Addison Wesley Longmans).

Matthews, A.M., and C.J. Rosenthal (1993) "Balancing Work and Family in an Aging Society: The Canadian Experience," in G.L. Maddox and M.P. Lawton (eds.), *Annual Review of Gerontology and Geriatrics: Focus on Kinship, Aging and Social Change* (New York: Springer Publishing): 96-122

Scharlach, A.E., and S.L. Boyd (1989) "Caregiving and Employment: Results of an Employee Survey," *The Gerontologist* 29: 382-7.

Stone, L., G.L. Cafferata and L. Sangl (1987) "Caregivers of the Frail Elderly: A National Profile," *The Gerontologist* 27: 616-26.

Wagner, D.L., M.A. Creedon, J.M. Sasala and M.B. Neal (1989) *Employees and Eldercare: Designing Effective Responses for the Workplace* (Bridgeport, CT: Centre for the Study of Aging, University of Bridgeport).

Discussion questions

1. What models of work and family balance characterize John Hamilton's behaviour in the past? What models of work and family balance now best describe John's situation?

2. What are the societal, organizational as well as personal factors that are contributing to John's current strategy of silence? What are the reasons for and problems around organizational silence?

3. What options are open to John Hamilton? What action should John take?

4. What course of action do you recommend for Barbara Verdun?

Teaching notes for this case are available from Greenleaf Publishing. These are free of charge and available only to teaching staff. They can be requested by going to:
www.greenleaf-publishing.com/darkside_notes

1.3

Hugh Connerty and Hooters
What is successful entrepreneurship?[1]

Mary Godwyn

On March 8, 2006, Hugh Connerty was invited to speak at Babson College by a student group, the Babson Entrepreneurial Exchange (BEE). His talk was advertised in an email sent to all faculty, staff, and students touting Connerty as "an entrepreneurial genius." Although Hugh Connerty's association with Hooters ended almost two decades before his talk at Babson, his connection with Hooters figured prominently in the Babson advertisements for his talk. The controversy around Connerty's invitation focused in part on timing: he was scheduled to speak during Babson's celebration of women's history month and on International Women's Day, and in part around BEE's categorization of Connerty as an "entrepreneurial genius."

This case is primarily about the Babson community's attempt to define successful entrepreneurship. Babson College's official definition of entrepreneurship is "a way of thinking and acting that is opportunity obsessed, holistic in approach, and leadership balanced." Hugh Connerty has been associated with a range of entrepreneurial enterprises. The two discussed in this case, and those predominantly mentioned in the advertisements for his talk and the *Babson Free Press* interview, are Hooters of America and Outback Steakhouse. Each is examined separately by Babson's ethical decision-making framework,[2] and evaluated against the definition of entrepreneurship in the surveys taken of the Babson community. Secondary considerations include:

1 This case was researched and prepared by Mary Godwyn as a basis for class discussion rather than to illustrate either effective or ineffective handling of an administrative situation. Funding was provided by Babson College and the Harold Geneen Foundation. © Mary Godwyn 2008.
2 Babson's ethical decision-making framework is included as an appendix to the teaching notes to this case, which are available to course leaders (see page 51).

- Exploring the complexities of being associated with companies that engage in unethical or illegal activities
- Recognizing the tendency to draw premature conclusions before having all the facts
- Demonstrating the respectful discussion of ethical quandaries
- Acknowledging the power of marketing to attract negative attention

This case is derived from actual events and issues involving Babson College and Hugh Connerty. All the interviews and quotes are from real individuals. There are many characters in the case—among them the Babson community, the Babson faculty that participated in an email forum to discuss Hugh Connerty's invitation, the students who created the advertisements for his talk, Hooters and Hugh Connerty himself. The case includes interviews, email correspondence, press coverage, and legal issues.[3]

Babson College is a business college in bucolic Wellesley, Massachusetts, a suburb of Boston. For 14 consecutive years, *U.S. News and World Report* named Babson the number one entrepreneurship college in the United States. Babson is also the only business college to have a Center for Women's Leadership. For three years in a row (2004, 2005, 2006), the *Princeton Review* ranked Babson's MBA program number one for "Opportunities for Women," and *Cosmo Girl* and *Seventeen* magazines have ranked Babson the top business college for women.

March is Women's History Month, and in 2006, March 8 was International Women's Day. To mark the occasion, Babson President Brian Barefoot sent a congratulatory email to the entire college community celebrating Babson's commitment to diversity. He specifically mentioned the increased number of tenured women faculty.[4]

Also on March 8, 2006, Hugh Connerty, an entrepreneur, was scheduled to give a speech at Babson. A Babson undergraduate student group, the Babson Entrepreneurial Exchange (BEE), had invited him to campus. Connerty's talk was advertised in an email sent to all faculty, staff and students. Large placards were placed around campus touting Connerty as "an entrepreneurial genius."

---

3 Hugh Connerty was not interviewed or contacted with regard to the content of this case study. However, he has reviewed the case after its initial presentation and generously allowed his personal response in the form of an email to the author to be included as an addendum (see page 47). Like all responses contained herein, Mr. Connerty's response provides important insights and undoubtedly contributes to the richness of the narratives. The intention is to represent the fullest range of perspectives with regard to the ethical issues discussed; therefore, the addendum should be considered a central part of the case.

4 Babson College faculty is organized in nine divisions, but more generally into business and liberal arts. Babson has 165 tenured and tenure track faculty: 32% female and 68% male. There are 48 full professors: 19% women and 81% men.

Connerty's business interests are in real estate and restaurants. He is the President of the Stokes Land Group, and his entrepreneurial credentials include founding Longhorn Steakhouse, being the original franchisee of Outback Steakhouse and being a founding partner in Hooters of America.

Most well known among his entrepreneurial enterprises, Hooters is self-described as "delightfully tacky, yet unrefined," and declares that "the element of female sexuality is prevalent in the restaurants."[5] The all-female wait staff, referred to as "Hooters Girls," wear a uniform of a white tank top and orange running shorts and, as part of their jobs, frequently compete in various beauty contests such as the Hooters "Dream Girl," model in swimsuits for posters and calendars sold at Hooters, and make appearances at various charity events. Hooters hires women "who best fit the image of a Hooters Girl to work in this capacity."[6] Though Connerty's association with Hooters ended over a decade ago, his connection with the restaurant was featured prominently in the campus-wide advertisements for his talk.

The initial response

Upon the announcement that Connerty would speak on International Women's Day, and that Babson, with its considerable clout in the world of entrepreneurship, had proclaimed Connerty an example of entrepreneurial genius, several female professors raised concerns. The following is an email exchange that circulated among some of the faculty (names have been changed and the emails have been edited for brevity).

Professor Anderson

I just noticed that Hugh Connerty, the founder of Hooters, is speaking on campus on Wednesday at 7 pm. Does anyone have any suggestions for productively examining the "cultures and values" content of this opportunity in and possibly out of the classroom? Entrepreneurially yours . . .

Professor Arendt

I just sat down to write a similar email myself—so thanks so much for getting the ball rolling. I saw the announcement this morning, and to be honest, my first reaction was real dismay. Several students in classes have mentioned this event, and I know that we need to discuss it. One student pointedly asked if we could devise a question or series of questions for Connerty. I would really appreciate a

---

5 www.hooters.com/About.aspx.
6 Ibid.

discourse among faculty, not necessarily only liberal arts faculty, on the implications and ramifications of the decision to have Connerty here. It would also be great to get a sense of what has historically happened at Babson in these situations as well, if anyone can speak to that.

Professor Nussbaum

It looks like the speaker has been involved in many businesses, but Hooters is certainly most notable.

One thing I will do is to talk again with the student leader of the club—I am not the advisor, but I can still ask about whether or not female entrepreneurs (and those of different color/races) are also speaking so that a variety of role models are being showcased.

As for questions, will have to think about this. My suspicion is that he will argue that his goal was money and sex sells.

Professor Fraser

Given the new diversity initiative announced by President Barefoot and a to-be-formed women faculty affinity group, I am copying other female faculty on this email. But given that this is also about who Babson endorses as entrepreneurs and how the endorsement is decided and advertised, this is NOT a woman-only issue.

I am certainly disturbed to see that an invitation has been extended to the founder of an enterprise such as Hooters and that a platform is being provided for him to talk about his success with this business.

Is it a teachable moment? Yes, undoubtedly it could be. Although I certainly object to the business being touted as an entrepreneurial success, the reality is that there is certainly a right to freedom of speech and association. So, it doesn't seem appropriate to try and censor this invitation, much as any of us might not like the business. Beyond the freedom of speech issue, there is an interesting ethical question as to where philanthropic dollars come from. According to the bio, Mr. Connerty is a philanthropist, active in South Africa and the U.S. as well as with both medical and educational institutions. What an interesting question to get students to think about—does the source of wealth matter if the wealth is being put to philanthropic use? (Trickle down economics in the Reagan era was a different approach to asking a similar question . . .) If Babson were to get a ginormous capital campaign gift from, say, Larry Flynt or a weapons dealer, would we accept it? Should we?

But, perhaps the larger question is one that has already been raised in this email trail as well as that Prof Arendt raised in her voice message to me. What kind of culture is created/reinforced by hosting such an event on Babson's campus? What messages to students, faculty and staff are sent or received (even if no message was intended)? Does it create a potential environment of discomfort, possible harassment, unease? Here again, is the teachable moment potentially on many levels.

I don't offer a particular solution on how to handle this but I appreciate the dialogue that has begun. What I wonder most is whether this is a question among our students. If it were, what I would most love to see is for them to feel empowered to attend the event and to ask questions of Mr. Connerty. We do not know what Mr. Connerty's views are about his business or what he would say about Hooters. Rather than having students shy away from engaging with him, it would be great to see them question him. I would certainly also love to see students approach their peers on the BEE club to ask them about this event and to express their concerns. If we don't have students who are concerned, then I'm really worried!!

Professor Leibniz[7]

I agree that this is clearly not a woman-only issue. It is an important conversation for the community.

I have taken the position that the students have the right and responsibility to choose and recruit the speakers. That does not mean I agree with inviting Mr. Connerty. I do not. That right is not unalienable and there is clearly room for debate. I would not feel comfortable tying funding to speaker "approval." I also hold that the community has the concurrent right and responsibility to make their voices heard before, during and after the event.

I also agree that learning moments are many. I believe the faculty and administration are likely to be of a consistent mind on issues like accepting philanthropy from what this community might consider unsavory sources, but, again, that is an important discussion.

Professor Foot

Hello!

I am actually not opposed to having Mr. Connerty on campus for several reasons. First, I believe that students should be allowed to hear and can benefit from discussions with people with a variety of backgrounds and beliefs. Second, I do like students to explore the benefits and issues of philanthropy. Third, I believe that, if handled correctly, this can provide a learning opportunity.

Just a note: Connerty, while one of the founders, currently does not own Hooters and has no connection to them.

It might be interesting to ask Connerty the following:

1. When and why did your association with Hooters end?

2. You seem very dedicated to giving back to society through your various

---

7 The only male professor to comment in the email exchange.

philanthropic activities. Have you ever found your business choices or decisions to be inconsistent with this mission? If so, would you make different decisions today?

3. Would you like to see your daughter, niece or other relative become a "Hooter's girl"?

Professor Freeland

In many ways I agree with Prof. Foot. That being said, I have three concerns.

The first lies more in the consistency in which we as an educational community address these issues pre and post event. I am not 100% confident that in all situations, student groups, student businesses or individuals are having the conversations with as broad a community as would be necessary to address all the issues in planning such an event. In this case, the student group does receive funding. Did the group present the pros and cons of the speakers' appearance at the College? Did they seek out the opinions of those who might be in opposition so as to better weigh their decision and be prepared for what might transpire? I strongly believe in supporting student actions and also allowing them to take ownership for them, but feel we have an obligation to help them see things from the lenses of many.

In this case, should these conversations have occurred, I am still concerned that the external world would not know of the process of rigorous examination that may have taken place. Might it not have been a good idea in the advertisement to note the opportunity to challenge the business plan, the impact on consumers, and society as well as discuss the apparent (monetary) success?

And finally, in light of this being Women's History Month, I am more concerned about the message it sends. Again, were the students aware of this as well?

I like the questions being posed by students from classes as well. Thanks.

Professor Okin

Everyone, thanks so much for this discussion.

I have to agree with Prof. Freeland. One problem with having Connerty on campus is that the announcement came after the invitation had been extended; there was no time for debate or discussion. Though we can ask Connerty questions when he arrives, there was little time to research Hooters in order to ask educated questions or to create a balanced presentation by providing other speakers at the same event. Though it may sound cynical, I can imagine that Connerty loses nothing by dismissing questions that challenge his decisions. Additionally, it is not clear to me that we as faculty and administrators have provided students the time, space and guidance to view Hooters as anything other than a very profitable business.

One consideration in inviting a speaker is what the invitation says about the relationship between the speaker and the institution. At Babson, we profess a commitment to cultural and ethical values in entrepreneurship that recognizes the relative ease of, and also condemns profiting by, the exploitation of various social definitions that often act as impediments to full access to the economy and to citizenship rights. In the case of Hooters, the business makes money providing a forum for the explicit valuation of women based only on certain physical attributes, and further requires that these women sign a statement acknowledging and agreeing to tolerate a work environment "in which joking and innuendo based on female sex appeal is commonplace."[8]

Sex is big business, but the phrase "sex sells" glosses over the fact that what is being sold is prurient access to women's bodies. Simply put, Hooters is a business where what women look like is more important that what they say or think. Women are valued so long as they are physically appealing and receptive to men; Hooters, and places like Hooters, therefore, can undercut women's ability to be taken seriously for talents and interests that do not depend on their physicality.

I admit that, though I had heard of Hooters, I didn't know much about the company. I began researching Hooters by putting "Hooters" and "Connerty" into Google. With these two keywords, the Babson Entrepreneurial Exchange website[9] appears on the first page of Google under the heading "Success in the Restaurant Business." Though Connerty is no longer an owner of Hooters, by emphasizing his role as founder of Hooters in the advertisement for his talk, Connerty, Hooters, and Babson have become intertwined. Does Hooters represent Babson's ideal of entrepreneurship? Is Babson saying that Hooters is a good example of success? Clearly, inviting Connerty to speak can be interpreted as an endorsement from Babson of his particular manifestation of entrepreneurship. As the number one college in entrepreneurship, Babson increases the credibility and prestige of a business like Hooters.

Here are some of the things that I found out about Hooters:

In 1991, the Equal Employment Opportunities Commission (EEOC) filed a complaint against Hooters on behalf of men (Hooters does not allow men to serve customers). The company argued that it was legal for the restaurant to have an all-female wait staff because, according to Hooters, "the women, not the food, are the product."[10] Hooters is based in Atlanta and protected by people in positions of power. Twenty-three male members of the 104th Congress, led by Representative Charles Norwood (R-GA), wrote to the EEOC requesting it drop this matter. On May 1, 1996, news reports announced that the federal agency would not pursue litigation. To date, Hooters has not received formal notification from the EEOC; however, it believes the matter is concluded.

---

8   From the Hooters' handbook found at www.thesmokinggun.com/archive/0915051hooters1. html.

9   www3.babson.edu/ESHIP/academic/co-curricular/studentorganizations.cfm.

10   74.125.47.132/search?q=cache:eE-lfJypk8QJ:www-cgi.cnn.com/US/9512/ hooters_eeoc/hooters+eeoc+women+are+the+product&cd=3&hl=en&ct=clnk&gl= us&client=firefox-a, accessed August 10, 2008.

Like most wait staff, servers at Hooters are paid below minimum wage and depend heavily on tips from the largely male clientele (men make up about 70% of the customers). At one time, women who worked at Hooters were hired on the condition that they sign away their right to sue for sexual harassment, with the understanding that the management would protect women from being harassed including, according to a Hooters statement, "unwelcome physical and verbal behavior."[11]

In 1996, Annette Phillips attempted to sue Hooters for sexual harassment. She alleged that a Hooter's official and brother of the manager of Hooters of Myrtle Beach sexually harassed her by grabbing and slapping her buttocks. After appealing to her manager for help and being told to "let it go," she quit her job. Hooters countersued Phillips. The company maintained that Phillips had signed an agreement stating:

> . . . the employee each agree to arbitrate all disputes arising out of employment, including "any claim of discrimination, sexual harassment, retaliation, or wrongful discharge, whether arising under federal or state law." The agreement further states that "the employee and the company agree to resolve any claims pursuant to the company's rules and procedures for alternative resolution of employment-related disputes, as promulgated by the company from time to time."[12]

In 1999, a South Carolina court overruled the arbitration agreement in Hooters of American, Inc. v. Phillips. The ruling found that it would be "unconscionable" to enforce the agreement and compel Phillips to arbitrate her claims under the Hooter's scheme. The court was swayed by Phillips' relative lack of bargaining power, Hooters' failure to disclose its arbitration rules, its attempt to severely limit Phillips' rights under federal discrimination laws, and the lack of neutrality in the selection of arbitrators. Even if the agreement had been properly entered into, the court noted, Hooters' idea of arbitration was "sham arbitration, deliberately calculated to advantage Hooters in any proceeding in which claims are initiated against it."[13]

In addition to the Phillips case, in 2004, Joanna Ciesielski, a former Hooters server in Chicago, alleged that the restaurant management did nothing to stop co-workers from "grabbing her and watching her change clothes through peepholes drilled in changing room walls."[14] She provided videotape footage of the holes in the changing room and break room walls. Another server, Melissa Frankfort, who also testified, supported Ciesielski's allegations. Also in 2004, five women in Los Angeles alleged that a Hooters manager "set up a camera to photograph them in a construction trailer while they were changing." The lawsuit

11   gcaa.collegiategolf.com/files/gcaa/MPC2004_hooters_iframe.html.
12   laws.lp.findlaw.com/4th/981459p.html.
13   library.findlaw.com/1999/Oct/1/130600.html.
14   www.nbc5.com/news/3933245/detail.html?z=dp&dpswid=2265994&dppid=65192, accessed August 10, 2008.

claims the Atlanta-based chain was negligent in its supervision of the manager. In February, authorities raided a trailer at the restaurant construction site and seized a computer holding 180 digital videos of women. Investigators believe there are as many as 80 other victims.[15]

Because Hooters has been so profitable, there have been a series of Hooters spin-offs. In October 2005, Larry Flynt announced he was opening a restaurant chain called Hustler Bar & Grille.[16]

I found the following statements online from women who worked at Hooters (or places like Hooters):

> I have worked in bars where I wore cheerleading outfits (something I would not have been caught dead in, in high school), a "cowgirl" costume, a French maid's uniform (need I go on?), etc. All of which were pretty humiliating, but I did it because it paid a lot more that I could make anywhere else with the same skills. Many of these places also employed men. Their uniforms were equally humiliating. Each of these places discriminated for a number of reasons. For example, the largest uniforms were size 9. Anyone who could not fit in the uniform was not hired. One of my employers said that he would hire any "guy who could fill out the uniform"—(it was a tight French maid uniform). Bottom line, Hooters is more insulting, but I doubt that the government or the plaintiffs (who no doubt were male feminists) had a case here.

> Not only would Hooters not employ males as wait staff, they would not employ me, although I am female. They would not employ me because I am too old (47) and am small busted. Where is the equity???[17]

> There was a time, almost thirty years ago, when I worked . . . in a couple of clubs in Missouri wearing provocative clothing and making sure customers drank and danced a lot . . . not unlike the dance hall women of the 1880s west. In Missouri, at the time and perhaps even today (apologies to happy Missourians) those jobs were the best paying for women. And I had a baby to support. I was probably no older than many of your students.[18]

The following is an excerpt from an article by John Henderson in the *Denver Post* (December 14, 2005):

> Wolfram, 24, a Hooters girl for five years in Kansas City and Myrtle Beach, SC, revealed some Hooters secrets that probably aren't very surprising. Management requires every Hooters girl to squeeze into no

15 www.nbc5.com/news/2964857/detail.html, accessed August 10, 2008.
16 blog.brandexperiencelab.org/experience_manifesto/2005/10/larry_flynt_to_.html
17 64.233.179.104/search?q=cache:Qtw_le3KTBYJ:cgi.cnn.com/US/9512/hooters_eeoc/ +hooters+feminist&hl=en&gl=us&ct=clnk&cd=4, accessed August 10, 2008.
18 www.h-net.org/~women/threads/disc-hooters.html.

bigger than medium shorts. To stay thin on lunch breaks, girls often brought in healthier food such as Subway. Are there weigh-ins? "No," she said. "A couple girls got heavy, but they don't last long. They don't make the tips the small girls make." Which is exactly why waitresses sit down and chat. I remember this happening to me once in a bar in Bangkok. "I only did it to the ones who tipped me good," Wolfram said. "If they tipped good the first time, and I saw their face again, I'd pull them to my section."[19]

I also found the following on the web:

I was a Hooters girl for 5 hours last week. All these years, I thought it was simply a tank top and orange hot pants. No. It's not that simple. To even get into a Hooters tank top, you need help from friends. The material appears to be stretchier than it is, and they have XXS and almost every girl, regardless of the size of her boobs, wears the XXS. I always wanted an official Hooters shirt, but it's not comfortable enough for every day life.

They have regulations.

The nude colored pantyhose are the worst. They're super tight and very thick and compounded in their disgustingness by having to be worn with thick white crunch socks circa 1992. Luckily, the feet are cut off. For those of you that worried about having a girl whose vag was nearly exposed next to your food, the pantyhose ease all those fears. Not a single microbe of DNA can escape these pantyhose. So pull up a chair and order up all the buffalo wings your heart desires. The shorts? Well, those are bright orange and would be cute if you were allowed to wear them one size bigger. But instead, it may just be a requirement that you wear them up your butt even though the "up your butt" look has a big red X through it on the Hooters Regulations poster. Every girl I saw had them up her butt. And most of the girls were telling me to "fold the top of the shorts over" to achieve this look, but I said "No thanks." They sweetened the offer by saying they'd give me a mini apron to put around my waist to hide the camel toe that folding the shorts over would cause. I still said, "No thanks . . ."

Did you know that a Hooters girl is not allowed to have one thing in her hair? Your hair must down and natural. Not a single bobby pin, not a ponytail, nothing. And I thought, but isn't that a health/food violation? No, it's not because Hooters girls don't ever go into the actual kitchen. They just deliver the food to the table of men that stare at your boobs and look at your butt as you walk away. Now, your hair must be all natural but you can wear as much makeup as you like. As a matter of fact, the girl on the regulations poster had on dark lipliner

---

19 www.denverpost.com/food/ci_3303763, accessed August 10, 2008.

and light lipstick. If you're doing that right now, in this day and age, you better steer clear of your windows and doors, duck down because I might come and shoot up your place. Drive-by!

A Hooters girl must wear white athletic shoes, much like the ones that standup comedian dudes always wear. Those aren't so bad when your feet don't hurt after entertaining beer-guzzling patrons all night. Being there for just 5 hours, the job actually appears to be strenuous and hard. I commend a girl that can handle all the emotional and physical tolls all at once. Not only must you just get over the fact that your ass is out while you work with no airbrushing or lighting tricks or glamour or perks like free Merlot or designer shoes, but you must walk around, being all chipper and happy to serve men who would have the nerve to hand you their helmet and then look at you crazy when you didn't take it. One guy did this to me as if I was some kind of coat check whore. I looked at him like he was out of his ****ing mind and then proceeded to say in my most professional voice, "I don't work here" and rolled my eyes, quickly followed by surveying the room to make sure the security man was close by. I wanted to take the helmet and bust him upside his head with it, but I held it all in. What a ****ing ***hole. Granted, I did have the uniform on so it would appear that I did really work there (even though I stuck out like a sore thumb), but even still, a girl that works there shouldn't have to deal with this kind of idiot. Most unfortunate, but it probably comes with the territory.

You can only wear a white or a nude colored bra, and your straps must be hidden. You can't have long nails, no excessive jewelry and no visible tattoos.

The outfit is so constricting, I could feel my insides conjuring up some kind of infection. Yeah, that probably sounds disgusting, but it's true. To be all jacked up for an 8-hour shift with humidity in the air is out of control. It was like wearing a mildly wet bathing suit all day. Gross, I know. But if you're into that, more power to you.[20]

In 1991, Justice David Souter reasoned that nude dancing could be regulated because of the harm of "secondary effects," namely rape, prostitution, increased crime generally, and decreased property values. There are also "secondary effects" of Hooters. In addition, there is the physical and verbal behavior of customers and management at Hooters, behavior that often constitutes sexual harassment, and many of the women are told by Hooters management they are expected to tolerate it. Hooters reinforces the definition of women as compliant, obsequious, subordinate, and valuable only insofar as they are sexually provocative to men. Though women, understandably, choose jobs at Hooters (and places like Hooters) because they can make more money by conceding to the Hooters mentality than they can when they are not participating in prejudicial

20 www.princessmelissa.com/weblog/archives/2003/08/hooters_girl.html.

gender roles, the image of the subordinate, pliant women who exists to please men, dangerously jeopardizes alternative constructions of women as capable, intelligent professionals, and therefore undermines the ability for women generally to get paid for using their intelligence rather than because men enjoy looking at them.

It seems to me that to position Hooters as an entrepreneurial success is not only inconsistent with the celebration of diversity generally, Women's History Month, International Women's Day (ironically March 8), but to Babson's commitment to women's leadership.

Professor Fraser

Professor Okin, could I share this email from you with an MBA student I briefly spoke to about this yesterday? I asked her what she thought about the speaker and she scoffed it off, said she'd often eaten [at Hooters] with friends because the food was cheap, and that the women who work there choose to do so and isn't it good that we're so liberated now that we can enjoy the laugh. Not at all what I would have expected to come out of her mouth—a Wellesley grad no less!

Addendum

From: Hugh H. Connerty
Sent: Wed 7/9/2008 10:46 AM
To: Mary Godwyn
Subject: Re: Hugh Connerty and Hooters

Dear Dr. Godwyn,

Thank you for sharing the study with me.....I have taken the time to review the materials and would like to make the following observations if I may. Please feel free to use any of my thoughts or opinions as you wish. First of all I wanted to say that I completely enjoyed the exchange that took place with the students at Babson. A number of students contacted me after the presentation in the ensuing weeks and I found the dialogue to be most interesting and engaging. Jacob Levinson .....is the young man who contacted me about coming to Babson to speak as a part of the lecture program. I have known Jacob for many years....my son Cameron and Jacob went to school together for a number of years and I have always enjoyed being around Jacob and loved his enthusiasm for business...so when he called and asked if I would come speak.....I said yes. Jacob asked me to come and speak about being an Entrepreneur......would I share my personal experience regarding my career. I have had the opportunity to speak for many years (several times per year) as a guest speaker at Emory University's Goizueta School of Business......about the same topic. My purpose in coming was to do as I have in the past and that is be willing to discuss the more personal side of entrepreneurship....the prices that are sometimes paid for building a company... any company. It is not the easiest thing to do...to stand up and speak about "personal failures" such as alcoholism or parenting.......but I honestly felt that these issues were a relevant and important aspect of life to share with young people who are excited about getting out into the "real" world and testing there own metal.

My involvement with Hooters was a small portion of my overall presentation. Anyone who attended would have to attest to that point.......I have been blessed to enjoy many successes in business and I attribute them all to hard work and living a life of dignity and integrity. .....in fact I emphasized to all that were there ...that they possess the one thing that will prove to be there most important asset in business...there reputation. I am proud of my reputation. What disturbs me about the study is that my name will be featured as the architect of a company who's policies are portrayed to be extremely discriminatory and degrading. It is my feeling that you could not be any further from the truth. Without exception....every example of sexual harassment ..or discrimination took place long after I was no longer a part of the Hooters Company. Yet I am portrayed clearly in your study as if I am the responsible party......perhaps you have read the actual EEOC findings......I certainly have, and as you will note.......I am the ONLY person that was part of Hooters past and present that is NOT named in the findings as having any part of the proposed findings of the EEOC regarding discrimination.

Several references are made by a number of people who responded to you that I was billed as "an entrepreneurial genius".......I would like to make something perfectly clear about this point.......I had nothing to do with this title, I had nothing to do with the posters that were put up around campus or the content of those posters. I can assure you Dr. Godwyn that I am a far more humble man.....I would NEVER tout any achievement of mine as such. Perhaps the student body that extended the invitation should explain such headline billing. Special note was made of the fact that although I have not been associated with Hooters for over a decade....my connection was featured prominently in the campus - wide advertisements. Therefore I must still be "connected" or tied to Hooters??

Although I would consider it an honor to be endorsed by an institution as well respected as Babson as an example of entrepreneurial success.....it certainly disturbs me to think that such an accolade upon me has caused such concern and that furthermore may have tarnished the impeccable reputation that Babson has earned. Once again, I was only asked to come and speak by a student forum....not given any "official" recognition by the institution itself.

When I read such expressions as "real dismay"....."implications and ramifications of the decision to have Connerty here"....."my suspicion"...."I am certainly disturbed to see that an invitation has been extended"......"I can imagine that Connerty loses nothing by dismissing questions that challenge his decisions" ....(most successful people do NOT employ such practices in my opinion).......I must seriously question the open mindedness of those who profess to provide the most open and free exchange of ideas between students who are eager to learn and those that are entrusted with the responsibility to provide real world experiences for honest exchange. Perhaps a more "censored" environment would be more conducive?? Some of your colleagues seemed to be more open minded about this issue......I was certainly encouraged by this. Nothing in my opinion should EVER be presumed regarding what any speaker will do or not do until put to the test. It is my own personal style of leadership to challenge my peers, partners and co workers to shoot holes in any idea presented.....it promotes creative thinking in my opinion.

In your Instructor's manual I took note of the section "Hugh Connerty and Hooters: What is Successful Entrepreneurship? will represent the first shared text for use in business and liberal arts classes." So much is highlighted in the other sections of your study regarding the moral and or offending issues of Hooters...... any "problem" that made its way to the press seemed to be the basis of most comments that were to portray the "dark side"........what I find disturbing is that I was the person who founded Hooters of America.....I was NOT the person who originated the idea "Hooters"....I made this point very clear in my presentation. I identified an idea that I felt American consumers would embrace.....and built an organization around that idea. There is no mention of this very important issue anywhere in your entire body of work. So, I beg the question, is successful entrepreneurship about creating and Idea or can it not also be about taking an already existing idea and building a bigger better mouse trap? If anyone has any leadership skills and can muster the financial backing.....and has an idea that has ALREADY been proven to the public to be successful.......building a company is NOT as difficult as one might think. Fortunately for Arthur Blank and Home Depot.....the "hardware" store concept had been embraced by the American people long before he and Bernie built a better mouse trap.

The Central Ethics Issue: This seems to be the cornerstone question you wish to have students think about. Regrettably in my opinion you have turned the question "Does Hugh Connerty represent the Babson Community's definition of a successful entrepreneur?" into an issue that is completely biased to the business practices of a single company named Hooters. There is no mention of the many other businesses that I have been involved in (and they number many).........How anyone can read what I have read and think that THE CENTRAL ETHICS ISSUE relates to the question you pose about ME representing The definition of successful entrepreneurship and NOT come to the conclusion that this entire study is NOT really about the business life of Hugh Connerty but really his brief tenure at a company that is 25 years old.......(my involvement was from 1984 to 1989) strikes me as being totally and completely unfair as it relates to me and my experiences in life and business as well as the Central Ethics Issue. Perhaps a study should have more appropriately be completed on the subject of Hooters itself...the company and its controversial issues.

Finally, I would like to comment about the issue as it relates to what has been presented in these pages.......I do not understand why no effort was ever made to speak with me about this study and solicit my opinions regarding facts that are presented.....there are numerous errors in fact presented in my opinion. You have taken the liberty to use my name in the title of this study.......I would have given "me" the courtesy of discussing this issue and how you wished to use this tool as "the first shared text for use". For years I was honored to be an invited speaker at Emory University on the subject of Leadership and Entrepreneurial Enterprise......a number of years I was selected by the faculty and students as the "best speaker" ......I find the presentation being put forth here to be unrepresentative of who I am as an entrepreneur......this is NOT a paper that addresses the question "Does Hugh Connerty represent the Babson Community's definition of a successful entrepreneur?"....but more of a dissertation to express the overall disapproval of the Hooters business.

With so many unanswered questions posed by your associates and yourself, I wish to say in closing that I would welcome the opportunity to address them face to face in a forum of your choosing. I have a great deal of respect and admiration for the work done in our many fine universities and support them to the best of my personal ability.......I encourage you as well Dr. Godwyn to continue to explore the boundaries of Ethics in business and wish you much success on your journey thru life.

With Kind Regards,

Hugh H. Connerty Jr.

Discussion questions

1. Should Connerty be allowed to speak at Babson? If so, under what conditions? If not, why not?

2. If Connerty does come to Babson, what questions should he be asked?

3. Does this situation call for changes in Babson policies on speakers? If so, what changes? If not, why not?

4. Babson's marketing of Connerty as an "entrepreneurial genius" can easily be interpreted as an endorsement of Connerty's entrepreneurial

enterprises. How could this affect Babson's brand as the leading entrepreneurship college?

5. As the college that has held the number one spot in entrepreneurship for over a decade, does Babson have a responsibility to define the parameters of what it means to be a "successful entrepreneur"? How should this definition be determined? What is a successful entrepreneur? A successful business?

6. Though there is clearly a range of opinions among women about Hooters and Connerty's visit, if this is not a "women's issue," why were so few men involved in the discussion?

7. As Professor Fraser asked, would Larry Flynt or a weapons dealer also be considered examples of successful entrepreneurs? Why or why not?

8. Is Babson's endorsement of Connerty's entrepreneurial history relevant to International Women's Day, Women's History Month and Babson's commitment to diversity generally?

9. What assumptions did the students in BEE make about why Connerty would be a good speaker? What assumptions did the faculty make about Connerty?

Teaching notes for this case are available from
Greenleaf Publishing. These are free of charge
and available only to teaching staff. They can be
requested by going to:
www.greenleaf-publishing.com/darkside_notes

1.4

Antiquorum Auctioneers
Building brands on ignorance?[1]

Benoit Leleux

The case was designed to discuss a grey zone between ethics and marketing, a common area of contention and debate in modern management theory. How far can marketing go to create perceptions of value in mostly ignorant consumers? What constitutes outright manipulation?

Over the years, many of the most reputed auction houses and galleries have apparently been promoting a strategy in which the producer of the product to be auctioned (cars, premium watches, even modern art pieces) would bid anonymously against other buyers, thus driving the price significantly higher. High prices at auctions would translate into the appearance of a "hot" product, and help drive prices up on the street for the products.

The case is based entirely on documented facts that emerged late in 2007 in Switzerland in the rarefied world of antique watch auctions. In this case, Antiquorum and Omega joined forces in a series of thematic sales which generated record prices for antique Omega watches. The results of the sale were hailed in the watch collector press as extraordinary and served to re-establish the pre-eminence of Omega as a premium watch maker. It later emerged, through a whistleblower during a management coup at the auction house, that the buyer for the most acclaimed pieces was actually . . . the firm Omega itself, supposedly buying pieces for its own museum. Omega's participa-

1 The case was written by Professor Benoit Leleux, with the assistance of Research Associate Nir Berger, as a basis for class discussion rather than to illustrate either effective or ineffective handling of a business situation.

Copyright © 2008 by IMD, International Institute for Management Development, Lausanne, Switzerland. Not to be used or reproduced without written permission directly from IMD.

tion in the auction was of course not known to the participating public, nor was it disclosed later by the auction house or the buyer. The top prices were reported to have been paid by an "anonymous Swiss buyer" . . .

> I do not approve of anything that tampers with natural ignorance. Ignorance is like a delicate exotic fruit; touch it and the bloom is gone.
>
> *The Importance of Being Earnest*, Oscar Wilde (1895)

Auctions have been presented as the ultimate mechanism to sell scarce goods to a public with various means or willingness to pay. From a seller's standpoint, it permits the extraction of the highest value for the goods, with a minimum of strategic gaming. For the buyer, it offers the promise of a fair market, where the dynamics of pricing are for the most part visible. But is this really the case, or have auctions been turned into the most insidious marketing game in town? Have auctioneers created new smoke-and-mirror environments to take naïve investors to ignorance nirvana? Has the essence of auctions been sold to the gurus of brand marketing?

Imagine you fancy a vintage watch, hand-picked from the catalogue of a vintage watches auction and for which you are willing to pay a substantial amount of money. The auction is organized by a most reputable auction house. You travel to Geneva, dress up appropriately and savour the opportunity to mingle with similarly minded enthusiasts, exchanging opinions and views on horology. The auction starts; tension is in the air, you place your initial bid, followed by many others . . . A fierce bidding war erupts, the watch price goes sky-high, eventually making history for the watch manufacturer. The watch finds its new home . . . but it is not yours. A few days later, coincidentally, you find out that the object of all your attention was actually acquired by none other than the watch manufacturer itself, also the organizer of the auction . . . Cynical manipulation? Grand marketing ploy? Unethical perversion of the auction process?

The above storyline is not fiction but reality. In April 2007, at an auction held by the reputable Antiquorum auction house in Geneva, an all-time price record was reached for a timepiece belonging to a brand mostly known as a relatively large producer of timepieces vying to gain some respectability, namely a 1953 Omega Platinum Constellation Grand Luxe watch which fetched the astonishing price of $351,000.[2]

---

2 Connolly, M. (2007) "Auctions' Role in Watch Prices Raise Ethical Concerns", *Wall Street Journal*, 8 October 2007.

1950s Omega watch
sold for **$351,000** at
auction at Antiquorum
last month.
BUYER: Omega

Source: Connolly, M. (2007) "Auctions' Role in Watch Prices
Raise Ethical Concerns", *Wall Street Journal*, October 8, 2007

Source: Antiquorum press release

Watch magazines and retailers hailed the sale. Omega trumpeted it, announcing that a "Swiss bidder"[3] had offered "the highest price ever paid for an Omega
watch at auction". The sale itself, appropriately labelled "Omegamania", was:

> ... organized by the world's leading horological auctioneers Antiquo-
> rum, and generated the total of SFr 6,536,911 ($5,540,000) (€4,010,375),
> selling all 300 lots for three times their presale estimates. Several world
> records were set, including the highest price ever paid for any Omega
> at auction and additionally for a non-complicated self-winding wrist-
> watch.[4]

The specialized press was quick to draw inferences from the auction results.
Osvaldo Patrizzi, founder and chairman of Antiquorum, summarized the buzz:

> Many, many lots doubled, tripled or made ten times and more their
> presale estimates. Two original Speedmasters, the watch that became
> the first and only model ever to be worn on the moon, were sold for 30
> times more than the current retail price ... Omegamania has confirmed
> the arrival of Omega in the top echelon of collectors' brands. Omega's
> most collectable timepieces now join Patek Philippe and Rolex.[5]

---

3 Antiquorum press release, 16 April 2007 (www.antiquorum.com/eng/press/2007/13_04_07/
   p_release_results_eng.htm).
4 Connolly, op. cit.
5 Ibid.

Vincent Ferniot, a renowned French journalist, added the perspective of Omega collectors:

> Omega collectors like me always felt a little discredited by other watch brand collectors. We knew that the prices of our vintage Omega watches were underestimated. From now on we might even be envied. I have been an Omega fan for years and after the weekend in Geneva, I shall now proudly consider myself as a real Omegamaniac.[6]

Stephen Urquhart, president of Omega, would not be left behind:

> We are extremely happy at the outcome of the auction, which exceeded all our expectations. It has shown all watch fans the fantastic richness and scope of the brand and its heritage. Today's auction will remain as a milestone in Omega's history.[7]

FIGURE 1 Auctioneer Osvaldo Patrizzi, president and co-founder of Antiquorum (left), and Stephen Urquhart, president of Omega, at the Omegamania auction, 15 April 2007

Source: www.antiquorum.com

What Omega failed to mention, of course, was that the buyer was Omega itself . . .[8]

---

6 Ibid.
7 Ibid.
8 Connolly, M. (2007) "How Top Watchmakers Intervene in Auctions", *Actualités Horlogères*, 8 October 2007.

Antiquorum Auctioneers

Antiquorum claimed to be the world's leading auction house specializing in the field of horology. Established in Geneva in 1974, Antiquorum had successfully achieved impressive world records for the sale of exclusive "grandes complications"[9] watches, wristwatches, clocks, marine chronometers and regulators at auction. Of the 62 watches ever sold publicly by major auction houses around the globe with auction prices above SFr 1 million ($900,000), Antiquorum claimed an impressive 44 as their own.

To become the undisputed leader of the antique watch auctions, Antiquorum relied on a number of innovations. During the early 1980s, when auctions were relatively rare, Antiquorum, led by Osvaldo Patrizzi, pioneered the presentation of wristwatches at auction, launching also thematic auctions—sales devoted to a single subject.

The first thematic sale was held in 1989, focusing on the "Art of Patek Philippe". It could not have come at a better time since the sale was celebrating the 150th anniversary year of this brand, one of the most prestigious in the watch-making world. Patek Philippe and Antiquorum clearly found the magic formula, with this and subsequent similar sales breaking world records for watch prices.

Since the first Patek Philippe thematic auction, prices for this manufacturer have surged. In 2002, Antiquorum established the all-time world record price for a wristwatch at auction when it sold a (probably . . .) unique 1939 platinum Patek Philippe World Time Reference 1415 for an astounding $4,026,524 (auction costs not included). This record-breaking price more than doubled the previous world record price for a wristwatch at auction (see Exhibit 1).

In 2004, at the 30th anniversary April auction in Geneva, the similarly unique white gold Calibre 89, by Patek Philippe, heralded as the "most complicated watch in the world" sold for $5,002,652, beating the 2002 record (see Exhibit 2). From there on, even more mundane wristwatches would fetch surreal prices (see Exhibit 3 for a Patek Philippe Ref 5712T "Nautilus Titanium").

The Mastermind behind thematic auctions—Osvaldo Patrizzi

Osvaldo Patrizzi, 62 years old, had gone to work at a watch repair shop in Milan at the age of 13 after his father's unfortunate death, dropping out of school. Later in his career Mr Patrizzi moved to Geneva, considered to be the watch-

---

9 Grandes complications—or high-complexity mechanisms—are the summit of the watch-making hierarchy, representing one-of-a kind exceptional feats of micro engineering and innovation. Because of their scarcity and their exceptional workmanship, they represent the equivalents of van Gogh or Manet for impressionist paintings.

making centre of the world, to practice the arts and crafts of watch trading. In the early 1970s, Osvaldo Patrizzi co-founded Galerie d'Horlogerie Ancienne— later to become Antiquorum. At the time, auctions of used watches were rare, in part because it was hard to authenticate them. But Mr Patrizzi, described by his friends as a rare intellectual in a market with many coarser types, knew how to examine the watches' intricate movements and identify whether they were genuine.[10]

Osvaldo Patrizzi struck gold when he discovered a rare defect in a Rolex Daytona owned by Guido Mondani, a book publisher and watch collector. The Rolex's dial was sensitive to ultraviolet rays and could change colour. Mr Patrizzi became an informal adviser to the collector, directing him to interesting pieces to add to his growing collection. He also started to write reference books on collectible watches, books that Mr Mondani was all too happy to publish. Antiquorum eventually ended up auctioning off Mr Mondani's entire Rolex collection in 2006 for about $9.4 million at prevailing exchange rates, close to ten times the pieces' reported original retail prices.

At first, prominent watchmakers were wary. Mr Patrizzi approached Philippe Stern, whose family owns one of the most illustrious brands, Patek Philippe, and proposed a "thematic auction" featuring only Pateks. The pitch: Patek would participate as a seller, helping drum up interest, and also as a buyer. A strong result would allow Patek to market its wares not just as fine watches but as auction-grade works of art. The first Patek auction in 1989 featured 301 old and new watches and fetched some $15 million. Mr Stern became a top Patrizzi client, buying hundreds of Patek watches at Antiquorum auctions, sometimes at record prices. The brand's retail prices soared. Over the next decade, the company began charging about $10,000 for relatively simple models and more than $500,000 for limited-edition pieces with elaborate functions known in the watch world as "complications".[11]

Patek began promoting its watches as long-term investments.

> You never actually own a Patek Philippe. You merely look after it for the next generation.[12]

Mr Stern said he bid on used Patek watches as part of a plan to open a company museum in 2001. Building that collection, he said, was key to preserving and promoting the watchmaker's heritage, the brand's most valuable asset with consumers. "Certainly, through our action, we have been raising prices," he admitted.[13] Auctions gradually became recognized as marketing tools. Brands ranging from mass producers like Rolex and Omega to limited production names

10 Connolly, M. (2007) "How Top Watchmakers Intervene in Auctions", *Actualités Horlogères*, 8 October 2007.
11 Ibid.
12 Patek Philippe advertisement
13 Connolly, M. (2007) "Auctions' Role in Watch Prices Raise Ethical Concerns", *Wall Street Journal*, 8 October 2007.

like Audemars Piguet and Gerald Genta flocked to the auction market with Antiquorum and other houses. Cartier and Vacheron Constantin, both owned by the Compagnie Financière Richemont SA luxury goods group in Geneva, also starred in separate single-brand auctions organized by Mr Patrizzi.

"Patek opened a lot of doors for us, but we also opened a lot of doors for Patek," said Mr Patrizzi.[14]

Brands began to vie for his attention, sending Mr Patrizzi watch prototypes to assess and, they hoped, occasionally wear. They hired his assistants at Antiquorum as their auction buyers, cementing ties. "He was a kind of spiritual father for me," says Arnaud Tellier,[15] who worked under Mr Patrizzi before becoming Patek's main auction buyer and director of the Patek museum.

The auction game you cannot lose

The Omega name appeared in 1894 when it was trademarked. The brand—easy to read and equally easy to pronounce in nearly every major language throughout the world—gradually supplanted other brands and became up until the 1970s, as prestigious as Rolex in the eyes of collectors and consumers alike. Omega built a reputation for providing innovative watch mechanisms in famous series such as the "Constellation" or the "Speedmaster". It also received worldwide recognition for becoming the Winter Olympics' stopwatches provider of choice, forever associating its name with leading sportsmen and their achievements.

During the 1980s, confronted with massive imports of cheap electronic quartz watches from Asia making inroads into its markets, Omega completely re-engineered its strategy. It closed most of its production facilities of fine mechanical watches,[16] for which Switzerland was famed, and developed leading-edge, quartz-based electronic watches. This choice of strategy, which dragged the brand down-market, would tarnish its image for generations. When it became clear that competing in the quartz world would only inflict pain and suffering, Omega decided to return to its roots by reintroducing high-end mechanical models, hoping to revive its brand . . . but with limited success. Collectors had clearly longer memories than watchmakers. Omega was desperate to find original ways to rebuild its foregone lustre.

When Omega and Antiquorum joined forces in the end of 2004, Mr Patrizzi definitely seemed to have a plan in mind . . .

14 Ibid.
15 Ibid.
16 The most prestigious mechanical watch factories are referred to as "manufactures".

> The choice of Omega is obviously not by chance. For quite a while we have discussed, amongst ourselves, the historical and technological merits of this manufacturer, which can be easily compared to that of the "sophisticated" collectors' brands . . . It is our contention that many of these facts have gone unnoticed by the majority of collectors. This hypothesis was confirmed when we tried to find a comparable brand to Omega; we found a strong parallel between Omega's and Rolex's products.[17]

Mr Patrizzi brought to Omega a proven formula, one that did marvels boosting Patek Philippe to the pinnacle of mechanical horology. When buyers saw antique Patek Philippe watches fetch extraordinary prices at auction, they inferred that the brand appreciated over time, very much like a good investment. Auctions, by providing the appearance of liquidity in the market for antique premium watches, very much validated the product as an asset class in itself, one with solid return potential, not unlike other "trophy goods", such as diamonds, supercars, vintage property wines, etc. So paying $225,000 for a brand new Grande Complication Patek made complete sense if it would command a nice premium ten years later.

To bring back Omega's brand from its death bed required shock treatment. And Mr Patrizzi knew how to administer it. The first Omega thematic sale came to the industry as a surprise, as explained by Augostino Veroni, one of the most revered Italian horological journalists:

> The Omega thematic auction came as a surprise, for, apart from a few rare exceptions, the brand had not been a favourite of collectors, who had tended to prefer the usual group of brands found at all auctions.[18]

But for the treatment to really cure the patient, the watches on offer had to fetch mind-boggling prices, which could then be converted into higher retail prices for contemporary Omega models. Apart from a very careful selection of pieces offered for sale and a superior communication job to present these pieces and attract both the rich and famous and the biggest world collectors, it seemed difficult to guarantee prices in the auction. Unless one was willing to "organize" the auctions a bit more . . .

---

17 Interview with Osvaldo Patrizzi, Antiquorum Omegamania, by Augustino Veroni, January 2007.
18 Ibid.

Reinventing auctions or unethical marketing?

As any luxury goods manufacturer knew, one of the pillars of premium pricing was to wisely manage the supply in such a way that equilibrium would not be reached. Maintaining a supply shortage was the traditional key to "creaming" a market.

Some luxury brands, such as Ferrari, did one better on the shortage storyline. Not only did they keep production low (below 5,000 cars a year in that case), even if that led to 3–5 year waiting periods for new cars, but they also gave "priority rights" in the queue to existing Ferrari owners. In other words, two queues were effectively in effect at all times: one for esteemed owners of a Ferrari car and one for first-time buyers. One sure way to jump the second queue (and often save 1–3 years on the waiting period) was to get a hold of a second-hand Ferrari. So supply shortages on new cars led to shortages on the second-hand market as well, where even non-functioning cars were guaranteed high valuations.

The question for Omega was a bit more complex. Omega was part of the Swatch Group (see Exhibit 4 for a short history of the Swatch Group), the largest watch producer in the world with a global market share in excess of 25%. Omega was the crown jewel in the Swatch galaxy, representing 32% of the total sales and generating earnings before interest and tax (EBIT) margins of close to 47% (see Exhibit 5 for the Swatch Group sales mix and Exhibit 6 for traditional watch market price segmentation). The group had spent a fortune marketing itself around the world. Organizing a real production shortage did not seem like an enticing proposition, and did not guarantee a strengthened brand image. Clearly, a lot more would have to be done to build credibility as a premium producer . . .

The business of auctions for collectibles was not a model of transparency. The identities of most bidders were often known only to the auction houses themselves. Sellers commonly put "reserve" or minimum prices, and, when the bidding was stuck below that level, it was common for the auctioneer to anonymously bid the prices up on the seller's behalf. Ramping up the value of merchandise on offer made sense for the auctioneers for a number of reasons. First and foremost, their fees were set as a percentage of the sales price. Second, the specialized press would often evaluate the "success" of a particular auction by how much it surpassed the estimated total sales estimates. To the extent that the pre-auction price ranges often came from the specialists retained by the auction houses themselves to organize the auction catalogues, it seemed relatively easy to underestimate the initial price range . . . only to boost it during the sale itself and create the impression of a booming market for the auctioned items.

Auctions provided the silver bullet Omega had been looking for. Instead of letting the ever unpredictable "market" set the price in the auctions, Omega decided to get into the bidding action for its own account. But of course doing so anonymously . . . To build interest, Mr Patrizzi and Omega officials travelled to 11 cities, hosting events such as a party at the Beverly Wilshire Hotel with celebrities such as actors Charlie Sheen and Marcia Gay Harden. Antiquorum and Omega joined in publishing the huge, glossy auction catalogue. When the sale, dubbed "Omegamania", took place in April 2007, it was shown on jumbo screens at the Basel World watch fair and streamed live on the Internet for online bidding. It brought in $5.5 million. Besides the $351,000 platinum watch, Omega outbid collectors on 46 other lots, including many of the most expensive. Mr Patrizzi estimated Omega bid on 80 lots in all, out of 300 (see Exhibit 7 for some of the company-purchased watches).

A Singaporean collector, told of Omega's role, called it "heinous". Melvyn Teil-lol-Foo, who bid over the Internet and bought a few pricey watches, added: "If it turns out they bid against me and got me to $8,000, I would be ticked off."[19]

> The auction is boosting retail demand just as Omega is introducing pricier models. My top-selling Omegas used to be $1,400 models, but Omegas costing three times that are selling now. Customers are conscious of the fact that an Omega watch sold for $300, 000 at auction, but they have no idea who bought it.[20]

Omega, in its defence, said it was buying the watches for its museums (the same argument was used earlier by Patek Philippe). Omega's president, Stephen Urquhart, said:

> The company is not hiding the fact that Omega anonymously bid and bought at auctions. Omega bought the watches so it could put them in its museum in Bienne, Switzerland. We didn't bid for the watches just to bid. We bid because we really wanted them. [21]

An opposing ethical view is expressed by an industry leader, Georges-Henri Meylan, chief executive of Audemars Piguet SA, a high-end Swiss watchmaker:

> A lot of the public doesn't know that the biggest records have been made by the companies themselves. That is a bit dangerous.[22]

---

19 Connolly, M. (2007) "Auctions' Role in Watch Prices Raise Ethical Concerns", *Wall Street Journal*, 8 October 2007.
20 Steven Goldfarb, Seattle watch retailer.
21 "Message from Stephen Urquhart, President of Omega", Antiquorum Omegamania press release, January 2007.
22 Connolly, M. (2007) "Auctions' Role in Watch Prices Raise Ethical Concerns", *Wall Street Journal*, 8 October 2007.

Opening the Pandora's box

These auction practices would have never emerged into public scrutiny were it not for power struggles and internal conflicts within Antiquorum Auctioneers. On 2 August 2007, Antiquorum's board noted Mr Patrizzi out of his chairman and chief executive positions. His lieutenants were forbidden to enter the Geneva headquarters and were also relieved from their executive roles.

On 8 October 2007, the *Wall Street Journal* summarized the internal strife as follows:

> Named interim chief was Yo Tsukahara, an executive at Artist House Holdings, a Tokyo company that owns 50% of Antiquorum. Artist House then formed a different Antiquorum board. Mr Tsukahara hired auditors from PricewaterhouseCoopers to scour Antiquorum computers, financial records and inventory.
>
> Mr Patrizzi's "thematic auctions" for a single brand of watches weren't an issue, Mr Tsukahara says in an interview. They were a "win-win" situation.
>
> Mr Patrizzi's relations with Artist House had been worsening for a year. One issue was his resistance to adopting more rigorous accounting in compliance with the Tokyo Stock Exchange. Mr Patrizzi opposed an Artist House push to replace Antiquorum's accountants, according to Leo Verhoeven, a Patrizzi ally and an executive at Habsburg Feldman, a Geneva company that owns 43% of the auction house.

Auction or manipulation?

Through the auctions, Swiss watchmakers had found a solution to a challenge shared by makers of luxury products from jewellery to fashion: getting their wares perceived as things of extraordinary value, worth an out-of-the-ordinary price. When an Omega watch can be sold decades later for more than its original price, shoppers for new ones will be readier to pay up.

> If you can get a really good auction price, it gives the illusion that this might be a good buy. [23]

Niche watchmakers had used the auction market for years to raise their profiles and prices, mainly among collectors. As mainstream brands like Omega embraced auctions, increasing numbers of consumers were affected by the higher prices.

Real questions remained:

23 Al Armstrong, watch retailer.

- Are auction manipulations of the type used by some watchmakers just another sophisticated marketing ploy, not better or worse than many other means to influence people's perception of the value of goods?

- Would it make sense to require the disclosure of the buyers' identities when conflicts of interest are evident? Clearly, this would be a two-edged sword. If it was public knowledge that Omega was bidding on a rare Omega watch for its own museum collection, it could either (1) kill the auction cold if other participants anticipate that they cannot win against the deep pockets of the Swatch Group or (2) offer the watch seller opportunities to bid the price up in the knowledge that the buyer is willing to go to extreme levels.

- The willingness of the watchmaker to pay higher prices is linked to company-specific externalities, i.e. the known impact a high price at auction has on the perceived value of watches from the brand today as investments. As such, these externalities are public knowledge and should be incorporated by the public. The price paid for the watch is a combination of the intrinsic value of the watch and the pricing benefits derived by the watchmaker as buyer.

- If auctions were to be further controlled, what would prevent those antique watches to be sold through private transactions, where the reported transaction prices communicated to the specialized press are even more fallacious and often have no connection to reality?

Ignorance is indeed a very delicate exotic fruit . . .

EXHIBIT 1 The 1939 platinum Patek Philippe World Time Reference 1415

No. 929693

Case No. 656462, Ref. 1415 HU (Heures Universelles). Extremely rare and probably unique platinum "World Time" gentleman's wristwatch with a platinum Patek Philippe buckle. Accompanied by original fitted box and the Extract of the Archives.

Patek Philippe & Cie, Genève, No. 929693, case No. 656462, Ref. 1415 HU (Heures Universelles). Production of this reference started in 1939. Extremely rare and probably unique platinum "World Time" gentleman's wristwatch with a platinum Patek Philippe buckle. Accompanied by original fitted box and the Extract of the Archives.
C. three-body, solid, polished and brushed, hand-engraved revolving reeded bezel bearing the names of 41 cities in the world, teardrop faceted lugs. D. matte silver with applied white gold Arabic numerals, concentric, revolving dial in 24 hours for the nocturnal and diurnal hours. White gold fancy hands. M. Ca 12'''-400 HU, rhodium-plated, "fausses côtes" decoration, 18 jewels, lever escapement, cut bimetallic balance adjusted for heat, cold isochronism and 5 positions, Breguet balance spring, micrometer regulator. Dial, case and movement signed. Diam. 31 mm.

EXHIBIT 2 White gold Calibre 89 Patek Philippe, the "most complicated watch in the world"

Patek, Philippe, Genève. The most complicated watch in the world with a total of 33 complications. A spectacular and unique, keyless three-barrel, double dial, astronomical and astrological 18K white gold watch with sidereal time, second time-zone, time of sun-rise and sun-set, equation of time, perpetual calendar, century leap year correction, century, decade and year indication, four year cycle indication, season, equinox, solstice and zodiac indication, star chart, phases and age of the moon, date of Easter indication, split-seconds chronograph, hour and minute recorders, Westminster chime on four gongs, "Grande and Petite sonnerie", alarm, up/down indicators for the going and striking train, three way setting indicator, winding crown position indicator, thermometer and Tourbillon regulator. Accompanied by an Extract from the Archives and a fitted hardwood box.

C. four-body, "bassine", polished. D. Front: cream with applied white gold Breguet numerals, retrograde date sector, hour and minute recording dials combined with the power reserve sectors for the going and striking trains, moon phase, year, month, day and four year cycle apertures, second time-zone, thermometer, winding-crown position indicator, alarm indicator, outer 1/5th seconds scale with five minute/seconds red Arabic markers and subsidiary constant seconds. Blued steel and white gold hands. Back: Silvered with hours of sidereal time, date of Easter sector, sun-rise and sun-set dials, subsidiary sidereal seconds, equaeion of time sector, sun hand and aperture for the star chart. Blued steel and white gold hands. M. Cal. 89, three-barrels on four levels, maillechort, 600grams. "fausses côtes" decoration, 126 jewels, 1728 parts straight-line lever escapement, Gyromax balance, blued-steel Breguet balance spring, adjusted to heat, cold, isochronism and five positions, tourbillon regulator. Dial side main plate: mechanisms for the chime, alarm, 12-hour recorder and the power reserve indicators, the. Reverse main plate, mechanisms for mean time, the chronograph, the 30-minute recorder and the tourbillon regulator. Plate 2: mechanisms for sidereal time, the season, solstices, equinoxes and solstice, the times of sunrise and set, the equation of time, the date of easter and the star chart. Plate 3: the mechanisms for the secular perpetual calendar, the second time-zone, the phases and age of the moon and the thermometer. Dial, case and movement signed. Diam. 88.2mm, 41.07mm thick (with the crystals), total weight 1100 grams

EXHIBIT 3 Lot 26 at Only Watch Auction, Monaco Yacht Show, 20 September 2007, €725,000

Source: Antiquorum auction website (catalog.antiquorum.com)

LOT 26

Patek Philippe, Ref 5712T "Nautilus Titanium", Genève, Pièce Unique.

Patek Philippe Ref. 5712T-001 wristwatch in titanium. Caliber 240 PS IRM C LU. Self-winding. Date. Moon phases and power-reserve indication. Seconds subdial. Sapphire-crystal case back. Water resistant to 60 m. After its thirty-year success story, the NAUTILUS watch has become a cult object among the brand's collectors and enthusiasts. As a guardian of a long-standing tradition and as a model of technical and aesthetic innovation, this exceptional timepiece was entirely crafted in titanium for this occasion. At the heart of this complicated NAUTILUS beats the self-winding Caliber 240 featuring subsidiary seconds, a power-reserve indicator and a calendar with moon phases. The movement can be admired through the sapphire-crystal case back. The epitome of casual elegance, this unique watch features a two-tone rhodium and charcoal-gray dial with an embossed horizontal relief pattern accented by luminescent "baton" hour markers. This timepiece also stands out with its saddle-stitch rubber strap and its double-security titanium fold-over clasp. It is water resistant to 60 meters and, as the original advertising campaign emphasized, it "works as well with a wet suit as it does with a dinner suit."

Estimate: On request

Grading system

| C | 1 | D | 1 | M | 1 | *A* |

Click here for written condition report

EXHIBIT 4 Omega and the Swatch Group: a short history

Source: company website and annual report

The Swatch Group Ltd is a Swiss company and the biggest watch manufacturer in the world, with a global market share estimated at about 25%. It was formed in 1983 through the merger of the two Swiss watch manufacturers, ASUAG and SSIH, and took its present name in 1998. The Group employs more than 20,000 people in over 50 countries. Gross sales in 2006 increased by +12.3% from the previous year to SFr 5.05 billion, net profits by +33.7% to SFr 830 million. In 2007, gross sales were reported at SFr 5.94 billion.

SSIH originated in 1930 with the merger of the Omega and Tissot companies. Swiss watch quality was high, but new technology such as the Hamilton Electric watch introduced in 1957 and the Bulova Accutron tuning fork watch introduced in 1961 presaged increasing high technology competition. In the late 1970s, SSIH became insolvent due to a global recession and heavy competition from inexpensive Asian-made quartz crystal watches. Although it had become Switzerland's largest and the world's third largest producer of watches, the creditor banks assumed control in 1981. ASUAG, formed in 1931, included the Longines and Rado brands. ASUAG was the world's largest producer of watch movements but was caught in the same maelstrom in 1982. SSIH and ASUAG were reorganized and merged into the ASUAG-SSIH Holding Company in 1983, then taken private in 1985 by CEO Nicholas Hayek, who was born and raised in Lebanon, and renamed SMH in 1986, and ultimately Swatch Group in 1998.

The launch of the new Swatch brand in 1983 was marked by bold new styling and design. The quartz watch was redesigned for manufacturing efficiency, with fewer parts involved. This combination of marketing and manufacturing expertise restored Switzerland as a major player in the world wristwatch market.

The Swatch Group operates 156 production centres, primarily in Switzerland, but also in France, Germany, Italy, Thailand, Malaysia and China. Active in the manufacture of finished watches, jewellery, and watch movements and components, the Group produces nearly all of the components necessary to supply its 18 watch brand companies and the entire Swiss watch-making industry, and operates its own worldwide network of distribution organizations. The Swatch Group is also a key player in the electronic systems sector.

It offers watches in all price categories, with leadership positions in most market segments:

- Breguet, Blancpain and Glashütte-Original at the very top end
- Léon Hatot, Jaquet-Droz, Omega, Longines, Rado and Union in the luxury market
- Tissot, ck Calvin Klein, Certina, Mido, Hamilton and Pierre Balmain in the mid-range market
- Swatch and Flik Flak in the broad consumer segment
- Endura in private label watches

Sports timing and measurement technologies, although not a core business, play a key role in terms of brand and Group visibility—a number of Swatch Group companies serve as official timekeepers at a variety of international sports events, including the Olympic Games.

The 16 brands of the Swatch Group are presented below.

EXHIBIT 5 Sales mix at Swatch Group

Source: Bottger, P. (2006) "Nicolas G. Hayek and the Swiss Watch Industry: Business Leadership over Two Decades" (IMD-3-1648; IMD International).

	Sales mix	EBIT
Low price segment (inc. Swatch)	24%	7%
Medium price segment	15%	15%
Prestige watches (excl. Omega)	29%	31%
Omega	32%	47%

EXHIBIT 6 Price segmentation and competitors in the watch industry

Source: Turpin, D. (2006) "Relaunching the Alpina Brand: High Precision Watches since 1883" (IMD-5-0713, IMD International).

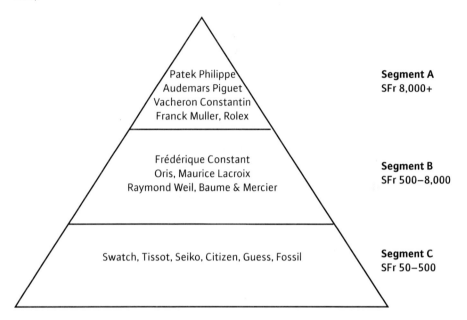

EXHIBIT 7   Timepieces that have gone at auctions

Source: Connolly, M. (2007) "Auctions' Role in Watch Prices Raise Ethical Concerns", *Wall Street Journal*, 8 October 2007.

Going Once ... Going Twice ...

Some examples of the timepieces that have gone at auction

1939 Patek Philippe Platinum Minute Repeater*, sold at an Antiquorum auction for **$1,658,730**. **BUYER:** Philippe Stern, owner Patek Philippe

1923 "Officier"gold Patek Philippe wristwatch sold for **$1,918,387** at an Antiquorum auction. **BUYER:** Middle Eastern Collector

A 1930s Patek Philippe platinum wristwatch sold for **$228,900** at an Antiquorum auction. **BUYER:** Philippe Stern, owner Patek Philippe

Eugène D. Hirsch Patek Philippe wristwatch sold at an Antiquorum auction for approximately **$350,000**. **BUYER:** Philippe Stern, owner Patek Philippe

Triple date Patek Philippe wristwatch sold at an Antiquorum auction for **$1,169,555**. **BUYER:** Philippe Stern, owner Patek Philippe

Patek Philippe 18K gold wristwatch sold by auction house Phillips de Pury & Co for **$1,911,770**. **BUYER:** Philippe Stern, owner Patek Philippe

1950s Omega watch sold for **$351,000** at auction at Antiquorum last month. **BUYER:** Omega

Photos: Patek Philippe Museum unless otherwise noted   *NOTE: Picture does not depict original platinum band

Discussion questions

1. As a recent buyer of a prestige Omega watch, how would you react to the publication of the fact that the inflated Omega watch prices at a recent auction were essentially the result of Omega buying its own watches?

2. As a bidder in the auction, who ended up losing in a bidding war to Omega, how would you feel?

3. Was Omega's behaviour unethical? If so, what aspects of the behaviour would you label unethical and why? Or was this simply sophisticated, if aggressive, marketing to build a brand?

4. Can the practice of shilling be supported? Why has it been declared illegal in many locations?

5. What aspect of the story did you find most disturbing? Why?

6. Could the behaviours observed and documented be reconciled with normal marketing practices? Are they any worse than other tactics to build up the buzz around a brand? What other tactics would you put in the same category?

7. Where are the limits of ethical marketing? When is marketing overstepping its bounds and bordering on manipulation? Is marketing inherently manipulative since it aims to change your perceptions of products and purchasing behaviour?

8. Once the information became public, how should Omega have reacted?

9. Do you perceive the material in the case as indicating a need to change auction rules? What would be the costs and benefits of requiring disclosure of the parties' names?

Teaching notes for this case are available from Greenleaf Publishing. These are free of charge and available only to teaching staff. They can be requested by going to:
www.greenleaf-publishing.com/darkside_notes

1.5

The Lidl international career opportunity
From dream to nightmare in eight weeks[1]

Matt Bladowski and Rosemary A. McGowan

This case chronicles the experiences of Matt Sosnowski, a management trainee with Lidl, a German-based European food discounter. Matt, a multilingual business school graduate accepted a management training position with Lidl on the understanding that, within two years, he would be part of the executive team in Lidl's planned Canadian expansion. The culture and work load at Lidl were extremely harsh; working weeks of 80–100 hours, an autocratic culture marked by mistrust and disrespect for employees (and customers), and a failure by the organization to procure a visa for Matt's bride, Larisa, created a hostile work environment. Written primarily in the first person, the case provides students with an opportunity to assess how Matt found himself in this situation, to analyze the organizational cultural and structural factors that contributed to the hostile work environment, and to develop a plan of action for Matt.

The case has four primary objectives.

First, the case provides students with an opportunity to assess the interview and hiring approach at Lidl. The students can also consider the factors that drove Matt to accept the management training position, despite some reservations.

Second, the students can analyze the organizational culture of Lidl, an organization with troubling employment practices. Students can identify the strengths and limitations of the bureaucratic control mechanisms at Lidl, as well as the strengths and limitations of mechanistic organizational structures.

Third, students can discuss how Matt makes sense of his experiences during the training period. The case provides numerous examples of Matt's attempts to understand his situation and to develop an understanding of the organization's procedures. Students can address the question of what motivates Matt to stay with Lidl.

Finally, the case gives students the opportunity to put themselves in Matt's position and identify alternative courses of action and, perhaps more importantly, to identify a plan of action.

Introduction

It was a dream come true for Matt Sosnowski. In October, 2003, Matt had been chosen as a candidate for the management training program at Lidl[2]—a giant German food discounter with plans to expand into the Canadian market. As a management trainee, Matt was offered a salary and benefits package worth almost C$100,000. During the training period all of Matt's living expenses would be covered including accommodation, meals, an Audi A6 (including weekly car washes, gas, and repairs), and a return flight to Canada every six months. Matt was told that after a two-year intensive training period he would return to Canada to assume an executive position in Lidl's planned Canadian operations. It was the opportunity of a lifetime.

By the end of January 2004, the dream management training program was becoming a nightmarish test of endurance and wills. Matt found Lidl extremely autocratic. From his perspective, the company used a demoralizing approach to people management. He had seen even the most minor of mistakes severely and publicly punished. Grueling 90–100 hour work weeks were the norm. The most difficult issue for Matt to cope with, however, was the company's promise to secure a visa for his wife so that she could join him for the duration of the training period. The visa never materialized. Demoralized, exhausted, and frustrated Matt was faced with the decision—to stay or to resign?

---

2 The employee names have been disguised.

Matt Sosnowski

Pursuing a career in international business was Matt's passion. Matt grew up in Poland and spent almost two years in Germany before coming to Canada at age 11. Matt completed three years of the BBA program at Wilfrid Laurier University (Waterloo, Ontario). He then worked for two months in Germany before completing his bachelor's degree at the University of Alicante in Spain. In December 2000, only a few months after graduation, Matt landed a market research/sales job with a German company which allowed him to travel around the world. Already fluent in Polish, German, Spanish, and English, Matt learned French, Portuguese, and Italian. At 24 years of age Matt was on top of the world. Every month he was on a different continent gaining priceless international experience. Not to mention the fact he was back in Europe with 40 days of paid vacations and two flights home to Canada a year. While studying at Laurier, Matt met and fell in love with Larisa, a dentist who had come to Canada from Colombia to study English for a month. He was looking for somebody to help him practice his Spanish and she was looking for someone to help her with her English. Not long after they met, Larisa returned to Colombia and Matt was getting ready for his final year in Spain. They did not see each other for 16 months, but kept in touch. Over the next three years Matt and Larisa would see each other twice a year, summer vacation and Christmas holidays, and each time they traveled— through Europe, Colombia, or North America.

Matt spent 2½ years working in Germany. His plans to have Larissa work in Germany did not work out. Matt resigned his job in Germany in order to get married in Colombia and bring his bride to Canada to start a new life together. Quitting that job was a difficult decision, but Matt was convinced that he made the right choice. Leaving Germany was even more difficult. He was leaving a job he loved, and leaving Europe meant that he was giving up the opportunity to work in a multilingual environment.

In May 2003 Matt and Larisa came to Canada. Starting over in Canada was not an easy task. Matt believed that his experience in international business and language skills would land him at least a middle-management-level job. After three months of searching, Matt was still unemployed. He was stuck in a trap between being overqualified and underqualified, and the only jobs he was getting were in the fields of door-to-door sales, insurance sales, and telemarketing. Despite having over three years of international business experience Matt was forced to dramatically lower his salary expectations. In August 2003, Matt finally secured a position with a company he liked. It paid $36,000, less than a half of what he was making three years ago when he first graduated. Doing phone interviews was not his favorite activity, but it gave him the opportunity to use his foreign language skills. Meanwhile, Matt kept his eyes open for other opportunities.

The Lidl opportunity

It was late October when Matt found a posting on the Internet:

- A large German food discounter is looking to expand to Canada. We are looking for young and energetic individuals to be area managers. There will be a two-year training period in Germany, and upon completion the candidates will receive a substantial increase in salary

- We offer a very high salary and a car for the duration of your training. Upon the return to Canada, the candidates will also have a company vehicle

- Requirements:
  - A completed university degree
  - Knowledge of German a must. French an asset
  - No previous experience necessary. We will train

Matt did a quick check on the Internet and learned that the grocery discounter, Lidl Stiftung Lp., was Germany's second largest retailer. Their stores are comparable in size to Shoppers Drug Mart. By 2003 there were approximately 5,600 stores employing 80,000 people throughout Europe with half of them in Germany. Lidl offers a limited range of good-quality products at a low price. Lidl was planning an aggressive expansion to Canada—400 stores in Quebec and Ontario in the first few years. They were planning to offer a hybrid between large grocery stores (Zehrs, No Frills, Dominion) and convenience stores. Lidl sought Canadians who spoke German to fill key management positions.

Matt emailed his resume to the company. Lidl scheduled an interview for early November.

The interview: November 10th—Mississauga

Matt recalled his feelings as he drove to the interview.

Was I nervous? No way, I was too excited to be nervous. There were two things I was sure of: I had the qualifications they were looking for, and there was no one who wanted this job more than I did. My international experience and my knowledge of foreign languages, things that seemed of little value to Canadian employers, were finally going to be recognized. The opportunity to live and work in Europe was very attractive.

Shortly after he arrived at Lidl's offices in Mississauga, just west of Toronto, Matt was greeted by two tall men in their 40s.

"Herr Sosnowski, Guten Tag. Ich bin Herr Backer." *(Mr Sosnowski, good day. I am Mr. Backer).*

The entire interview was conducted in German. Precise, professional, and straight to the point—just the way I recall the German approach to business. They only asked me three questions: "Why I want to work for Lidl? What was my previous work experience? How soon could I start?"

The entire interview lasted 25 minutes. I asked them specifics about the company and the training program. I didn't ask about the weekly hourly commitment, I didn't think it was an appropriate question for an initial interview. Besides, Germany has very strict laws that prohibit employment of over 50 hours per week.

It was a two-year management training program. In year one, I would be a store employee (six weeks), a store manager (two months), involved in general training in the areas of purchasing, sales, and marketing (two months), substituting store manager (two months), and, finally, area manager (five months). In year two, I would be involved in training at the headquarters in Neckarsulm. This portion of the program was unique to the Canadian trainees since I would be one of Lidl's Canadian pioneers.

Four days after the interview there was a contract in my email inbox. After carefully studying the contract, I had no doubt this was the job of a lifetime. A week and a half later I was back in the same office in Mississauga to discuss employment details.

Herr Gopp, the vice-president of Lidl Canada welcomed me with a firm handshake. He had a stack of papers ready for me to sign.

"In Germany you will be given an Audi A6. All expenses for the car including gas, repairs, carwash are paid by the company. In Germany we will provide you with a hotel where you can stay for the duration of your work. If you want to move to an apartment you may, and the company will pay for it. We will give you an additional $60/day (tax-free) to spend on food or whatever else you need to buy. Any other expenses, including phone (for business purposes), medical expenses etc. you will pay, and send us a receipt and we will reimburse you. Two times a year a company will pay for a return trip to Canada. Any questions?"

"Herr Gopp," I started. "I am married and would like my wife to come with me for the duration of my contract. Do you foresee any difficulties?"

"Herr Sosnowski, that's your life, you can do whatever you wish. She can come, but Lidl will not cover any of her costs."

"That's understandable. The problem, though, is that she is a landed immigrant from Colombia. I've already found out how to apply for her visa, but I know it can take some time. I know from experience that if Lidl applies for visas for my wife and I at the same time it will be a much easier and faster process. I will of course cover all of her costs."

"Don't worry about it. We have advisors in Germany and they will take care of it."

"OK, thank you. So when am I flying out, so that I can make a reservation for her?"

"You will be flying out on November 28th at 16.00. Here is your flight schedule. There will be a car waiting for you at the airport."

"But that's in 12 days! I haven't resigned my job yet."

Of course I wasn't going to quit my job until I was 100% sure I was going. And besides, from experience I know that it can take a company a few months to get a work visa for a potential employee. That's why I was surprised with such a quick turnaround. I didn't understand the rush, but I did not question it.

"Herr Sosnowski, you said you could start in two weeks. We have a training program already for you in place and we need you there starting December 1st. Here is the airline ticket. If you can't make it, we'll find somebody else who can."

"I understand Herr Gopp. I will be on that plane. Please do your best with your advisors so that my wife can join me soon."

"Don't worry. There are people from many countries that come for the training in Germany. Our people have dealt with much more complicated issues. This is their full-time job."

I left the meeting with mixed feelings, I liked my current employer but I was very happy about going to Germany. I still didn't know where exactly in Germany I was going, but with a fast car and autobahns without speed limits, I couldn't be any further than six hours from my beloved Düsseldorf. I was going to be back in Europe, again be able to use all my language skills and this time I will be with Larisa. And, above all, this was a beginning of an amazing career. This is the break I was looking for. The fact that the total package was worth close to $100,000/year was a bonus.

Departure for Germany: Friday November 28th, 2003

"Was möchten Sie zum Trinken?" (*What would you like to drink?*)

"Coke with red wine" (this was also known as Calimocho—a popular drink in southern Spain). To my left sat Anas. We met earlier this morning in Mississauga, and he too was going to Germany for the training. Anas was going to work in Stuttgart, and I to Hermeskeil, a small town between Saarbrucken and Trier. I was happy with my location. Being close to the French border meant going to France whenever I wanted and practicing French. We both thought it was odd that they were in such a rush to send us to Germany. And at the same time they waited until the day of the flight to tell us where we were going. We knew that this program involved more Canadians, but any further details were secret. We agreed this was not a typical behavior for German companies, but we were too excited to worry.

The Lidl experience: week 1

Monday, December 1st—Neckarsulm

In the morning I drove to the Lidl's head office. The building was impressive. The parking lot was full of beautiful new cars, almost all of them Audis. When I entered the building I noticed that everyone was impeccably dressed in expensive suits and polished shoes. "This is where I will make a career," I said to myself. I was ready to give 100%, no matter the cost. Larisa and I agreed that the following two years were an investment in our future. Ms. Langnbruner, my boss's assistant, took my passport and my contract and told me to come back the next day. It was 8.03 in the morning and I had a whole day to myself.

Tuesday, December 2nd—Neckarsulm

It was 8.00 am and I was ready to meet my boss. Instead, his assistant Ms. Langnbruner greeted me. She told me that my work visa has not been issued yet, and that I needed to come back the following day. They were in such a rush to get me over to Germany and they don't even have a work visa for me? Why were they in such a rush? Ms. Langnbruner told me I would need to move to a different hotel; my hotel was fully booked for that evening. Upon returning to the hotel (ten minutes later) there was a message on my phone from Ms. Langnbruner to call her back and tell her if I already found another hotel. "What's the rush? It's not like I won't find another hotel by myself." I stepped out for a few minutes and when I returned there were three more messages from Ms. Langnbruner and the phone was ringing—it was Ms. Langnbruner.

Wednesday, December 3rd—Neckarsulm

8.00 am. When I arrived at work, Ms. Langnbruner showed me into my boss's office. I smiled and was just started to introduce myself when I was interrupted in mid-sentence . . .

"Herr Sosnowski, you have to show more initiative. It is expected of you, just like the rest of the employees here at Lidl. When you are told to do something like for example find a hotel, you should do that immediately."

Well, that was a little different from a standard introduction I was used to.

"We have some difficulties getting you the visa, but don't worry, we have a representative at the government level, and he will get it done. Now, we can't waste any more time. Did you check out already?"

"Of course."

"Good, so get in your car and start driving. You are already one day late with your program!"

As I drove westwards I wondered what was going to happen next. I failed to make good first impression, but I knew that through hard work I would make it up.

At 11.30 am I arrived at Friedrichstal (Lidl's western headquarters). Just like the main headquarters, this office was the size of three Canadian Costco stores. I was introduced to Miss Schmidt who right away took me downstairs and gave me the blue and yellow work uniform along with safety boots.

"I'm so excited," I told her. "I always wanted to work in a store but never had the chance."

She looked at me in disbelief. "It's hard work. Monday until Saturday, early morning till evening."

I thought she was joking. We drove to the store in the little town of Hermeskeil, my home for the next few months. After checking into the hotel, Miss Schmidt took me for a ride in her Audi. We went to a few stores and I was told that I was to test the cashier. I was to try and steal a chocolate bar by hiding it in the cart underneath a carton of juices. This was the standard test they conducted on the cashiers. I felt sorry for the women working at the cash register. I am sure most Canadian cashiers would have failed this test. How can you tell the customers to lift up the carton in their shopping cart? This seemed so rude. At Lidl, every cashier was supposed to do this. If not, they received a warning. A few warnings and they were gone. I was thankful the cashier passed the test.

Miss Schmidt explained how the store should look.

"It will be your responsibility Mr. Sosnowski that the store *always* looks great. There can be no dirt, all products must always be displayed in a nice and presentable fashion and the shelves always have to be full. This will be controlled, and if something doesn't look perfectly tidy, there will be trouble. The worst thing you can do is to take a lunch break when the store is not perfect. So what are you going to do?"

"Well, first get to know my co-workers and find out about the culture in the store. I need to find out how things are done first."

"No, you don't have time for that. You are in charge, and the things will be done the way you like them to be, regardless of the past."

"But isn't this authoritative approach demoralizing?"

She grinned. "If you want to be successful at Lidl, you had better forget that word. 'Morale' is not a Lidl word."

End of week 2

Thursday, December 11th—Hermeskeil

Miss Schmidt wasn't joking when she said I would be working Monday to Saturday morning till evening. I had worked 85 hours in my first week and I was exhausted. None of the employees worked more than eight hours a day, or more than five days a week. There was clearly some mistake. I talked to the store manager Mrs. Schlieman and she did not have any information on my schedule. So I called Lidl Canada.

"Herr Gopp, this must be mistake. I need a work schedule. I have worked 85 hours. I think they are trying to kill me."

"Herr Sosnowski, you were warned in the interview that it was going to be hard work."

"But if I work so much, I can't even go shopping, nor get any personal things done. The only day I have free is Sunday, and Sunday everything is closed."

"That's your problem Mr. Sosnowski. You are being paid to work and not to go shopping nor do your personal things. If you can't get your shopping done, find someone else that can do it for you. You have food and place to sleep. What else do you want?"

I was left speechless. I thought about quitting but quitting was not an option. Soon it became clear to me—it was all a test of my endurance, physical strength, initiative, commitment, and perseverance.

They can't have me working like this forever. Nobody works like this—they would burn out. My only concern was that I still didn't have my work visa—a basic requirement for my wife to apply for a visa. I was confident though that the company would take care of it.

Friday, December 12th—Lebach

I was invited to the Lidl Christmas party. Before the party, all area managers had a training session that was led by Mr. Mikorai and Ms. Milock—the regional sales coordinators. I was still working in a store but was invited to the meeting as I was considered a district sales coordinator in training. Most of the district sales coordinators were around my age, some of them even younger. The meeting was anything but friendly. It was not intended to promote a group discussion, but rather delegate what needed to be done and point out what wasn't done correctly. Only last names were used, and two-way communication and suggestions were *not* welcomed . . .

"But Mr. Mikorai, the way you wanted the coffee displayed in the aisle isn't appealing," suggested Mr. Muller, of the district sales coordinators.

"Mr. Muller, when I tell you to nail a yogurt to the wall, you do it! Understand? It will be done as I say. Any other suggestions?"

"Yes, are we going to get computers in the stores? A computerized system would save us a lot of money."

"No!! No computers."

This is Germany, a fast-paced technically sophisticated country. And here is Lidl—no computers, nothing. Just recently they installed a scanner at the checkout, and it works only for some articles. All of the bookkeeping is done with old paper (recycled so many times that it looks gray), and a black pen. Other colors are not acceptable. Each store has an old fax machine and phone, both of which break down frequently.

Over the last week I had worked like never before, and met some of the most unpleasant people. I missed my wife and the visa process was stalled. I was told my working visa was ready a week before coming to Germany. Three weeks have passed and the visa was not there yet. I was frustrated and close to burning out.

And then the strangest thing happened. I felt that I really liked what I was doing. There was something about the company and the people that I admired. Whether it is the sense of power, strength, or dominance, I don't know, but one thing was clear—Lidl was an amazing organization.

Christmas and New Year came and went; I was in Germany and Larisa was in Canada. It was not a good holiday. The relationship with my wife was on a slide. I was confident that by the middle of December Larisa would have received her visa.[3] Under that assumption we gave up our apartment in Toronto and Larisa moved in with my parents in Barrie, Ontario (a small city approximately one hour north of Toronto). The relationship between my wife and my parents was strained, and soon Larisa was desperate to return to Colombia. Our evening phone conversations were increasingly marked by conflict. After 16-hour workdays, I was simply too tired to listen and to be supportive of my wife.

Week 6

January 5th—Hermeskeil

I had been a Lidl employee for just over one month. As time went on, my responsibilities increased, and now I was averaging 93 hours a week. In order to save money the stores were terribly understaffed. In a 16-hour workday, I rarely had more than a one-hour break. I was in fear that Miss Schmidt would come when I was on break. She said that in order to go for lunch the store needed to be perfect. With 50 customers in the store and three employees (including me), it was nearly impossible to keep the store in perfect condition. But for Lidl, I soon learned, customer service was not as important as saving money. Physically I

---

3   According to the German rules, I was not allowed to invite my wife until I had an apartment, not a hotel. The company prohibited me from getting an apartment, because they needed me to be mobile. Thanks to my good relationship with the store manager, Mrs. Schlieman, I was able to get her to sign a document stating that I was living in an apartment at her home. I could finally start the application for Larisa's visa. Since I was working Monday to Saturday morning to evening I had no opportunity to find an apartment. I talked to the regional sales coordinator Ms. Milock and asked for a free day to look for an apartment.

"Mr. Sosnowski, we don't think it is a good idea. You shouldn't look for an apartment, because at any time the company can change their mind and send you to another part of the country. You need to remain flexible and remain in the hotel."

"Ms. Milock, for me it doesn't matter, I can stay in the hotel. But if I don't get an apartment, my wife can't come."

"That's your problem, Mr. Sosnowski. But understand, we all have personal problems, and we don't let it influence our work. You are not any different."

was doing fine except for the fact that my lower back was killing me from lifting heavy items. I addressed my concerns of heavy lifting to one of my co-workers.

"You just need to get needles and you'll be fine. I get them all the time."

That's not the answer I wanted to hear. I was under a constant pressure to work faster and faster, and each time Miss Schmidt or Ms. Milock came, they had something negative to say.

"You're too slow. Mr. Muller, when he was working here, he was on his knees unpacking boxes. He would sweat so much he needed to change his clothes twice a day. That's expected of you. If you are not sweating and falling on your face, you are not working hard enough. If at the end of the day you still have strength left to watch TV, you are not working hard enough. If you don't spend the whole Sunday sleeping, you are not working hard enough," commented one of my co-workers. And that was perfectly true and perfectly normal at Lidl. That night I called Anas. His situation wasn't any different. We both came to the conclusion that this is the Lidl world. Until you worked there, you can't imagine that something like this exists.

At Lidl you always felt like a thief. I addressed this issue with Miss Schmidt, and she replied it was the only way to control so many stores. At Lidl, there was on an average $300 worth of food thrown out a day. A farmer would come each morning and take the food. An employee taking anything would be considered misconduct. One former employee took an old bun to feed the sea gulls and was fired on the spot. Any employee purchase had to be accompanied by a receipt. The receipt had to be signed by two different co-workers with a black pen (any other color of ink was not acceptable and could lead to reprimand) and the receipt had to be taped to the item with transparent tape. This wasn't a bad idea but the process became ridiculous. I purchased a cooking pan that I used at work every day for a month; I had to keep on re-glueing the receipt. If you bought more than one apple, to which apple do you attach the receipt? Failure to meet the rules on product receipts led to trouble.

As area manager I had the right to search the employees' pockets, any personal belongings and their personal vehicles at any time without any justification. Checking lockers and employee vehicles was a routine exercise the area managers were expected to do. After a month of work, the company would leave me alone every evening to count the money. The store made on an average of €10,000–20,000/day. Any money missing would come out of my pocket. I had the right, though, to fire any employees suspected of stealing money.

What morale and motivation is to other companies, fear and mistrust was to Lidl. The customers were treated similarly. The customers were expected to put everything from the basket on the belt. One time there was a man who bought eight bags of dog food (10 kg each), and placed only one bag on the belt. I had to ask him to place all of the bags on the belt to see if maybe he was hiding a 20 cent chocolate on the bottom basket. When I first started I felt really uncomfortable asking customers to remove every single item from their grocery cart, but after a month at Lidl shame wasn't an issue. If the customer is upset and never came back, too bad, I did my job according to the rules. So, what's the upside?

Well, I did prevent the possibility of theft. I had no choice but to act in this way, because any of these customers could be a Lidl employee doing a test on me. If I failed the test, I would be in serious trouble.

Week 7

January 12th—Hermeskeil

With six weeks of work experience at Lidl I was adapting. Now Ms. Schlieman would leave me alone with the employees and the store was my sole responsibility. My weekly work hours reached 102 hours. But I was healthy and physically fit. I estimated that I walked or ran about 140 km each week through the store and lifted a few tons of product. I was overworked, but knew that soon Larisa and I were going to be together. The conversations in the evenings were on an upward turn again.

Although I considered myself physically fit, my brain was not responding. I was so overworked that even basic arithmetic was difficult. I had to count cans in a box: six across, five wide and three high plus four extra. How many cans were there? It took me a minute and I still had it wrong. In the evenings I had to count the money, and that was the worst. To not make a mistake, I would do everything extra slowly and triple-check it. As a result I was at the store until midnight; the next day at 5.45 am I was back, unpacking vegetables.

The curious thing was that none of the district sales coordinators was married. I wasn't sure if it was because working at Lidl consumed all of their time and energy, or because their personality changed while working at the company. To be successful at Lidl, you had to be—pardon my language but there is no other way to describe it—a total selfish bastard, and treat others like crap. If you didn't have this personality, Lidl wasn't a place for you. I've worked and lived in Germany before, and let me tell you this has nothing to do with Germany. It is not the German culture, it is the Lidl culture.

January 14th—Hermeskeil

As soon as I got to the hotel (11.30 at night) the phone rang. It was my father. My wife and my mom had been in a car accident. Larisa was driving. The car was demolished and my mom was in hospital. I was deeply conflicted about where I should be and what I should be doing.

Week 8

January 20th—Neckarsulm

Today I was in Neckarsulm again. It was a meeting for all Canadians involved in this program. I was looking forward to sharing my experience with others. I didn't know how many Canadians were in Germany or their locations. When I got there, I didn't see anyone. We all had our interviews at different times so that we wouldn't meet each other. I entered the office and a warm smile greeted me. Mr. Leonard sat me down and talked to me like I was a human being. He asked me how I was, so I brought up the issue with my wife. He promised to look into it. He asked me if I have been overworked, and then said not to worry.

"They just want to see if you can work, that's all. In your second year of training you will be here at head office, then it becomes more normal—60 to 70 hours max."

I left Neckarsulm convinced that this training marathon was just a test. Only a test! I knew it was all going to be good. Larisa will soon be here. I trusted Mr. Leonard to get the things done. The next ten months were going to be difficult, but after that I will collect dividends. I will work at the head office, I will be an executive, I will perfect my German and we will live in Europe. Ten more months to go! Despite sleeping only two hours (again), I was pumped, I was ready and loving it

January 21st—Hermeskeil

I called Mrs. Morchett at the Trier City Hall to find out if the papers for my wife's visa were ready. Not yet. This night I called Larisa and we got into another fight. She wanted to go back home to Colombia, and I told her to stop acting selfish. She said she doesn't want to stay in my parents' house any longer. My response was: "That's your problem. You've got food, you've got a place to sleep. Smarten up, it is expected of you." She called me a bastard and slammed down the phone. This has never happened before. Then I realized that I had changed. I was becoming part of Lidl culture. I was becoming a "Lidl person." But I was too tired to think about it, and in three hours I had to be up.

January 22nd—Hermeskeil

I called Mrs. Morchett seven times to finally get hold of her.

"Yes, your papers have arrived."

"Is everything OK? Can you send them to Canada?"

"No, I can't, Mr Sosnowski. Your work permit doesn't permit you to invite your wife."

She started explaining me details, but I was too furious to understand. In addition the area manager Mr. Zimmer came in and gave me a dirty look.

"Mr. Sosnowski, look at all these unpacked boxes. They needed to be unpacked at 12.00. It's now 11.45 and you haven't started."

I wanted to jump into the car and see Mrs. Morchett. There was nothing more important in this life than going there right now. I told the store manager I had to go, but she refused. She said they needed me to help with the boxes, but that I could go tomorrow. I was devastated. I didn't know what to do. In the morning I was motivated, but after this phone call I felt flat. Shortly after the call, I cut my finger to the bone with a knife while cutting one of the boxes. I needed stitches. My co-workers looked at it and laughed:

"That's nothing. Get back to work."

I taped my finger and put a coke bottle cap on top of it to shield it from any type of pressure. For the rest of the day I was slow. Later in the afternoon the store manager told me that there were serious complaints from head office that my *personal* problems are getting in the way of my work, and if this continued I would be fired.

This was followed by a phone call from Mr. Backer from Canada with the same message. I didn't want to beat around the bush. I explained to him, it is not personal problems that are affecting my work, but rather Lidl's inability to get their things done. He was blunt in his comments:

"Mr Sosnowski, we don't feel it is a good idea that your wife comes over. She doesn't speak German and being in a foreign country will not be easy. With you working all the time, you won't have any time for her and she will get very lonely. And this will not have a good effect on your work."

"Whether my wife comes or not is my decision, and not Lidl's."

"Well, that's your opinion. It's not Lidl's responsibility to help your wife come over."

January 23rd—Hermeskeil

In the morning I drove to meet Mrs. Morchett. She explained to me that the work permit I have authorizes me to work, but not to sponsor my wife. I asked to see my file. She didn't want to show me, and hinted that she was given instructions not to show my file to me. I was furious.

"This is my file, my information and I want to see it. I don't care about the instructions you were given. I have a right to look at my personal records!"

She showed me the file. It weighed about 2 kg and had all of my information, much of it confidential in nature. They had all the information about me, including addresses of all of my previous employers and my home addresses. I had no idea they had all this information about me. She wanted to get me out of the office fast, but I wasn't going to leave until she answered all of my questions. At this point she was the only person I trusted. She saw my determination and my hopelessness and became cooperative. She explained that, with the work visa that I have, my wife will never be able to come, and that all the work I had done up to this point was useless.

"How hard would it have been for Lidl to make my contract in such way that she could come?"

"Not hard at all. All they needed to do is request it at the time your visa was issued in December."

I left the office devastated. There was no doubt in my mind Lidl did it purposely. They didn't want my wife to come, and they had done everything that they could so she wouldn't. They pretended to be helpful, understanding and tricked me to give up all I had in Canada. Lidl has a department that deals with getting visas for foreign workers, and they have their own people in the local governments. One phone call from Mr. Gopp from Canada to the local government and Larisa would be on the plane to Germany. But that's not what they wanted to do. Mr. Gopp said he would talk to the people in Germany to help with my wife's visa, and said that my visa was already done. In reality, my visa took over a month, and there was nothing done for my wife. Mr. Leonard's role was to be the "good cop" and delay the process. Mr. Muller in the city hall at Neckarsulm knew that all the paperwork I was doing was totally useless, but he kept his mouth shut. And the regional sales coordinator at Friedrichstal was supposed to keep me so busy that I wouldn't have time or means to get anything done like find an apartment or visit the city hall. What were they thinking? That I am going to give up my marriage for Lidl? Some Lidl managers have gone down that path.

As I came out of the city hall I was welcomed by a nice warm and sunny day. I sat on a rock to think about what has happened. It was 11.00 am. They were expecting me back by 10.00 am, and I was going to be in trouble. I was devastated, not angry, but sad. I saw a young couple with two children walking through the park. I felt tears in my eyes. That's what I wanted. That was why I was here, so that I would have a future where I could walk through the park with my wife and children. Why don't I have the right to do this?! Why can't I have a normal life?

Everyone told me to quit, that I wasn't going to make it, that I was going to be in the 80% that don't make it. I was so determined to prove them wrong. Two months ago I left Canada as a winner. Larisa and I had plans to work extremely hard over the next two years, do whatever it takes, and in two years buy a house and have children. Two years from now I was going to be an executive, and would make our dreams come true. If I quit now, I will shatter our dreams. If I go back to Canada, I will be a loser. I will have to move into my parents' house with my wife and sit in my parents' basement for the next few months and look for a job. What job am I going to land? Another telemarketing job for $13/hour? Or admit defeat and return to my old job? They would probably take me back, but I don't think I would be able to go back. What am I going to say to my family and friends? That I quit, that I didn't make it because the work was too tough? Mr. Leonard said that the second year will be normal working hours. It is all just a test, only a test. I can still win this. I can physically stand working the 90–100 hour weeks. As far as mentally, as soon as the problems with my wife are solved, my mind will be clear. We'll make it through the first year, and the second will be easier. Upon return to Canada, we will have enough money to buy a house in two years. We can still make this dream reality.

As I was driving back to Lidl I shifted between anger and hope. I knew that upon my return to the store there would be a group of people to "greet me." What should I say? I've been lied to and felt used. Mr. Zimmer's black Audi was at the Lidl parking lot in Hermeskeil. Surely he had a speech ready for me. A showdown would occur. What should I do? What would you do?

Discussion questions

1. Describe the interview approach used by Lidl. How did Matt manage himself in the interview? How would you characterize Matt's effectiveness in the interview? What questions could he (should he) have asked? How can people such as Matt "do their homework" far more effectively before they take on "expat" assignments around the world?

2. With respect to organizational culture, identify the underlying values and beliefs at Lidl. What are the effects of this culture on employee morale?

3. What form of organizational control does Lidl use? What are the strengths and limitations to this form of control?

4. Describe Matt's attempts to make sense of his situation. What motivates Matt to stay with Lidl?

5. What courses of action are open to Matt? What do you recommend that he do?

Teaching notes for this case are available from Greenleaf Publishing. These are free of charge and available only to teaching staff. They can be requested by going to:
www.greenleaf-publishing.com/darkside_notes

Part 2
**Business and
local communities**

2.1
Food Lion vs. the UFCW
Time for a change?[1]

Paul Michael Swiercz

Delhaize America is the nation's fifth largest supermarket company. Its three subsidiaries, Food Lion, Kash n' Karry and Hannaford Bros. Co., employ more than 109,000 associates in more than 1,400 stores on the American eastern seaboard. Within the industry, Food Lion is the largest of the three Delhaize subsidiaries. For most of its history, it has been distinguished by its very high growth rate, exceptionally low cost structure and aggressive non-unionization stance. Its non-union status has been a major source of competitive advantage relative to its primary and highly unionized competitors (Kroger, American Stores, Safeway, and Giant).

In 1992, the United Food and Commercial Workers (UFCW) began using a "corporate campaign" strategy in its long-running effort to organize Food Lion workers. Coincident with this campaign, the ABC network news show *Prime Time* broadcast a highly critical and controversial exposé of the company. The impact of the program was devastating. Tom Smith, the man who had led the company through three decades of interrupted success, resigned abruptly, the company withdrew from south-western markets, and stockholders lost a million in equity.

After seven years of stagnation, the company was reorganized by its parent, the Delhaize Group of Belgium. New leadership was appointed and with it came a new competitive strategy. The previous strategy was built on four pillars:

- Extremely efficient operations using Food Lion's proprietary "effective scheduling" system

---

1 This case was prepared under the direction of Paul Michael Swiercz, PhD of The George Washington University, Department of Management Science. The case was developed solely for the basis of discussion rather than to illustrate either effective or ineffective management practice.

- Conservative financing with few external obligations
- Entry into high-growth suburban areas using a "cookie cutter" approach to store design
- An assertive non-union operating preference taking full advantage of the advantages afforded by the status relative to its unionized competitors

In contrast, the new strategy focused on:

- Growth through acquisition of successful competitors in non-traditional markets
- Use of riskier financing strategies
- A willingness to experiment with new store designs customized to customer preferences

What isn't new about the new strategy is Food Lion's commitment to remaining a low-cost leader. The present leadership faces the difficult challenge of reconciling the conflicting demands of its new strategy with the realities of the contemporary market. Food Lion has virtually exhausted the growth potential of its south-eastern base and, in order to grow, it must penetrate unfamiliar geographic areas. The UFCW showed that its power cannot be treated lightly. Food Lion's leaders must find a way to retain the cost advantages derivative from its non-union-dependent low-cost strategy while simultaneously lowering the level of conflict with its long-time protagonist, the UFCW and its allies.

Profit margins in the grocery industry are razor-thin with the industry average now estimated to be only one penny on the dollar. Because of this tight margin, profitability is tied to high volume and low costs. As the Food Marketing Institute notes: "Supermarkets would rather sell a $1 item 100 times, earning a penny on each sale, than a ten-cent item ten times."[2] Virtually all the major players in the industry seek competitive advantage by coupling high volume with low wholesale food, selling, and general administrative (SG&A) costs.

Food Lion has traditionally been a high-volume–lowest-cost leader. As such, for many years, it served as an excellent investment for Belgium's "Le Lion" group following its purchase of 52% of the company's stock during the mid-70s. However, a 1992 ABC television *Prime Time Live* report destroyed this long record of uninterrupted success. Using undercover reporters and hidden cameras, the controversial report showed employees of the chain repackaging and selling out-of-date meat and violating other food safety and handling practices. In the seven years following that broadcast, Delhaize's Food Lion investment

---

2   Spencer, P. (1996) "Is your supermarket good enough? Questionable trade union accusations against supermarkets," *Consumers Research Magazine* 79 (February 1996).

decreased in value by 42%, while Standard & Poor's (S&P) 500 stock index moved up 195%.[3]

Before his unexpected and sudden departure in April 1999, Tom Smith served as chief executive officer of Food Lion for 30 years. As CEO he engineered the growth of Food Lion from 317 stores with sales of $1.9 billion to 1,223 stores with sales of over $10 billion. Tom Smith was known for his hard-working, penny-pinching, and innovative management style.[4] He was also known for his strong desire to keep Food Lion union-free.

Since the early 1990s Food Lion has claimed that the United Food and Commercial Workers Union International (UFCW) has been waging a sophisticated "corporate campaign" against the firm. During this period, the UFCW and its affiliates have been involved in numerous charge and counter-charge disputes with Food Lion. The conflict has involved such issues as:[5]

- Alleged violations of food safety and handling laws
- Several forms of pattern discrimination in hiring and employment
- Alleged conspiracy to violate state wage and price laws
- Alleged illegal organizing efforts
- Conspiracy to libel and slander

Following the abrupt April 1999 departure of Food Lion CEO Tom Smith, a new leader was assigned responsibility for improving firm performance. Pierre-Olivier Beckers, a 38-year-old MBA and CEO of Delhaize "Le Lion" Group, was appointed the new chairman of Food Lion.

Beckers knew he had to formulate a new strategy to regain shareholders' confidence and put the stock price back on track. As part of the effort to get the company again moving in the right direction he found himself having to address three questions:

- Was the cost advantage of non-union labor worth all the problems Food Lion was having with the UFCW?

- Would a break with the Tom Smith precedent of keeping the unions out put the spark back into the company and its stock price?

- Was a union-free workplace one of Food Lion's strengths or actually the thorn in foot that was preventing the company from achieving its goals?

He knew he would have to get a handle on this issue before he made his recommendations to the Delhaize Board of Directors.

3   Reed, T., and A. Williams (1999) "Food Lion CEO to retire after seeing firm through boom times, slide," *Charlotte Observer*, April 8, 1999.
4   "Tom Smith puts aside Food Lion mantle," *Herald Sun* (Durham, NC), April 8, 1999.
5   "Wrestling with the Lion," *Progressive Grocer*, June 1, 1997.

Industry overview

The grocery industry includes supermarkets, food stores, and grocery stores primarily engaged in the retail sales of all sorts of canned goods and dry goods, such as fresh fruits and vegetables, fresh and prepared meats, fish and poultry, etc. The grocery industry includes the following functions:

- Obtaining goods from distributors and manufacturers,

- Marking up the price to cover costs and to allow for profit, and

- Reselling the merchandise to the general public

In 1996, there were altogether 130,000 establishments in the U.S. retail grocery industry, with total sales of $412.5 billion.[6]

Supermarkets are the biggest component of the grocery industry. In 1996, the number of supermarkets exceeded 29,800 and the total sales volume was $311.7 billion, accounting for 75% of the total industry sales. The supermarket industry is further subdivided into affiliated independents and corporate chain supermarkets, with corporate chain supermarkets as the dominant sector. Corporate chain retail supermarkets are company-operated, and include such well-known companies as Safeway, Giant, Kroger, A&P, Winn-Dixie, Jewel, Publix, Acme Markets, and Food Lion. However, no single corporate chain supermarket dominates the national market, and none has operations in all 50 states.

A slowdown in growth

The corporate chain supermarkets enjoyed moderate sales growth during the late 1980s and early 1990s. According to the U.S. Bureau of Census, the industry growth rate between 1987 and 1992 was 22%.[7] Growth after this period began to slow. To remain competitive and to maintain the growth rate, supermarkets introduced a variety of new initiatives, including horizontal and vertical integration, expansion of private label brands, non-traditional marketing, introduction of larger stores, development of specialty services like delicatessens, and corporate cost-saving programs. Nonetheless, intensive competition and relatively flat sales characterized the industry during the 1990s. As a result of this competition, the profit margin of the industry was reduced to the current industry average of one penny on the dollar.

Accompanied by the increasing competition, research and technology became more important in helping the industry reduce costs and increase efficiencies. New technologies in accounting, ordering, receiving, and scheduling systems are being introduced. Scanning technology, such as UPC bar codes used at checkouts, has become nearly universal. Other innovations like electronic payment

---

6 Gale Business Resources (1999) "Grocery Stores" (industry analysis).
7 Ibid.

systems and customer clubs have enabled faster and more accurate payment and massive data banks to track customer buying habits.

A labor-intensive industry

With more than 3.7 million workers, retail grocers employ a significant portion of the U.S. working population. It is therefore not surprising that labor costs represent the single biggest variable cost in the industry. According to the U.S. Bureau of Economic Analysis, wages and benefits of employees represent about 13.2% of total industry sales on average.[8] Despite the increasing total number of grocery stores in the United States, the industry's total workforce has remained stable during the recent years, which may be indicative of productivity gains and the industry's efforts to reduce labor costs. Employee turnover rate in the grocery industry is relatively high. According to the Food Marketing Institute, turnover for full-time grocery workers in 1995 was 12.9% and 69% for part-time workers.[9]

Organized labor

The United Food and Commercial Workers International Union (UFCW) is the primary labor union representing employees in the industry. Most leading industry players like Kroger, American Stores, Safeway, and Giant have contracts with UFCW locals. However, unionization rates as a percentage of total employment have declined in the industry in recent years. Although supermarket workers remain unionized at many major chains, the entry and the expansion of non-unionized competitors like Food Lion, Winn-Dixie, and Publix have weakened the bargaining power of UFCW member employees.

Non-union chains have a considerable competitive advantage over union chains in controlling labor costs by offering lower wages and benefits to employees. Wages of employees of Food Lion are about a third lower than that of the industry average. In 1993 the *Washington Post* compared some of the labor costs at Food Lion to those at Safeway and Giant, both paying workers under a union contract. It found that experienced, part-time stockers in Food Lion earned $6.60/hour, while employees doing the same job in Safeway and Giant earned $12.90/hour.

Partially because of the competitive advantage of lower labor costs, non-union chains have successfully expanded their market shares and extended to new regions at the cost of unionized chain companies. Food Lion, as one of the most aggressive non-union competitors, grew to become the seventh largest national chain supermarket. Likewise, Winn-Dixie and Publix have also succeeded in moving themselves on to the top industry player list. Figure 1 shows the largest firms and their relative market share.

8 Ibid.
9 Ibid.

FIGURE 1 Relative market share of major grocers, 1997

Source: *Supermarket News*, January 20, 1997

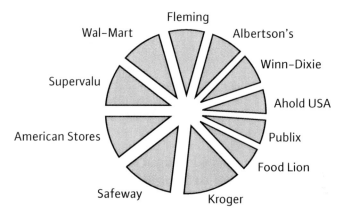

Faced with these aggressive non-union new entrants to the industry, the UFCW redoubled its organizing efforts. Conflicts between the UFCW and non-union companies intensified, with the struggles between the UFCW and Food Lion and Publix being widely publicized.

Food Lion overview

Food Lion, Inc. (Food Lion) is the seventh largest supermarket chain in the United States. It was incorporated in North Carolina in 1957 and maintains its corporate headquarters in Salisbury. Its greatest presence is in the southeast but also extends to the mid-Atlantic region as far north as Pennsylvania and as far as Florida to the south. The Food Lion stores, which are operated under the name of "Food Lion" and "Kash n' Karry," sell a variety of groceries, meats, dairy products, seafood, frozen food, deli/bakery, and non-food items such as health and beauty aids and other household and personal products. As of March 31, 1999, there were 1,223 supermarkets in operation in 11 states employing over 90,000 employees.

Growth strategy

Food Lion is a company well experienced in the art of generating high growth rates. The average annual growth rate was more than 20% from the late 1960s through the 1980s.[10] According to the company's management, Food Lion's success is the result of a growth strategy built upon:

10 Gale Business Resources (1999) "Food Lion—History" (company profile).

- **Extra low prices**. Food Lion is recognized as the low-price leader in the retail food supermarkets industry. According to an industry survey, Food Lion prices are 8% lower than the industry average. This 8% gap is the key factor in Food Lion's success in increasing its market share and expansion

- **Convenient, fast and friendly service**. Food Lion's low overhead makes it profitable to locate more stores in each market, so that Food Lion stores are convenient to more customers

- **Successful customer loyalty card program**, There are more than 5.8 million households shopping with Food Lion's "MVP" card, and an estimated 70% of sales are card-related. This program also serves as marketing research, which helps Fool Lion develop its marketing strategy

- **An aggressive capital expansion plan**. In 1998, the company opened 79 store and remodeled 141 stores. In 1999, the company plans to spend $390 million on capital projects, including the opening of 80 new stores and remodeling of 140 stores

- **Strong financial position to finance growth**. Food Lion has a strong balance sheet and an investment grade debt rating, which enables the company to continue its expansion program and finance future acquisition opportunities[11]

Arguably the most important element leading Food Lion's history of competitive advantage is its low labor cost. In the retail food supermarket industry, labor costs are the largest component of SG&A expense. The industry's average SG&A expense is approximately 20% of sales, while the SG&A of Food Lion is only 14% of sales.[12]

As part of its strategy for competitive advantage through controlled labor costs, Food Lion created a sophisticated and controversial operation and management system called "Effective Scheduling." Under Effective Scheduling, the number of items to be processed or stocked by an employee during a particular week is established according to weekly sales projections, then a certain amount of hours for the employee are specified to complete all tasks. Employees are expected to finish assigned tasks within the allotted time; failure to do so could result in a negative performance review.

Under the Effective Scheduling program, overtime work was strictly controlled. At a hearing on Capitol Hill in 1992, several former and current Food Lion employees testified that their supervisors told them to do whatever is necessary to "get the job done," while at the same time warning workers that they would be fired if they worked overtime or "off the clock."[13]

---

11   Food Lion (1998) "Investor Facts."
12   UFCW (1993) "Food Lion Over the Line."
13   Ramsey, J. (1992) "Workers testify Food Lion forced off-the-clock labor," *Supermarket News*, March 30, 1992: 6.

Lower wages and Effective Scheduling have contributed greatly to the company's competitiveness and market share gains. However, lower wages and Effective Scheduling, especially the latter, have been the focal point to the long and oftentimes acrimonious conflict between Food Lion and the UFCW. Employees in unionized companies enjoy higher wages and benefits, as well as other protections. In an effort to redress this imbalance, the UFCW has been trying to unionize Food Lion for more than two decades. For many years the UFCW has charged Food Lion with enforcing an "anti-union" policy, which the union defines as taking "all possible" measures to prevent Food Lion workers from organizing and becoming members of the UFCW.

Corporate campaign

Food Lion's unblemished track record of avoiding organizing success by the UFCW led the union to adopt a new organizing strategy. The effort, known as "corporate campaign" (also known as a comprehensive or coordinated campaign) within the labor movement, is designed to discredit a company by exposing illegal work practices and bringing pressure on employers.

Designed to be comprehensive and intense, it uses everything from boycotts and proxy fights to lawsuits in an effort to alienate corporations from their suppliers, customers, lenders, and shareholders. In addition, it includes lobbying against the company in legislatures, opposing company bids for government contracts, filing complaints with a spectrum of government agencies at various levels, provoking bad publicity and litigation costs, and rallying community, religious, environmental, and other activist groups.[14]

This aggressive and multifaceted strategy was born out of frustration with low overall unionization rates (only about 10% of the private sector labor force is unionized) and efforts by new leaders to revitalize the union movement. In his acceptance speech in October 1995, John Sweeney, the AFL-CIO's newly elected president proclaimed: "We will use old-fashioned mass demonstrations, as well as sophisticated corporate campaigns, to make worker rights the civil rights issue of the 1990s."

In response to the new aggressiveness, business reacted with proposed legislation and lawsuits charging unions with racketeering and defamation. Food Lion, for example, filed a $300 million lawsuit against former employees and the UFCW for allegedly violating the Federal Racketeer Influenced and Corrupt Organizations (RICO) Act. According to Food Lion's complaint ". . . a corporate campaign is essentially a sophisticated method of extortion."[15] Within the labor movement, lawsuits of this type are labeled as SLAPP suits (for "strategic litigation against public participation").

14 Tyson, J.L. (1996) "As strikes lose potency, unions turn to tactics outside the workplace," *Christian Science Monitor*, February 16, 1996: 1.
15 Skolnik, S. (1995) "Food Lion's spoil for a fight—suit tests limits for 'corporate campaigns'," *Legal Times*, August 7, 1995: 2.

Jeffrey McGuiness, president of the Labor Policy Association Inc. in Washington, DC, observed that if one of these suits prevails ". . . it would force corporate campaigners to make sure they are on really solid ground with the charges they level."[16]

The new conflict begins: the UFCW vs. Food Lion

The Bryant case

A "cold call" received by the United Food and Commercial Workers Union in 1989 from the wife of Ricky Bryant, a former assistant store manager for Food Lion in West Columbia, SC, led to an intensified confrontation between the union and Food Lion. Bryant, who had been a nine-year employee for Food Lion, complained to the UFCW that Food Lion had unfairly fired him for "gross misconduct."

According to Bryant, he was issued two warnings a week apart in December 1987, and discharged in March 1988 for reasons unrelated to his performance. He claimed that Food Lion laid him off nine months short of ten years intentionally for the purpose of preventing him from becoming fully vested in the company profit sharing plan. According to Food Lion's policy, an employee becomes eligible only after a full ten years. In Bryant's case, eligibility would have meant $67,000. Al Zack, UFCW spokesman and assistant director of organizing, remarked:

> What Food Lion calls "gross misconduct" involved having a messy
> back room and not having some of the product properly lined up on
> the shelves. Anyone who works in the supermarket business knows
> that this is almost impossible to keep from happening.[17]

After interviewing other Food Lion employees and investigating public documents, the UFCW concluded that Food Lion's top management was denying full profit-sharing and health benefits to thousands of employees. The union decided to help finance a class-action suit Bryant filed against Food Lion. The union stated ". . . that through 1987 only 81 Food Lion employees, most of them high-level officials, were eligible for full benefits," and related this number to the approximately 21,000 employees enrolled in the plan.[18] When an employee leaves the company prematurely and receives only part of the profit sharing, the

---

16 Ibid.
17 D'Innocenzio, A. (1990) "UFCW sues Food Lion over benefits plan," *Supermarket News*, March 19, 1990: 4.
18 Albright, M. (1990) "Fired employee sues Food Lion," *St Petersburg Times*, March 13, 1990: 2E.

remaining amount is reallocated to the accounts of the other participants. The suit argued that this evidenced a conflict-of-interest for the fund's managers.

Mike Mozingo, Food Lion's spokesman, denied the charges, saying that they were based on outdated statistics. He dismissed the suit as just another attempt by the UFCW to discredit Food Lion. Vincent G. Watkins, Vice President of Special Projects and Development, added that had the union picked 1988 figures—when Food Lion switched to a five-year vested plan—instead of 1987 numbers, the figures would have been much higher. The profit-sharing plan was changed after federal law changed and required that employees can cash in their full benefits if they leave the company after one year.

Department of Labor case

In September 1991, after helping Ricky Bryant file his law suit against Food Lion, the UFCW represented a group of about 400 employees who filed a complaint with the Department of Labor (DOL). The employees charged Food Lion's Effective Scheduling policy with requiring them to work "off the clock" to avoid costly overtime payments.

Food Lion's Effective Scheduling plan allocated a set number of hours for employees to complete assigned tasks. The complaint argued that required tasks could not be completed within the hours assigned. Therefore, employees felt forced to work off the clock to avoid violating the Effective Scheduling plan and risking a negative performance review or worse.

Food Lion settled a similar case with the Department of Labor in 1989 involving off-the-clock complaints in 1987 and 1988. Back then, the Department initially proposed fining the company $1.2 million, but eventually charged $300,000. Food Lion promised to never do it again.

This time, the DOL initiated an extensive investigation, including on-site inspections at 85 stores and reports from 150 other stores. In addition to the union's complaints about off-the-clock work, the DOL found violations of child labor and overtime rules that it called "widespread." Most of the violations related to hazardous conditions involved workers under the age of 18 putting cardboard into non-operating bailers.

Food Lion started negotiations with the DOL that lasted for eight months. The result was the largest settlement ever reached by the federal government in a wage and hour case involving a private employer. Food Lion was required to pay $13.2 million in back pay to over 30,000 current and former employees who had not received proper overtime pay. Additionally, the company agreed to pay $2 million for civil penalties arising from overtime and minimum violations and $1 million for child labor violations.[19] The settlement also included a compliance plan, which required regular internal audits of the Fair Labor Standards Act. Fur-

---

19 Battaile, J. (1992) "Supermarket chain to face child-labor case," *New York Times*, November 8, 1992: 35.

thermore, a labor ombudsman was appointed to oversee and coordinate company-wide compliance and provide a procedure for internal dispute resolution for employees.[20]

The company never admitted to any violations. According to its president, Tom E. Smith:

> ... rather than spend considerable resources and years in litigation, we decided to resolve our differences with the department now, and invest our dollars in our work force.[21]

Prime Time Live

On November 5, 1992, ABC *Prime Time Live* broadcast its extremely damaging news report. The ABC report, using hidden cameras, purportedly showed Food Lion "employees" repackaging aged, even rotten, meat for sale. The report suggested employees covered up the spoilage by bathing meat in bleach.

According to complaints filed by Food Lion in lawsuits against both ABC and the UFCW, the union helped pitch the story to *Prime Time*, and provided the producer with training and employment credentials at union-operated stores. UFCW's Al Zack readily acknowledged the union encouraged reporters to look at Food Lion, but said the UFCW was not responsible for what ABC found in its independent investigation.[22]

Asked about charges that the UFCW was "behind" the ABC broadcast and that ABC had edited its footage to entrap Food Lion, Zack said:

> Obviously only part of the tape was shown. My understanding is that they [ABC] have something like 53 hours of tape on file for that story. As to the other point, we [UFCW] had no role in ABC's decision to go undercover at Food Lion. We had no role in picking the stores they went into. We had no role in attempting to target particularly bad stores. We helped provide information to ABC, and ABC chose to pursue their story. We did not participate in any of the newsgathering or editing decisions made by ABC. In terms of supplying [ABC staffers with] references so they could get their employees hired, yes, we did get them references, but I don't know that that has anything to do with the price of oranges.[23]

20 Southerland, D. (1993) "Food Lion to settle claims it violated U.S. labor laws," *Washington Post*, August 4, 1993: A1.
21 Ibid.
22 Mathews, R. (1993) "Union leader says Food Lion and Wal-Mart are to blame for media woes—Al Zack of the United Food and Commercial Workers International Union," *Grocery Marketing* 5 (February 1993): 40.
23 "Wrestling with the Lion", *Progressive Grocer*, June 1, 1997.

Food Lion sued ABC and eventually won a $5.5 million judgment. A US District Court Jury in Greensboro, North Carolina, ruled in 1996 that ABC had committed fraud and trespassed, though a federal judge later reduced the award to $315,000. Food Lion says that 43 hours of outtakes (the footage not broadcast) of the *Prime Time*'s undercover video clearly exonerates Food Lion and shows the producer setting up the eight minutes of damaging footage. However, portions of the videotape shown during the trial revealed that the two women, while purportedly working for Food Lion, were actually attempting to capture sensational footage for the news magazine show. "Their own tapes showed them scouting locations for other hidden cameras, attempting to violate Food Lion's food-handling policies and expressing frustration—to the point of swearing—when attempts at sensational footage were foiled by conscientious Food Lion employees," said Chris Ahearn, Food Lion's Manager of Corporate communications.[24]

Following the ABC report, Food Lion saw its earnings drop by half over the next six months. By 1997 Food Lion decided to close and sell its 61 stores in the Southwest. Food Lion claims this was largely due to the effects of a negative publicity campaign generated by the UFCW. "The union activity made it difficult for us to be able to establish a customer base there," said Food Lion's Chris Ahearn.[25]

The baby formula story

Following the ABC investigation, media-oriented campaigns against the company continued. In July 1995, the Consumers United with Employees (CUE), an independent activist group sharing offices with a unit of the AFL-CIO, publicized the results of its investigation. The group claimed that, during a canvas of 166 Food Lions in 78 cities and 14 states, it found more than 8,000 products with overdue expiration dates, particularly baby formula.[26]

In response to these allegations Food Lion issued a press release. In a prepared statement, released on April 4, 1995, the chain explained that:

> Food Lion acknowledges, as does every other retail food company, that even the best quality control systems may not function perfectly ... This is a fact of life in this industry, which handles billions of items each year.

24 Tosh, M. (1997) " 'Prime Time' replays Food Lion tape. ABC's 'Prime Time Live' rebroadcasts 1992 report on Food Lion's sanitary practices," *Supermarket News*, February 17, 1997: 4.

25 Zwiebach, E. (1997) "Food Lion blames union for Southwest exit, decides to close and sell its 61 stores in the Southwest," *Supermarket News,* September 29, 1997.

26 Spencer, P. (1996) "Is your supermarket good enough? Questionable trade union accusations against supermarkets," *Consumers' Research Magazine* 79 (February 1996).

"Just this past weekend," the statement continued, "in an ad hoc survey of stores in the Greater Washington, DC area, there were 742 out-of-date items of infant formula and over-the-counter drugs in 50 Safeway, Giant and Magruder stores, all located within the Beltway. The items we found included infant formula, children's medicines, children's laxatives, allergy medicines, and many other items. Out-of-date items were found at all of the Magruder stores checked, as well as at significant numbers of Safeway and Giant stores."[27]

Supermarket industry associations strongly criticized CUE's claims as irresponsible. The associations indicated that CUE's tie to labor unions as a motivating factor in the targeting of the non-union Food Lion. "We find it suspicious that Consumers United with Employees continues to focus on one specific company, which happens to be non-union," said a statement from the Food Marketing Institute. "Their attempt to disguise a labor dispute with a consumers issue is a disservice to the consumers," argued a spokesman for the National Grocers Association, Reston, VA.[28] And an unprecedented evaluation by the Food and Drug Administration and six state health agencies found Food Lion food safety and sanitation practices to rate an "excellent" score.

The union vote

During the early 1980s representatives of the UFCW contacted Food Lion employees in North Carolina and conducted some hand-billing in front of Food Lion stores in an effort to gauge the interest employees had in organizing. According to UFCW officials, "the workers were not ready." Unionization rates tend to be much lower in the southern United States than in northern states. The furthest north that Food Lion owns stores is Pennsylvania.

Food Lion's rapid growth offers greater opportunity for advancement then many slower-growing chains. Food Lion also instituted a profit-sharing plan for employees where employees directly benefit when the firm is doing well. Food Lion feels that these and other benefits keep employees happy and therefore curtails their interest in union membership.

The UFCW feels differently. Al Zack, chief organizer for the Food Lion campaign, said in an interview that intimidation from management is the primary reason Food Lion workers have not organized. He points to Food Lion's $300 million lawsuit naming two former Food Lion employees, among others, as an example of one of their tactics of intimidation.[29]

27 Mathews, R. (1995) "Can five wrongs make one right? Food Lion defends its sale of outdated items by identifying competitors that do the same," *Progressive Grocer* 74 (June 1995): 53.
28 Spencer, P. (1996) "Is your supermarket good enough? Questionable trade union accusations against supermarkets," *Consumers' Research Magazine* 79 (February 1996).
29 Interviews with Al Zack and Nicholas Clark of UFCW, April 15, 1999.

The financial situation

Food Lion derives most of its competitive advantage from very efficient management of its operating SG&A expenses. Historically, the SG&A of Food Lion was about 14.5–15% of Food Lion's net sales—the second largest cost component after cost of goods sold.[30]

Operating expenses consist of management and employee remuneration, rent expenses, lease, utility, distribution, etc. About 80% of the SG&A expenses consists of labor compensation. Food Lion's operating expenses average one-third below the industry average of 19.45%.[31] In an industry where profits are generally 1% of net sales, a one-third advantage in a cost component is huge.

A comparison of the SG&A expenses of Winn-Dixie and Publix, two other major non-union grocery retailers, shows Food Lion to have approximately 6% lower costs (13.3% vs. 19.4–19.9%).

In an interview discussing these cost comparisons, UFCW representative Al Zack stated that Food Lion's low SG&A expenses are primarily due to Food Lion's implicit policy of not paying the employees for all the work that is done, and not hiring people to do the extra work. According to Zack, the $16 million settlement for the off-the-clock violations in August 1993 still left Food Lion in charge of monitoring itself. After the settlement Mr. Zack said:

> ...[Food Lion's] Effective Scheduling system is still in place. That leaves the lion in charge of the hen-house.

Despite the challenges, Food Lion's expansion has been impressive. Between 1988 and 1997, the number of stores increased from 567 to 1,157, more than double over a nine-year period. During the same time period, the number of workers increased from 35,531 to 83,871, a more than 136% increase.

The company financed most of its expansion using conventional lease agreements, advantageous because it is an off-balance-sheet method of financing assets. Thus, the impact of expansion on liquidity of the company is minimal. Capital expenditure for 1998 was planned to be $360 million, with $150 million for store expansion and new store construction, and $150 million to equip those stores. The company planned to finance 1998 capital expenditures through funds generated from operations. The advantage in relatively low-cost non-union labor helped the company not only to maintain its policy of "extra low prices" but also to fund this aggressive expansion as well. Other sources of expansion funds include existing bank credit and credit lines.

The company maintains a revolving credit facility with a syndicate of commercial banks providing $700 million in a committed line of credit. As of January 3, 1998, the company had no outstanding borrowing on this account. The company also maintains additional committed lines of credit of $35 million, which are

---

30 1997 Food Lion Annual Report.
31 UFCW (1993) "Food Lion Over the Line."

available when needed. Outstanding borrowing on this account as of January 3, 1998 was minimal. The company also had $250 million in commercial paper program of which no borrowing was outstanding. Apart from these facilities, the company also had some periodic short-term borrowings under informal credit arrangements.[32]

Stock price

The price of Food Lion stock was $6.25 at the end of 1988. The stock price rose to over $18 by the end of 1991. However, after the broadcast of ABC's *Prime Time Live* report, Food Lion's stock price sharply plunged to below $6. Although the stock has rebounded since then, the pace was slow reaching only slightly above $10 by the end of 1998.

FIGURE 2 Ten–year trend of the stock price of Food Lion

Source: www.bigcharts.com

Compared to other major competitors' stock performances, Food Lion's dull pace of stock growth is made even more dramatic. Figure 3 shows the comparison of Food Lion's stock growth along with two competitors, Kroger (unionized) and Winn Dixie (non-unionized), as well as the S&P 500 index. Since the end of 1988, the annual average rate of return of the stocks of Kroger and Winn Dixie was 29.85% and 15.10%, respectively, while Food Lion gained a 5.45% average return. For comparison, the S&P 500 index had an average return of 16.04%.

32 Matthews, R. (1993) "UFCW vows to fight in face of Food Lion settlement," *Grocery Marketing* 59 (September 1993): 42.

FIGURE 3 Comparison of growth rate of stock price

Source: www.bigcharts.com

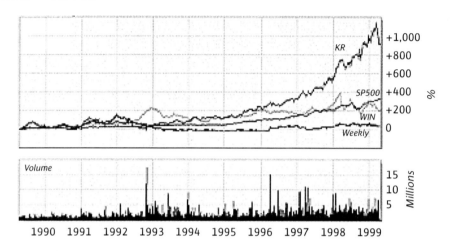

Pierre–Olivier Beckers' decision

By the time of Pierre-Olivier Beckers arrival, market forces in the industry were causing major consolidation. The Kroger Co. signed a merger agreement in October with the 800-store Fred Meyer chain of Oregon, vaulting them to the nation's largest food chain with more than 2,200 stores. Albertsons, Safeway, and Ahold USA also completed, or were in the process of completing, their own major mergers. Food Lion's last major acquisition was in 1996 when it bought the 100-store Kash n' Karry chain of Florida for $340 million.[33]

Mr. Beckers' financial analysis showed Food Lion's strength, but he knew it would take more than a continued low debt ratio to turn Food Lion's stock price in the right direction. He also knew the Delhaize Board of Directors was expecting a recommendation and they were expecting it soon. What was the key to putting the company back on track?

---

33 O'Brien, C., and Speizer, I. (1999) "Food Lion goes shopping," *News and Observer* (Raleigh, NC), April 9, 1999.

Epilogue

Formation of Delhaize America—a new management for Food Lion

In August 1999, the Delhaize "The Lion" Group created a new umbrella structure named Delhaize America as the parent company for Food Lion, Kash n' Karry, and Save 'n Pack.[34] It also announced Delhaize America's acquisition of Hannaford, a successful chain of 153 Northeastern US supermarkets. The acquisition made Delhaize America the fifth largest US food retailer.

Like Food Lion, Hannaford is a regional "every day low price" chain. Despite their similar low-cost strategies, Delhaize America announced that it anticipated significant cost-saving synergies by increased purchasing power, operational cooperation, and efficiency gains in procurement, category management, distribution, loyalty cards, marketing, and training.[35] Total cost savings were anticipated to equal $40 million in 2000. In conjunction with the reorganization, Delhaize America began trading on the New York Stock Exchange. All Food Lion shares were reverse-split and converted one-for-three into Delhaize America shares and listed on the New York Stock Exchange under the new symbols DZA and DZB.

Food Lion's new strategic focus

The retirement of Tom Smith was a telling moment for Food Lion. At an annual meeting in May 1999, Food Lion's new CEO Bill McCanless announced that Company plans included:

- Maintaining a strong customer focus

- Concentrating on its strengths of low prices and convenient supermarkets

- Enhancing the business through new stores and the aggressive pursuit of acquisitions[36]

The new strategic focus had three key elements. First, an aggressive hunt for acquisition candidates to increase shareholder value as evidenced by the Hannaford acquisition. Second, experimentation and possible abandonment of its cookie-cutter approach to internal growth. In a surprising move, for example, the company announced plans to experiment with new, more market-responsive store formats. In November 1999, it opened up a Village Market in Virginia Beach, a neighborhood market concept catering to customers' desires for convenience, quality, expanded fresh departments, and style.[37] And, third, a quiet declaration

---

34 Meyer, S. (1999) "Food Lion to Buy Hannaford," *MMR* 16.18 (September 3, 1999): 1+.
35 corporate.delhaize-le-lion.be/en/press/180899.html.
36 "New Food Lion CEO unveils strategic focus," May 6, 1999; www.foodlion.com.
37 "Food Lion unveils new store concept in Virginia Beach," November 17, 1999; www.foodlion.com.

of peace in its battle with the UFCW. In an unprecedented move, the company assured union leadership that they would not interfere with the relationship between the UFCW and Hannaford, at least with regard to a unionized Hannaford warehouse recently organized in Maine.[38]

Industry trends—the move toward consolidation and flexibility to markets

In recent years the wave of consolidations in the supermarket industry has picked up. Since 1994, supermarket chains made 169 acquisitions, with the two largest being the Albertsons' purchase of American Stores and Kroger's $13 billion acquisition of Fred Myer in May 1999.[39] Kroger, now the nation's largest retail grocery chain, reported that the estimated combined synergy savings from the merger with Fred Myer were $160 million for fiscal 1999. This total exceeded the company's previously announced projection of $155 million. Kroger expects to meet or beat its combined synergy savings goals of $260 million in fiscal 2000, $345 million in fiscal 2001, and $360 million in fiscal 2002. Kroger's fundamental strategy is to leverage its size while, at the same time, allowing divisional operators the freedom to respond to local communities and markets.

Kroger and Winn–Dixie

In November 1999 Kroger and Winn-Dixie announced an agreement under which Kroger purchased 74 Winn-Dixie grocery stores in Texas and Oklahoma. "This acquisition is a very good strategic fit for Kroger," said Joseph A. Pichler, Kroger chairman and chief executive officer.

> The addition of these stores will significantly strengthen Kroger's position in the highly competitive Dallas/Fort Worth market and provide expansion opportunities in new markets. It will also allow us to better utilize our purchasing, information technology and manufacturing across a larger store base in that region.

Mr. Zincke said that subject to approval by the Federal Trade Commission (FTC), the stores acquired from Winn-Dixie will operate as full-service supermarkets under the Kroger banner. He also said Kroger planned to remodel and upgrade the stores.

Food Lion and Hannaford

Food Lion did not receive a friendly market response to the acquisition of Hannaford. Its shares plummeted 35% following the Hannaford announcement.[40] One

38 Personal interview with Al Zack, Director of Strategic Planning, UFCW, February 11, 2000.
39 Weir (1999) "A search for staying power," *Supermarket Business*, September 15, 1999.
40 Giblen, G. (1999) "How not to start an acquisition," *Grocery Headquarters*, November 1999.

reason was the price, which was 12 times Hannaford's next 12 months' operating cash flow. This made the acquisition 22.5% dilutive of Food Lion's earnings per share (EPS). Also, unlike the Kroger/Fred Myer acquisition, the risk for only modest synergies dissuaded investors. Hannaford is already a super-efficient, high-margin, and well-managed company. There is little overlap in geographic markets so it is not likely that there will be the usual in-market acquisition savings from cutting redundant advertising, field supervision, and overhead.

The financial situation

Food Lion has historically derived most of its competitive advantage from very efficient management of its operating, selling, general, and administrative expenses. Historically, the SG&A of Food Lion was about 14.5–15% of Food Lion's net sales, the second largest cost component after cost of goods sold.[41] Operating expenses consist of management and employee remuneration, rent expenses, lease, utility, distribution, etc. About 80% of the SG&A expenses consist of labor compensation.[42] Food Lion's operating expenses average one-third below the industry average of 19.45%.[43] In an industry where profits are generally 1% of net sales, a one-third advantage in a cost component is huge.

In 1999, Food Lion's SG&A rose to 17.65% of net sales. Table 1 presents a set of recent figures for most of the big players in the industry. The table illustrates the level of competitiveness in which Food Lion operates and the investment community's attitude toward its attractiveness as an investment. The companies with an asterisk are non-union companies.

TABLE 1 Summary of financial performance of major US supermarket chains

	Delhaize/ Food Lion*	Hannaford	Winn- Dixie*	Kroger	Ahold	Safeway	Publix*
Sales ($ billion)	10.9	3.46	14.1	43.6	31.7	28.9	12.9
Price/earnings	8.83	31.35	19.71	17	20.09	20.67	20.84
Return on assets	8.05%	7.62	3.81%	4.99%	13.86%	7.96%	11.26%
Operating margin	5.2%	5.31%	1.1%	2.3%	4%	3.2%	6.9%
Current ratio	1.29	1.08	1.10	0.89	0.88	1.12	0.86
Return on equity	18.62%	14.4%	8.68%	65.5%	61.98%	26.92%	17.46%

41 1997 Food Lion Annual Report.
42 Matthews, R. (1993) "Union leader says Food Lion and Wal-Mart are to blame for media woes—Al Zack of the United Food and Commercial Workers International Union," *Grocery Marketing* 5 (February 1993): 40.
43 UFCW (1993) "Food Lion Over the Line."

Stock price

Figures 4–6 trace the performance of Delhaize America (Food Lion) stock over the last decade compared with the S&P 500. For comparison, the S&P 500 comparative performances of Kroger and Food Lion's new purchase, Hannaford, are traced over the same period.

Over the last ten years, Food Lion has fallen from a top performer compared with the S&P 500 to a poor performer; its performance worsened in 1999. In the same period, Hannaford tracked and recently beat the S&P 500. Kroger, as a fully unionized company, has consistently outperformed the S&P 500 over the same period.

FIGURE 4 Performance of Delhaize America (Food Lion) over the last decade compared with S&P 500

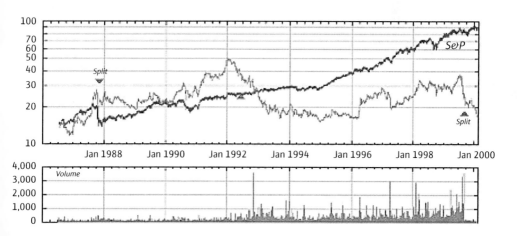

FIGURE 5 Performance of Hannaford over the last decade compared with S&P 500

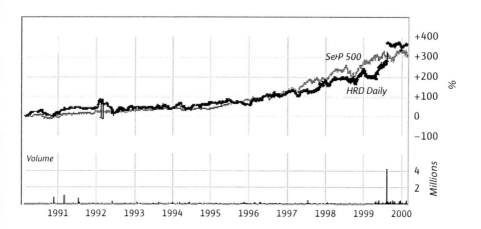

FIGURE 6 Performance of Kroger over the last decade compared with S&P 500

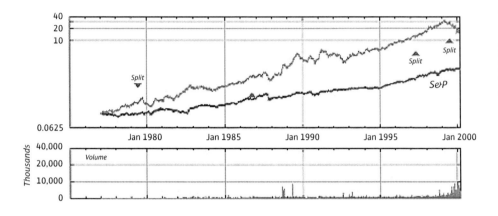

Discussion questions

1. Has non-union labor been the source of Food Lion's SG&A advantage? What about it's other questionable labor practices?

2. Why have the employees of Food Lion not "voted" to organize and join the UFCW despite their comparatively lower wages?

3. Is the cost advantage of non-union labor worth all the problems Food Lion is having with the UFCW? Could there be other means to gain a similar cost advantage?

4. What recommendation should Mr. Beckers give to the Delhaize Board of Directors regarding the future of Food Lion's employee relations strategy?

5. Is there meaning to be drawn from Food Lion's CEO Tom Smith's sudden retirement when most major companies usually publicly announce a succession plan months in advance?

Teaching notes for this case are available from
Greenleaf Publishing. These are free of charge
and available only to teaching staff. They can be
requested by going to:
www.greenleaf-publishing.com/darkside_notes

2.2

Manipulation, placation, partnership or delegated power

Can community and business really work together when surface mining comes to town?[1]

Sherry Finney

This case describes the issues faced by a community group in their attempt to form a working relationship with a company that plans to conduct surface mining operations in their hometown. John MacDougall is a member of the local Community Liaison Committee (CLC), a group set up to work with the mining company so that community interests were represented throughout the project. The case provides an account of the evolution of the group—in particular how they moved from a position of full opposition to a position of support, and then opposition once again. The role of the provincial government in its encouragement of this partnership is also considered.

Although they were initially opposed to the company's plans to surface mine within the town limits, John MacDougall and the CLC had relented and had tried to work with the company. They had been sold on a plan to create a new kind of partnership structure for surface mining where the community would play an active role and would be a stakeholder with influence.

1 This case was written by Sherry Finney of Cape Breton University, Nova Scotia, Canada. It is intended as a basis for classroom discussion and is not intended to represent either correct or incorrect handling of administration issues. This case may not be reproduced without permission of the author. Reprinted with permission. Names of the persons and the company are disguised to maintain confidentiality. Copyright © 2005 Sherry Finney.

Now it was 2005. The local mining company, MineCo Ltd, had finished the first stage of its mining project and the site hadn't been reclaimed to the community group's expectations. There had been issues with the manner in which some of the work was done and there had been broken promises. The CLC had decided that it would no longer provide any support for the mining company. The work completed to date had been part of a bulk sample test, and in the view of John and the committee, it was also a chance for the company to prove its capability and willingness to truly work with the community. In their views, the company had failed. Now the company was contemplating plans to expand the operation. John was wondering if the CLC ever really did have a significant role in the partnership or if there was anything that could have been done differently by any of the stakeholders to ensure a more positive outcome.

Main issue/problem

The planned community/business/government partnership has failed. What contributed to its failure and on what level did the community participation process fail?

Significance of the case topic

Corporations need to adopt socially responsible practices by developing close ties with the communities in which they operate and treating each other as partners, so that the communities are made to feel they are part of the whole process. By so doing, the company will feel obliged to care and invest in the community.

The rise of community partnerships also reflects a growing realization that individual entities—governments, non-profitmaking organizations and businesses—which may have acted independently of one another in the past, can often create better results when working together. There is an urgent need for business leaders to examine themselves and their corporations' activities to bring about positive change in all areas, taking into account the concerns and interests of shareholders, employees, customers, communities and corporate advocacy groups.

Teaching objectives

- Increase knowledge about the importance and role of citizen participation in business projects of which the community is a stakeholder
- Create an opportunity for students to learn and demonstrate their understanding of levels of community participation
- Develop an understanding of the role of the government employee in facilitating or discouraging citizen participation
- Create an understanding of the factors that influence the success or failure of community participation
- Learn how to consider a given situation from the differing perspectives of stakeholder groups

Introduction

As he headed to work on a frigid January morning, John MacDougall glanced out the window of his pick-up truck and took in the sight of the former surface mining operation near his home. John lived in a small town of approximately 7,000 in Nova Scotia, Canada. No matter how many times he looked at the scene, it still didn't appear any better. He and the other members of the community group weren't happy with the way things had unfolded. Although they were initially opposed to the company's plans to surface-mine within the town limits, John and the rest of his committee had relented and had really tried to work with the company. They had been sold on a plan to create a new kind of partnership structure for surface mining in which the community would play an active role and would be a stakeholder with influence. Well, the plan sounded good in theory, but, as John quickly found out, plans don't always become reality.

Now it was 2005, the local mining company, MineCo Ltd, was finished with the first stage of its mining project and the site hadn't been reclaimed to the community group's expectations. Further, there had been other broken promises. John and the rest of the Community Liaison Committee (CLC) had decided that they would no longer support the mining company. The work completed to date had been part of a sample test, and, in the view of John and the committee, it had also been a chance for the company to prove its capability and willingness to work with the community. In their view, the company failed. Now the company was contemplating plans to expand the operation.

As John pulled into the parking lot at work, he shook his head once again; he couldn't understand why the company had let them down the way it did. Some part of him wanted to believe that the company would fulfill its commitment and that they could work together. He knew that before the provincial government would approve any kind of license for a full-scale mining operation, a complete environmental assessment would be required, and part of that required that the company engaged in community consultation. Emotions were running high among John and his committee members as they thought about how they had been disillusioned. They would be ready for the public meeting when a date was announced. As he sat in his truck, he picked up his cell phone and made a call to Pat Young, one of the other committee members: "Pat, are you free tonight? I really think we need to have a meeting to decide our next steps."

Background—coal mining's legacy

John's hometown had a long and proud history of coal mining spanning nearly two centuries. It also had more than its fair share of abandoned shallow workings. The mine complex, located near John's home, consisted of several former mines in close proximity to each other on two coal seams. Mining in the early

1900s by the old room-and-pillar method left large pillars of coal to keep the roof from collapsing while miners worked. As time had passed, some of the workings had disintegrated, underground supports had deteriorated, and roof collapse had become inevitable in some areas. These mines, in addition to numerous bootleg mines, had left the area visibly scarred by subsidence, surface crop-pits, and mine-waste piles.

However, since the last mine was abandoned in 1940, the area had been slowly recovering, aesthetically. As well, not all of the area was disturbed. There were large tracts of land in the immediate vicinity that showed no signs of being affected by mining and had remained in a natural state, varying from thick woods to a large peat-bog and wetland. Despite visible disturbances by past mining, local residents had come to value the entire region as a recreational area and place to enjoy nature. People frequently hiked the trails and the woods were habitat to wildlife.

In recent years, the Province of Nova Scotia acquired the aforementioned property and numerous other similar parcels from the federal government. Along with these properties, it also received the liability associated with abandoned coal mining sites. These liabilities included threat to public safety due to undermining, and groundwater contamination caused by mine drainage. Not surprisingly, the Nova Scotia Department of Natural Resources (DNR) was receptive to a proposal by a local mining company to re-mine the land by open-pit method, effectively removing all liabilities along with helping to sustain the local coal industry. In a 2001 report entitled *Seizing the Opportunity*, the Nova Scotia Department of Energy (DOE) cited the need to encourage the use of indigenous coal where environmentally and economically feasible, as coal would likely be the principal fuel for electricity generation in the province in the near term (DOE 2001). In addition, the government also stood to earn a royalty fee for every tonne of coal that was mined.

MineCo Ltd

MineCo Ltd was a mining company owned and operated by Raymond Martell and his son, Kevin. They had operated previous surface mines in the region, and in the opinion of some, their standards of operation had not been acceptable. Residents who lived in the areas where they had mined in the past had complained about the destruction to the landscape and the mess that was left when the company was finished (see Exhibit 1). In their defense, however, the company stated that they had remediated the sites to comply with government standards. They didn't feel that they were in the wrong. However, MineCo had been blatantly remiss in other areas of their operations. In fact, the Department of Environment shut down one of its surface mine operations in 2004 because the business had not abided by environmental standards. The company was charged with allowing effluent from the mine operation to enter the ocean, thereby polluting marine life and, in particular, the local fishery stock. While Raymond and Kevin were largely responsible for the technical aspects of the mining, Gerald Martell, nephew to Raymond, acted as an independent agent for the company and was responsible for building and maintaining relationships with the community and government. The company had set its sights on the land in question, and, in the fall of 2002, they received a special exploratory license to prospect for coal on a 240-acre parcel of land in the area. The exploration license was the first of several approvals required before mining could actually begin.

Timeline of events

One day in November 2002, John and several of his neighbors noticed some excavation activity in the wooded area behind their homes. They made inquiries to their local Member of the Legislative Assembly (MLA) and municipal councilor, but they could obtain no information. Over the subsequent months, they continued to press the local politicians to find out what had been going on. Finally, in the spring of 2003, after consistent pressure for information regarding the activity on the site, the local municipal councilor supplied John with a draft copy of an application filed by MineCo Ltd for an excavation permit, and industrial approval for extraction of a bulk sample of 10,000 tonnes of coal. In the application, it was revealed that the said exploration and eventual surface mine was only the first phase of a much larger proposed development that could see the mining operation last as long as 5–7 years. At the same time, the neighbors learned of the exploration license that had been issued in December 2002. The application for exploration and subsequent approval was never made public. However, there was no legislation in Nova Scotia that required that it should be made public and that is why the company didn't do so.

Many of the neighborhood residents were furious. It was then June 2003, and, after repeated requests from neighborhood residents, the local MLA agreed to facilitate an information meeting with representatives from Departments of Natural Resources, and Environment and Labour. Prior to the meeting, John and some of his neighbors began circulating a petition as well as an information brochure to town citizens. The meeting was also announced to the public through a press release in the local newspaper issued by the local MLA. In the same article, a MineCo representative was quoted and mention was made of the remediation and employment benefits of the project.

On the night of the meeting, there were approximately 300 residents in attendance and of those who spoke out, the vast majority was strongly against the proposed project. They opposed the fact that this development would occur in a natural habitat adjacent to what was the main street of the small town and would border on the property of dozens of homeowners, churches, cemeteries and a wetland. Essentially, this activity would occur in the centre of a residential community. While the social impacts were significant enough, people also voiced concern over the environmental impacts associated with the burning of fossil fuels.

During the meeting, the MLA and officials of Department of Natural Resources gave a presentation on the mining approval process, as well as an overview of some of the benefits of surface mining. This presentation was later sent to all those in attendance. One of the more significant benefits mentioned was that this project could remediate the land, so that any danger due to former mining operations would be removed. This was something that many of the community members were aware of, but perhaps, didn't want to admit. Over the past decade, there had been several accounts of damage to buildings because of subsidence and there had even been instances of people falling into the old mine workings.

DNR officials also stressed to the public at this meeting, however, that the company had been approved for an exploration license, but without the excavation permit and industrial approval, they had no right to actually begin digging on the land; and they had yet to receive these approvals. DNR stated that these applications were currently being reviewed and nothing would happen on the site until they met all conditions. However, John and the others knew that, in fact, the company had already done some exploratory digging on the property in November 2002 without authorization. They wondered if this was an indication of how well the company could abide by government legislation.

Gerald Martell also spoke on behalf of the mining company and reported that the project would maintain nine jobs and create a further 5–11. Given that the town had been economically depressed for some time, it couldn't be denied that this was positive news. The presentations by the government and company were followed by a Q&A period. John felt that this was unsatisfactory, however, as the MLA placed a time restriction on the number of questions that would be allowed. Therefore, some people left the public meeting without having had a chance to ask their question.

Of those who did get an opportunity to speak, a wide variety of questions were asked about the particulars of the project including size, noise control, dust control, remediation plans, etc. Citizens were also concerned that the company would be able to get extensions on their bulk sample license and be able to mine a larger area. If the company could mine 10,000 tonnes without any environmental or community consultation, was there anything that could stop them from applying for extensions on the bulk sample approval so that they could mine adjacent parcels of land and avoid the environmental assessment process? DNR officials confirmed that, while there was not legislation to prevent this, the department's operating policies would not allow it to occur.

By the end of the evening, the general impression received by John and his neighbors was that the government officials and politicians were in support of the proposal. It was rumored that the company currently had nowhere to mine and several of their large clients, such as the provincial power utility and regional hospital, were in need of the coal resource. John wondered if this would be a factor for the government when considering approval of this bulk sample extraction.

Regardless of the government's motivation, John and his neighbors were still opposed. At the meeting that night and in days leading up to the meeting, a petition was circulating within the community. Following the meeting, a petition of 300+ names was presented to the local MLA requesting that he revoke the exploration license and declare the land unsuitable for mining. John and some others decided that they would continue to meet and work toward a resolution.

Initial opposition

A core group of approximately 15 people began to meet regularly over the summer months. All were individuals who lived in immediate vicinity of the proposed mining project. The first order of business of the group was to determine how they could create enough public awareness and, hopefully, resistance, so they could stop any further development. They didn't want to see even the bulk sample stage occur. They were worried that if the company managed to move ahead with the bulk sample, it would be easier for them to get approval for a full-scale plan.

The decision was made to create a website. On the website, information was provided about the social and environmental hazards of surface mining as well as details of the company's plans for development. An online email petition was set up so that supporters of the cause could email their concerns to the applicable government officials. The local public was made aware of the site by means of petition signs erected in the yards of neighborhood residents. The response to the website was encouraging. Within the first few months more than 500 individuals completed the online email petition. These email messages were forwarded to several provincial and municipal politicians and a letter of response was received from the Minister of Environment and Labour (see Exhibit 2).

John and some of his committee members were also in touch with residents of a nearby county, where another mining company had been operating. They had stated that, in their case, there were many violations of the mining permit during the operation, including a promise for ongoing remediation and disturbance of no more than 12 acres at any one time. Now there were excess of 200 acres of wasteland and there had been little or no remediation. They claimed that they had made repeated appeals to DNR for action to be taken. They had also made a request through the Freedom of Information Act to discover the amount of the performance bond posted by the company. The performance bond was money provided by the company that was held in reserve so that, in the instance that the company went bankrupt, the funds were available to remediate the land. The government denied their request citing that they could not make this information public because if they ever had to tender the remediation work, bidding companies would know the value of the fund.

John also came across a document prepared by E.L. Baudoux (Baudoux 2001) for the Department of Energy. It was a brief that addressed the need for a provincial energy strategy. What John found in the document was most disturbing. Baudoux's admittedly candid comments brought attention to the government's lack of fiscal accountability when dealing with resources that belonged, in Baudoux's opinion, to the people of Nova Scotia. He stated that the royalty fees that the government collected were a pittance compared to the profits earned by private enterprise. Further, it was the communities that suffered the most and they received nothing in return. Baudoux made the recommendation that a share of mining profits should be redirected to the communities affected. Baudoux also cited examples that have demonstrated how "ministerial discretion can bypass environmental procedures and thus make proper public examination redundant" (Baudoux 2001: 6). In his words, the granting of an environmental license was like an "in-closet charade" and some community members had considered such projects a "done deal" (Baudoux 2001: 6). As John and the others considered all of this, they became both angry and nervous.

Although the group was in full opposition mode, they were also meeting periodically with members of the Department of Natural Resources in an effort to educate themselves about the "One Window Process" (DNR 1997). This was the process that the government had established for reviewing, permitting and monitoring mine development projects in Nova Scotia.

Harvey Strickland, a senior DNR staff member, was very supportive of the group in their effort to become more informed. In particular, he wanted the community group to consider working with the company in coming up with a solution that would benefit all parties. He cited examples of how community liaison committees had worked successfully with mining companies in the past. He stressed again the subsidence dangers presented by the former mine workings. Further, MineCo Ltd had clearly indicated its interest in working with the group; it was left up to the residents to decide if they wanted to work with the company. DNR was also particularly interested in seeing this project succeed because they had dozens of other sites to remediate and they wanted to use similar methods. In Harvey Strickland's words, "We want this site to be a model for future remediation projects."[2]

During one of their meetings, Harvey, DNR staff members, John and his neighbors walked on the proposed mining site. Harvey admitted that, while there were still danger areas, the site was not as badly disturbed as he was led to believe by the mining company. It appeared to John and the others that Harvey was beginning to appreciate the views of the community and their fear of losing this recreational haven.

John and the other committee members considered their options. They realized that existing legislation did not require or allow for formal public consultation until an application for a full-scale mine had been made, and, based on this,

---

2   All quotes are taken from the interview with John MacDougall, February 14, 2005.

they knew that they really couldn't stop the bulk sample phase from occurring. Harvey Strickland also said "not in my backyard" was not good enough reason to stop this kind of project. Even though they had some reservations about the company and its willingness to work with them in good faith, they decided that they had nothing to lose by maintaining a level of involvement in the project.

Evolution of the Community Liaison Committee

The Community Liaison Committee was born, and over time, the role of the group evolved to include several goals:

- To act as a liaison between the community, government departments and the mining company

- To ensure the community was receiving accurate and up-to-date information

- To ensure the community's needs and concerns would be heard by government and the company as a plan for remediation was developed

By now, there were about seven active members in the group. Unsuccessful attempts were made to recruit others, and they could have benefited from a committee member who had some expertise in environmental matters. As well, John and another member, Pat Young, sometimes found that the commitment was overwhelming as they seemed to be the most involved of everyone.

After months of consultation and site investigation, it was determined by the citizens' group that the property posed a danger to the community and would continue to deteriorate unless action was taken to remove the hazards. The focus of the group shifted from opposition to monitoring and planning. It was important that the group played a key role in the development of the remediation project.

The group members now became focused on what could potentially become of the site. Now their emphasis was on not only fixing the "danger areas," but also working with the Department of Natural Resources on a full-scale remediation project that would see the cleaning-up of an adjacent auto salvage yard, as well as the construction of a passive-remediation bed that would clean the acid run-off from some of the other adjacent mine sites. There was a brook in the neighborhood that was red in color because of acid mine drainage; the source of this polluted water would be resolved.

DNR had conceptual drawings prepared in consultation with the CLC that showed how a full-scale mine operation would be mined in ribbons so that there would still be wooded areas remaining. These plans also included the development of a man-made lake that would be circled with a walking trail. DNR also began to search for other sources of funding that would cover the cost of the extra enhancements that would not be required work by the mining company. Several meetings were held between the CLC and DNR for the purpose of discussing the details of these plans. The CLC was very excited about the potential for the area. Harvey Strickland also appeared to be happy about the relationship that was forming among the stakeholders. While it was sometimes inconvenient and expensive for him and his staff to travel several hours to John's community, it was well worth it.

The CLC knew that there would be some inconvenience and discomfort in the short term, but, in the long term, the payoffs for future residents of the town and neighborhood made it worthwhile. It became their desire to develop a remediation project that would effectively remove all hazards on the property forever, but at the same time have a minimal effect on the environment and bordering community.

The project—the bulk sample

By January 2004, MineCo Ltd had met all government requirements and was ready to begin its bulk sample extraction. The bulk sample stage would allow it to mine up to 10,000 tonnes on a designated area within the 240-acre exploration block. The company's mining plan stated that this work was to be completed in a three-month timeframe.

According to company agent Gerald Martell, because the area had been previously mined, "We have to find out how much coal remains and the quality of the resource." DNR officials confirmed that the proponent was able to secure the necessary permits and post the required reclamation bond. This was an exploration (bulk sample) stage only. All parties realized the property in its current state posed a danger to the public and there was a need to reclaim the property to make it safe for public use.

Within the first week of the project, the CLC members were not pleased with MineCo's performance with the construction of the entry road. The actual width of the entry road was much more than what was stated in the mining plan documents. According to the members, it resulted in unnecessary clearcutting. Shortly after there were issues with the size of the settling pond, which was a catchment pool for water pumped out of the mine excavation. The CLC members became aware of these problems during periodic visits to the site to monitor the company's work. In a couple of instances, there were some uncomfortable moments with MineCo management and staff when CLC members questioned the manner in which work was done. Phone calls were made to Harvey Strickland of DNR to report the infractions and he immediately reacted and reprimanded the company.

After these occurrences, several of the CLC members decided that they no longer wanted to work with MineCo Ltd and they resumed full opposition mode.

John and two others, however, were still willing to give the company the benefit of the doubt and continued their relationship. During visits to the site, John was able to see the benefits of the work that was being done, as the underground workings were being backfilled. It was nice to know that, bit by bit, the area was becoming safer.

The community–business relationship really seemed to be paying off when Gerald Martell committed to a $2/tonne fee to be paid to the CLC. The money was meant to serve as a seed fund to allow the committee to leverage other funds. The group hoped to take advantage of grant programs that would allow them to further enhance the land beyond what the company would do as their required remediation. This promise of money was a sign of good faith and sealed the relationship. The seed money request had been made to MineCo Ltd after John had heard from DNR that other mining companies had made similar arrangements with community groups in the past.

By spring 2004, MineCo was complaining that it was not able to get its 10,000 tonnes in the designated area approved for mining by DNR. As a result, DNR approved expansion of the mine site. The CLC had no say in this decision and they weren't happy that the disturbed area ended up being much larger than what they were originally told. This decision by DNR also appeared to contradict directly with what they had been told at the June 3, 2003 meeting when community members addressed this exact issue.

MineCo Ltd continued to work in the area until September, and, by then, it reached its quota of 10,000 tonnes. The mining was supposed to be completed within three months, yet the company had been working at the site closer to nine. MineCo then, unexpectedly, removed its equipment and began mining in another area nearby. The remediation work was left incomplete and the CLC wasn't happy. The company had spread topsoil and done nothing more. The land still yet needed to be contoured, mulched and seeded. The conditions at that time were perfect for seeding, but, because the company didn't do it immediately, heavy rains began to wash away the topsoil.

Repeated attempts by the CLC to find out when the company would return were fruitless. They couldn't get MineCo to make a firm commitment. The CLC was also upset about the mine waste piles, and open holes left at the site. As well, there were rumours that the company had significantly exceeded its 10,000 tonnes limit. There was no way of verifying this, but it was very possible as the government required the company to self-monitor its tonnage. Therefore, who was watching?

But now the CLC had another reason for concern. Just before the bulk sample was completed, Kevin Martell began to mention development of a full-scale project that would see the company actually mining undisturbed areas, while avoiding previously mined areas, and therefore still leaving hazardous pits. This wasn't what had been talked about in the beginning. What would be the point of collaborating on this project if, at the end, the community was still left with hazardous sites? John knew that the CLC should have seen this coming, when, at a previous meeting of the group and the company, Raymond's son Kevin was overheard grumbling that all he wanted to do was dig coal and that there was no money to be made in filling holes. John decided it was time to get some of the group's issues addressed. He called a meeting of the committee, DNR staff and the company in November 2004.

The beginning of the end

The meeting was held at John's workplace late in November 2004. John and Pat Young were present along with Raymond and Kevin Martell, DNR's Harvey Strickland, and another staff member from DNR.

The meeting began with some discussion about the remediation efforts at the site. Harvey wanted a firm timeframe of when the work would be completed. It was DNR's job to monitor the work of the mining company and ensure that it was following the approved mining plans. Raymond said that they had to move their machinery so that they could mine elsewhere, but confirmed they would return. It was pointed out, however, that, according to the mining plan presented at commencement, all remediation was to be completed immediately.

Discussion then turned to the topic of the $2/tonne to be paid to the CLC. To everyone's astonishment, Raymond stated that he knew nothing about a prom-ise to make a contribution to the group. He said, "That promise was made by my nephew Gerald, and Gerald is only our agent, not part of our company." John became furious and continued to press Raymond about his awareness of the commitment. Finally, Raymond admitted that he knew about the promise but thought that the money was to come from coal mined during full-scale produc-tion, not from the bulk sample. John still wasn't pleased with this and presented Raymond with an ultimatum: "Regardless of what you knew, are you ready to make a commitment to us now of $20,000, as a sign of good faith that you are ready to work with our group. If not, we resume full opposition. I need an answer Raymond!" Raymond said, "No, I'm not. It might be something that I could con-sider for future mining, but no, I'm not willing to honour Gerald's commitment to you." John gave him a look of contempt, turned to the rest of the room and said that there wasn't any reason to continue the meeting.

Conclusion

That was over a month ago, and John knew from discussions with Harvey Strick-land that MineCo Ltd still had the area in its sights for possible full-scale mining production. While there currently might be more attractive sites for mining, this one was not forgotten. Harvey assured John that an environmental assessment would be required and the community would have their chance to be formally heard. John worried though that this still might not provide them with enough clout. He felt so disappointed. He really didn't believe that MineCo Ltd was the right company to do this job. If they were going to live with a surface mine in their backyards for as long as seven years, they needed to know that it would be a company they could trust and work with.

The CLC also felt let down by DNR. It had approved an expansion of the bulk sample site, and this decision directly contradicted earlier statements. As well, since the November meeting, there had been no more discussion about DNR's full-scale remediation plans for the site.

John wondered now if the promises by DNR and MineCo were just ploys to placate the group, so that the company could get at the site and get their coal. He wondered what could have been done differently by all the stakeholders (community, business and government) so that they could have had a positive outcome.

- Does the government need to change its legislation so that CLCs have real power?

- Perhaps their group needed to be larger and more formalized?

- Or maybe they left too much to trust and they should have had a more formal reporting relationship or perhaps a written agreement with MineCo Ltd?

John really wasn't sure. But, he knew that this issue wasn't going to go away and he wanted to examine some of these areas further so that the same mistakes wouldn't be made again.

Exhibit 1 Comments submitted to CLC website from residents living near former surface mine operations

"I lived near the site of one of MineCo's strip-mines for 12 years and I've seen the destruction of what a strip mine can do first hand. We had trucks going and coming all hours of the day; the dust and noise were terrible, not to mention the wildlife habitat being destroyed and our artesian well went dry, actually all the wells on the street went dry."

"I come from an area of Nova Scotia that has been ravaged by strip mining. Old mines that are no longer used are left as lumps of dirt and gravel. To allow this practice to continue is testament to ecocide."

"I am writing in regard to the proposed strip. After attending the public meeting regarding just what a strip mine would bring to our town (at best some 10 to 14 jobs), I am more convinced than ever that the very last thing our town needs is a strip mine. I stood and asked questions and am unconvinced that our town would reap any benefits from stripping the land and destroying natural animal habitat. We need only to visit the nearby community where MineCo has mined in the past to see exactly what strip mining does to any area. Thanks, but no thanks! Hopefully, the concerns of the town residents will be heard and not overlooked for the financial short-term benefits of a local business. It is time all Canadians look for ways to improve all communities rather than destroy what we have. Our town is trying to move forward with positive changes and improvements; surely stripping the land is a gigantic step backward. I say no to strip mining."

EXHIBIT 2 Letter sent to CLC from Minister of Environment and Labour

---

July 23, 2003

Dear Mr. MacDougall,

Thank you for your emails in which individuals expressed opposition to the development of a strip mine in the vicinity of [name removed for confidentiality reasons].

If the proposal reaches the stage where the proponent wants to move forward with an open-pit surface mine, then the Company will have to register the operation as an "undertaking" in accordance with the Environmental Assessment Regulations pursuant to the Environment Act. This process is designed to ensure that there is adequate information presented to the public to make an informed decision about the project, and to ensure the public will have a chance to express their views and feelings to the reviewers. The reviewers will then compile all of the material and present the package to the Minister for a decision.

Before the Company can even consider whether or not an open-pit surface mine is feasible, it must gather reliable data to support the venture. This exercise is crucial for a company to assess not only the viability of a proposed operation, but also to secure potential customers. It is common practice for firms to apply for an approval to extract a bulk sample to measure the quality of the mined material prior to making any application for a full-scale, open-pit coal mining operation.

An approval to extract a bulk sample is obtained by making application to the Department of Environment and Labour. The supporting documentation is reviewed by the engineering staff; and, if an approval is granted, there will be applicable terms and conditions which will restrict the size of the operation, the volume of coal to be extracted, and the amount of area to be disturbed. Once the bulk sample is extracted, additional terms and conditions of the approval will cause the proponent to rehabilitate the site to the satisfaction of the regulatory agencies.

The emails will be given to the appropriate staff for their perusal and consideration. I appreciate individuals bringing their concerns to my attention.

With personal regards,

Minister of Environment and Labour

References

Baudoux, E.L. (2001) "A Brief on Nova Scotia's Energy Strategy", www.gov.ns.ca/energy/documents/Baudoux.pdf, January 2005.

Nova Scotia Department of Energy (DOE) (2001) "Seizing the Opportunity. Part V: Coal", www.gov.ns.ca/energystrategy, January 2005.

Nova Scotia Department of Natural Resources (DNR), Mineral Resources Branch (1997) "A User's Guide to the 'One Window' Process for Mine Development Approvals", Information Circular ME56; www.gov.ns.ca/natr/meb/ic/ic56.htm#figure1, January 2005.

Discussion questions

1. Consider each of the stakeholder groups (community, business and government) and identify issues with each that may have contributed to the failure of the partnership.

2. (a) Define community participation. (b) List some of the different manners in which community members could have been involved in this project.

3. Review the stages of Arnstein's "Ladder of Citizen Participation" and provide examples from the case that demonstrate placement of the community at different stages of the ladder.

4. Find and read the following article: R.A. Irvin and John Stansbury, "Citizen Participation in Decision Making: Is It Worth the Effort?" *Public Administration Review* 64.1 (January/February 2004): 55. Now, place yourself in the shoes of DNR official Harvey Strickland. Using the advantages and disadvantages of community participation cited in this article, apply those that are relevant to the case.

2.3
The smell of power
Yves Rocher in La Gacilly, France[1]

Emmanuel Raufflet and Monique Le Chêne

Yves Rocher is a major brand of beauty products in France as well as the world's leading brand of vegetal beauty products. In all, Yves Rocher has about 13,500 employees worldwide and annual sales of €13 billion.

This case focuses on the relations between the multinational company and the town of its founder—La Gacilly in Brittany. The rise of the company as well as the local development of the town as a major regional economic and tourist magnet has been achieved by the mayor-entrepreneur Yves Rocher over more than four decades.

This case looks at the power relations of an industrialist, Yves Rocher, with a local community, La Gacilly, Brittany, France. This model of single industry economic success is based on a complete symbiosis between the town and the company, accomplished equally by the fusion of political and economic power and the fusion of images (the symbolizing of products using the land and vice versa: the representation of the land by the products).

The aim of this case is to invite students to examine and understand power relations at the heart of this town–company "symbiosis" and to illustrate a framework of power relations developed by three authors (Lukes, Clegg and Hardy) who use a three-dimensional conceptual model of power (decision, framing the decision, control of legitimacy). This theory of power sees three dimensions of power:

---

1 This case was first published in M. Le Chêne and E. Raufflet (2008) "Le parfum de pouvoir: Yves Rocher à La Gacilly", in E. Raufflet and P. Batellier (eds.), *Responsabilité sociale de l'entreprise: Enjeux de gestion et cas pédagogiques* (Montréal: Presses internationales Polytechnique): 131-40.

- Power as decision capability
- Power as ability to frame decisions
- Power as control of legitimacy

What makes this case relatively unique?
Cases about the relations between companies and their local milieus from a critical perspective are a rarity. This case illustrates the construction of local power relations. The theory application concerns an established tradition of critical management studies. This teaching case invites students to understand the construction of a consensus between a mayor-entrepreneur and the local population.

Teaching objectives
After using this case, students will have:

- Understood from a theoretical standpoint the construction of power relations based on a solid empirical case
- Become more acquainted with the theoretical definitions of power proposed by Clegg and Hardy
- Become acquainted with a theoretical perspective on the relations between firms and a local milieu that differ from the more classical corporate social responsibility or stakeholder approaches

---

A company–town symbiosis

> Imagine, organize, construct and realize—these are my goals! The people who follow us are those who want to live. One day, La Gacilly will be famous and prosperous. I give you my word. You will be the judge![2]

Forty years later, the Yves Rocher group employs more than 1,800 people at its plant in La Gacilly, Brittany, France. In the same period, the population grew from 1,100 in 1959 to 2,300 in 2000. The Yves Rocher Group meanwhile became the French leader in beauty products, with more than half its turnover coming from the international market, yet at the same time providing more than 3,000 local jobs. In 1977, the mayor-entrepreneur received an award for regional development and quality of life from the publisher of the financial journal *La Vie française*. The award had gone previously to major regional French urban centres such as Rennes, Poitiers and Tours.

---

2 Excerpt from a letter by Yves Rocher to the people of La Gacilly in 1959.

La Gacilly in 1959: a town in decline

La Gacilly is a Breton town situated some 60 km from the sea in the department of Morbihan. At the end of the 1950s, a local historian could write:

> Nothing unusual or original sets the region of La Gacilly apart . . . Although the countryside is rather more pleasant than in many other regions, nothing out of the ordinary distinguishes this part of the world (Guillet and Guillet 2000: 4).

The municipality of La Gacilly has been the capital of the canton since the French Revolution—a status that helped it develop more rapidly than its neighbours. And yet, far from major regional trade networks, the town—like many rural municipalities—was in a demographic and economic decline: the population went from 1,500 inhabitants in 1935 to 1,100 in 1959 and its prospects seemed limited.

An alternative plan for regional development

National and regional development policies in France began in the post-war period. They did not, however, respond to local needs. Indeed, they depended on the decentralization of industrial activity and mainly benefited regional urban centres. These policies neglected isolated rural areas such as that around La Gacilly.

In 1959, Yves Rocher, one of the area's native sons, refused to accept the economic and demographic decline that seemed to be La Gacilly's fate and drew up a rural industrialization plan.

Exhibit 1 The Founding Act

In 1959, Yves Rocher, a 29-year-old entrepreneur, sent a letter to the people of La Gacilly:

> As a descendant of one of the oldest families of La Gacilly, I feel, perhaps more than others who were not born here, a certain anxiety when I see the country heading towards a fatal destiny. The prosperity of a country depends on economic factors, and I am speaking to you now as a businessman. First, I rebel against those who, through lack of awareness, lack of ability, or lack of interest, claim that "there is nothing to be done". In the economic structure of the nation, which has until now been pushing industrial concentration, we aspire to a situation where, the commercial services of an enterprise having to reach across an entire region, being 15 km from the train station will no longer be a handicap if we are talking about light industry. To stay with what we know for certain, and without promising any miracles, La Gacilly will have,

by the end of 1959, 30 employees, and by the end of 1960, 150 employees. There is nothing extraordinary about this, and only gloomy thinkers will find fault with it. Even this effort will be not be enough to give La Gacilly the rank we want her to assume.

The plan has four characteristics. The first is the distribution across the territory of industrial facilities: Yves Rocher advocates job creation at the level of rural municipalities—an idea that goes far beyond the official policy favouring large-scale industrial facilities in regional centres. The aim of his approach is industrial development in harmony with the quality of life of small municipalities.

The second characteristic concerns the type of industrial activity recommended. The plan promotes light industries in rural areas, adapted to the limitations of isolated areas using mail-order distribution, with a postal service covering the entire region.

The third characteristic relies on local initiatives, and in particular on the activities of its own companies. In contrast to other local elected officials who try to attract businesses to the area with local tax incentives, Yves Rocher's strategy for regional development is to create the jobs himself that will keep the local area from dying. The choice of mail-order sales as the main channel for distribution and the "green" positioning of beauty products fit the aim of local development. At a time when only a small minority of women dared go into a perfumery, Yves Rocher undertook the democratization of beauty products, as much through affordable pricing (much less expensive than other companies) as through the method of distribution (solely by mail order at that time). At the same time, the image of the company and its products very quickly became associated with nature and plants. Beginning in the 1970s, people in La Gacilly grew flowers and vegetables that would be used to make beauty products.

Finally, the fourth characteristic of Yves Rocher's plan lies in its fusion of the political and economic spheres: the electoral promises of the politician contain the economic projects of the entrepreneur and job creator. The economic activities very quickly legitimize the political mandate, and the political mandate claims to be at the service of economic development. The politician's various electoral mandates align with local and then regional strategies for industrial job creation.

Yves Rocher became mayor of La Gacilly in 1963 after building his first plant there; this grew from 30 employees in 1959 to 334 in 1969, and from 1,200 in 1984 to some 1,800 in the 1990s. In 1982, he became departmental councillor for La Gacilly; his group set up production units in two of the canton's municipalities (Les Fougerêts and St-Martin) and participated directly in the setting-up of a printing plant in another of the canton's municipalities (Cournon). During his campaign for regional councillor, he promised job creation:

> In the first stage, we created 2,700 jobs between Ploermel and Redon.
> Today, with the Mini-Nord plan, we are entering the second phase. Very

> simply, what we're talking about is generating 2,000 additional jobs in
> Morbihan thanks to the development of mail-order sales within the
> Yves Rocher Group. And there you have my overall plan for the year
> 2000.[3]

As the political project became regional, it enlarged or created new units for production, storage, manufacturing and distribution networks in the region's municipalities including Questembert, Ploermel, Rieux, Sixt-sur-Aff, Guillac, Maure-de-Bretagne, Janzé and Saint-Marcel. We should also mention here that the administrative headquarters of Yves Rocher France, based in Rennes, employ more than 300 people.

In the same period that saw the widespread industrialization of the rural fabric, the municipality was developing the municipal space to make it more attractive to tourists:

> A village synonymous with nature, flowers and beauty, the municipal-
> ity where Yves Rocher was born offers Europe more than beauty prod-
> ucts, it offers the art of living. Because in the twentieth century, it still
> preserves its typically rural houses and flower gardens (*Livre vert de
> ma beauté*, 1991).

Indeed, since the 1960s, the municipality has been conducting a beautification project with the goal of making La Gacilly an "authentic town with a rich history" (Office du tourisme 2002a: 9). La Gacilly had been known as a natural, gently rolling site between the river and the hill behind it (Guillet and Guillet 2000). The local development policy deliberately constructed this village "of traditions" by supporting the arrival of craftspeople and the flowering and beautification of the town's streets, but also by creating tourist attractions directly tied to the company's activities, such as the plant museum at the Yves Rocher Foundation, and tours of the botanical garden and factory site.

For four decades, Yves Rocher has thus extended his activities as a politician/ job creator from his native municipality out into the canton and then across the entire region. This development project has transformed La Gacilly from a small, isolated rural municipality in decline into a major economic and tourism axis in the regional context. La Gacilly has indeed acquired the "rank" its native son promised it in 1959.

---

3 *Ouest-France*, 14 May 1992.

Creating a model town: La Gacilly—'city of flowers' and 'city of crafts'

One of the fixtures of municipal policy in La Gacilly since the 1960s has been the promotion of green tourism by creating a "harmonious and flowering" small town. This intention became clear in the 1970s with the setting-up of craftspeople in the town. These new artisans are weavers, glassblowers and etchers, potters, silk painters, sculptors in granite and wood, and calligraphers. They offer a variety of art objects designed for interior decoration and as gifts, aimed at the visitors to the town. These artists are the main actors in this model village. The municipality offers them incentives to move into the town such as a year's free rent and assistance in acquiring modern studios in renovated houses. In 2002, artisans were living in 22 studios.

Besides these activities, the municipality showcases the artisans in the streets, which become pedestrian malls and are given a neo-ruralist look. Asphalt is replaced by paving stones, house fronts are stripped of their roughcast, and benches and fountains appear, along with retro streetlamps, to create a crafts circuit. The municipality invites the local residents to join in the activities: in particular, to plant flowers that will add to the beautification of the town:

> Because we want to ensure the completion of our town's decoration, the Municipal Council has, at the suggestion of its mayor, decided to offer you again this year, free of charge, the plants you will need . . . I ask you all to continue to help in the beautification and development of our town in order to make La Gacilly a genuine "garden city".[4]

Related to the tourism policy transforming the face of the city is a prestigious and diverse recreation and leisure policy, supported by the municipality. In the late 1960s, a municipal tent containing around 500 seats was erected to accommodate shows by well-known variety artists. In the 1970s, the municipality began supporting prestigious events from time to time, appealing to a broad regional audience for horse racing, motocross events and an annual antiques show. It also pioneered the construction in the 1970s of a sizeable sports complex for a town of 2,000 people, including a games hall, pool, playing fields, covered outdoor tennis courts and a riding club. In the 1980s, the council began giving grants to an art gallery to host travelling exhibits of painting and photography; the gallery opened a major "mediatheque" (a public library including diverse media and Internet access) in 2002. This policy has allowed La Gacilly, with its leisure facilities and events, to stand out from the neighbouring municipalities, which are poorer and less well equipped.

In short, the beautification of the town and the prestigious recreation policy are a fixture in the municipality's activities. In a municipality that began with

4   Message to the people of La Gacilly in the municipal newsletter of May 1976.

no major tourist attractions, the municipality created a back-to-the-land space. It inserted the actors—artisans and local people—and showcased the town's streets. Finally, it invited visitor-spectators. And so appeared the new face of the "harmonious small town" promoted first in the Tourist Bureau's brochures, and then by the community of municipalities as well as the company's communications department (see Exhibit 2).

Its back-to-the-land aspect is both re-creation and recreation. It is re-creation inasmuch as it is a showcase for traditions: only the beautified and "typical" aspects of the past are showcased after being stripped of their practical or mundane characteristics. This ruralism is also recreation to the extent that it represents a leisure activity and a tourist attraction for visitors looking for a genuinely authentic model of the regional landscape.

Exhibit 2 Alignment of images of the town in municipal and company discourses

Municipality—"It is in this authentic village with its rich history that painters, engravers, silversmiths, glassmakers, craftsmen in marquetry and wood, sculptors, potters and coppersmiths have come to live. They work in leather, paint on silk, create *trompe-l'oeil*. They love furnishings and decoration, or make weathervanes. In the flowering lanes of La Gacilly, you can watch them work creating high-quality personalized crafts before your eyes. La Gacilly is the only village in France offering such a wide range of crafts, and it has been doing so for 25 years—proof that passion is not always fleeting" (Municipal tourist brochure, 2001: 9)

Company—"A village synonymous with nature, flowers and beauty, the municipality where Yves Rocher was born offers Europe more than beauty products, it offers the art of living. Because in the 20th century, it still preserves its typically rural houses and flower gardens" (*Livre vert de la beauté*, 1991)

The forgotten dimensions

Above anything else, however, municipal development policy enlivens the front of the stage—the old town—and ignores other neighbourhoods. In addition, it often excludes social and educational dimensions. The decision to build a new covered market illustrates the priority accorded to beautification to the detriment of less visible social dimensions. The public elementary school attended by more than 150 pupils is dilapidated. It has needed major investment for renovation or to put up a new building since the 1980s. At a 1991 municipal council meeting, the parents' association at the school submitted a request for investment in a building project. The project was refused. Yet, at the same meeting, the council approved a proposal from the mayor to construct a new municipal covered market that would re-create the weekly market the town had had 20 years before. The municipal covered market represents the most recent arte-fact resulting from a beautification policy based on neo-traditional styles and the showcasing of rural life. Every Saturday morning since 1994, the town has hosted a natural food market where fresh produce from the "terroir" is sold. Yet as of 2002, renovations to the public school still had not been completed.

In conclusion, from being a marginal entity in 1959, La Gacilly has become the centre of a major rural and regional economic development effort, as well as the symbol of harmonious village life—thanks to the municipality's tourism policy. Yves Rocher's 1959 promise has come true: La Gacilly will henceforth be famous and prosperous. The municipal council's projects represent the artefacts of the pride of a small town that has become great. The allocation of municipal resources reflects these concerns with beauty, greatness and fame—but often to the detriment of social and educational action.

Managing the town like a business

The mayor-entrepreneur's management of municipal policy assimilates in a very explicit way with that of a private company:

> The future of La Gacilly is tied to the choices the municipality will make. The latter considers the municipality as a true business. Its management must allow the raising of the quality of life at the local level . . . Tomorrow perhaps, the municipality will be seen as the kind of collective that was successful at expanding its economy thanks to the tenacity of a team of local men who knew it would not always be easy (Municipal brochure, 1976: 43).

The mayor-entrepreneur has played a central role in the modus operandi of the municipality for four decades. Mayor since 1963, Yves Rocher frames deci-sions in three ways. First, the mayor is the sole and uncontested creator of the town's master plan. It is a plan based mainly on job creation, the guarantor of the well-being and continued life of the region. For the mayor-industrialist, the town's economic development depends equally on an entrepreneurial manage-ment style and the holding of municipal powers by those able to ensure that management approach. The skill of the mayor and the entrepreneurial manage-ment style are thus mutually reinforcing. Moreover, the rarity of the mayor's physical presence in the municipality consolidates the perception of his effi-ciency and visionary ability. Indeed, he appears in public in La Gacilly only to make decisions at municipal council meetings, or for events inaugurating or commemorating the implementation of those decisions.

The mayor alone trains his team of intermediaries—the deputy mayors and, to a lesser extent, the other municipal councillors. This "team" of go-betweens are chosen to ensure that the mayor-entrepreneur's projects go through. The people interviewed in the course of our research stressed, however, that their role is confined to the daily business of the council and does not extend to more important decisions. One speaker mentioned the permanent indecision and lack of involvement of elected municipal officials—deputies in particular—in responding to citizens' requests. According to another speaker, the mayor surrounds himself with people:

> . . . with little charisma, who aren't very creative . . . underlings . . . financially tied hands and feet to the factory . . . and old boys [all the deputies are over 65] . . .

These choices are designed to avoid having elected representatives become involved or accountable. Besides, all of them "are afraid of his opinion swings". "The day after making a decision, Yves Rocher may have completely changed his mind." The contrast between the rare but crucial presence of the mayor-entrepreneur and the permanent but ineffectual presence of the deputies strengthens the constructed image of the demiurge.

The municipality tends to allocate grants and meeting space to the least disruptive groups, such as those constituted of elderly people and sports lovers, or to elitist cultural activities, at the expense of projects to improve society (children, youth). As an example, the municipality has rejected every proposal for youth shelters submitted to it since the early 1980s.

The erosion of civil society and local participation

This construction of power relations has had the effect of creating a climate that is not conducive to local initiative and, more generally, of creating apathy in local life.

The way in which the municipality refused, very recently, to open a locally initiated kindergarten is a good illustration of the effects of the mayor's concentration of decisional powers and the powerlessness of elected officials confronted with the needs of local people. In the late 1990s, an early childhood educator and the director of a day centre, along with several mothers of young families, identified some major gaps in services to pre-school children in the municipality. Citing a report by the agency responsible for the protection of mothers and children in the region (Protection maternelle et infantile du département; PMI), which confirmed the lack of services, they formed an association to design and implement a kindergarten project, in close collaboration with the deputy mayor for social affairs. One of the participants in the project recalls:

> Everything was going really well, the project was well put together, the budget drawn up, the location found—in the retirement home. The director was very glad to have them, and the old people even more so.

They had already set up a kind of small kindergarten with volunteer moms working a half-day once in a while. With the support of the mayor's secretary, the "early childhood" contract was agreed on by the town hall and the Caisse d'allocations familiales (Family Benefits). The only thing left was the council vote—a formality!

The council met in November 2000. The project was presented by the deputy for social affairs, and immediately and categorically rejected by the mayor with no discussion or justification. No one in the room dared come to the project's or the deputy's defence.

The categorical refusal of the mayor deeply affected the people involved. Those who had initiated the project were profoundly disappointed that a year and a half of community work had been rejected in that way—as they called it, "by one sweep of the broom". The director of the retirement home was deeply embarrassed. And most of the mothers in the association, whose husbands worked directly for the company to a greater or lesser degree, withdrew from the project. Finally, at the last elections in 2002, the deputy involved lost his job, despite doing extremely well at the polls.

Beyond this one example, this entrepreneurial management style, centred on the mayor-entrepreneur's personal vision and control over decisions, has had the effect of eroding participation in local political and social life. At the political level, no candidates list other than that proposed by the mayor-entrepreneur has been drawn up since 1968, and the last time an independent candidate ran for election was in 1980. Similarly, fewer than 30 people attended the counting of votes for the 2002 municipal elections. At the level of social activity, the municipality is strongly apathetic. The strongest associations are sports groups and those of elderly people who avoid politics.

Generally speaking, many Gacillians find the intervention of municipal power in society and the absence of dialogue hard to come to terms with. The stifling of collective demands by giving individual responses is especially criticized. Some speakers told us: "You can't do anything without the Mayor's Office." "Yves Rocher is Louis XIV in La Gacilly." This first observation—of economic success and improved quality of life alongside the political and social apathy of local people—is followed by a second: the absence of open conflict around the hijacking of how the town's affairs are run.

Building and sustaining consensus

There is genuine consensus around the fame and prestige the municipality enjoys thanks to its mayor. The mayor has been rewriting the local history so as to reinforce the legitimacy achieved through his actions. The discourse of Yves Rocher is delivered jointly by the company and the municipality. It does not confine itself to promoting the town or the programmes being run by the municipality or the Yves Rocher Foundation; it also extends to the construction of shared memories and a founding myth. For example, when the town's history is mentioned (the time before the plant was built), it is basically to remind people that the town was doomed to inescapable decline. That memory opposes two time periods: the time before-the-plant, which is dark and empty, and the time after-the-plant, a genuine golden age.

In 1988, a company museum, the Espace Yves Rocher, was inaugurated. Its mission is to educate people about the plants and to present the company's pro-environmental actions. It is also dedicated to preserving the memory of the company. This evocation of memory is in fact the jewel in the crown of the founding myth celebration. The story of Yves Rocher could be the simple tale of the "self-made man" but other elements have been added to it. The story resembles a legend, or at least displays some of those characteristics: the solitary child who loses his father, the meeting with the old woman who holds the secret of the buttercup pomade that would be the key to his future, and then the road strewn with obstacles all of which he overcomes. Other elements come into play: his transformation into the man who appeared just when the municipality needed him, along with his company's tremendous success and strong presence around the world.

This fictional narrative constructing the legend of the man continues in the reinterpretation of the history of La Gacilly, where an official memory has been forged. A selective past, the story told by the local press and the tourist bureau, is henceforth set in stone.[5]

For the Gacillians, the celebration of the memory of the company and the family of collaborators—sons of the "land"—consolidates the feeling of belonging to a unique adventure in big business. An identity is constructed out of this possibility of referring back to an established memory, and to a past everyone knows, much like that of other regions with a more legendary industrial past. Other elements, such as re-creating the past in a negative light, make the Gacillians feel that they have no alternative to the industry or the municipality's power, and this forces them to support it. The people of La Gacilly have transformed Yves Rocher into the man the whole town needed. As one speaker put it: "He's the one who saved La Gacilly from ruin."

For this reason, the period "post-Rocher" is cause for concern, since "he's the one who made and continues to make the land". The inhabitants are not sure his children will carry on his work. Some Gacillians think the sensible thing to do would be to relocate the plants, and that the rationale of "heritage" and "territoriality" does not fit with that of industry in general.

Furthermore, the support for the holder of municipal power happens outside the processes and content of decisions, whose specific aims are not directly

---

5 In 1998, the Espace Yves Rocher was replaced by the Végétarium. Dedicated to the knowledge of the world's plants, the museum no longer reserves space for the city. Recalling the town's and the firm's memories is now done at the plant site.

oriented towards the population. Essentially, this relates to the phenomenon of "environmentalism" and the municipality's tourism policy. The municipal discourse on improvements to the living environment is inseparable from the development of green tourism. The course of action on tourism policy is presented as an end in itself: it too must serve to support the development of the "land". That is its legitimacy. As a result, tourism policy becomes unassailable. Questioning its scope, based on what it actually involves and lacks, is not easy for the Gacillians.

The future of the model

Over the last four decades, Yves Rocher has expanded the scope of his actions as a politician/business entrepreneur from his native town to the canton, and to the region as a whole. This success has transformed La Gacilly's profile from a declining and isolated town to a major economic and tourist magnet in the regional context. La Gacilly has achieved the "rank" that Yves Rocher has promised to achieve in 1959. At the same time, some are concerned about the future of the model. Is the city really that well prepared for the future? To what extent does this successful industry–town symbiosis create winning conditions for the future?

References

Guillet, J., and A. Guillet (2000) *Commerçants et artisans en pays gallo, 1850–1950* (La Gacilly: éditions des Pins).

Office du tourisme (2002a) *Le pays de La Gacilly: Loisirs, hébergements, restauration* (La Gacilly: Mairie de La Gacilly).

—— (2002b) *La Gacilly, cité des métiers d'art* (La Gacilly: Mairie de La Gacilly).

Rocher, Yves (2002) *Le livre vert de la beauté: collection de 1977 à 2002* (La Gacilly: Yves Rocher).

Discussion questions

1. What surprised you in this case about Yves Rocher in La Gacilly?

2. Describe Yves Rocher's management style as a mayor.

Teaching notes for this case are available from Greenleaf Publishing. These are free of charge and available only to teaching staff. They can be requested by going to:
www.greenleaf-publishing.com/darkside_notes

2.4

Who takes responsibility for the informal settlements?

Mining companies in South Africa and the challenge of local collaboration[1]

Ralph Hamann

Among the mining companies in the case study area, corporate social responsibility (CSR) traditionally manifested itself as philanthropic initiatives premised on competitive efforts at gaining improved image and reputation. Not only did this manifestation

1 This case study is based on R. Hamann, "Corporate Social Responsibility in Mining in South Africa" (unpublished PhD thesis, University of East Anglia, Norwich, UK, 2004). Parts of the case study have been previously published in adapted form as an article; see R. Hamann, "Corporate Social Responsibility, Partnerships, and Institutional Change: The Case of Mining Companies in South Africa", *Natural Resources Forum* 28.4 (2004): 278-90. A version is also available in *The Business of Sustainable Development in Africa* (ed. Ralph Hamann, Stu Woolman and Courtenay Sprague), published by Unisa Press, 2008. The case study research consisted of semi-structured interviews with representatives from mining companies (28 individuals), local and provincial government and traditional authorities (11), unions, NGOs, and local community organizations (10), and consultants and analysts (5). Within the mining companies, the sampling strategy was informed by an initial interview with the corporate manager or director responsible for corporate or community affairs. At the operational level, managers for community relations, environmental management, human resources (HR) and, where possible, general management, were interviewed. In addition to the interviews, the research consisted of participant observation, document analysis, and a facilitated group discussion involving 16 participants from mining companies, local government, tribal authority and civil society organizations. Most of these interviews were conducted in 2003 but more recent discussions have been held with some of the original interviewees as well as others. I am grateful to the interviewees for their time and commitment to the research.

of CSR prevent a sincere, proactive engagement with the underlying causes of social problems in the area, but the competitive element also helped to obstruct the establishment of improved collaboration between local actors. Competitive pressures, even if seemingly supportive of CSR, can be at odds with the overarching objectives of CSR in the absence of a guiding institutional framework.

The CSR-as-philanthropy approach perpetuated an independent engagement with social issues around the mines and, most significantly, a reluctance to deal with underlying social problems. Hence, the companies considered the informal settlements—also known as slums or squatter camps—to be the responsibility of local government, disregarding the linkages between their own core business practices and the growth of these settlements. On the other hand, local government was constrained in fulfilling its constitutional mandate and furthermore expected the companies to be more proactive in addressing social challenges. The result of this vicious cycle of irresponsibility and lack of collaboration has been rapidly growing informal settlements and deteriorating socioeconomic conditions. The companies' recent modernization drive contributed further to the growth of informal settlements, thereby contradicting an underlying assumption in the business case narrative.

More recently, companies have been experiencing greater market-based pressures, especially from institutional investors and stock exchanges' corporate governance regulations. More significant changes, and greater alignment with national and local development needs, are the result of increasing pressures from the state's socioeconomic transformation agenda, premised on state sovereignty over mineral resources. Even the increasingly important pressures at the local level exerted by community groups or local government often rely on institutional changes at the national level spearheaded by constitutional rights and local government policy. The increasing commitment by companies to cross-sectoral collaboration is based especially on these local pressures.

Institutional changes—both in the market and the state—have led to increased commitment to CSR and cross-sectoral collaboration. The most powerful driver has been the state's mandate and its implementation through a licensing system based on state sovereignty over mineral resources. Over and above compulsion, however, institutional changes have brought about revisions in economic and competitive strategies. Community resistance, for example, has now become a much more significant risk. There has also been a change in what is legitimately expected of companies and in the manner by which corporate managers define their enlightened self-interest. The broader implication is that continued efforts are needed in shaping the public sector context for companies.

During 2003, the second largest platinum mining company in the world, Impala, planned a new open-cast mine adjacent to its established mines in the area around Rustenburg, South Africa, which employed over 20,000 workers. However, it was confronted with significant resistance from residents of Luka, a small village close to the planned mine. The fact that this resistance represented a formidable challenge to the company's plans was a manifestation of the changes that had been occurring in the international mining industry, with corporate social responsibility (CSR) and related concepts gaining in currency, and—more significantly—the far-reaching changes that had occurred in South Africa since the transition to democracy in 1994. More stringent environmental legislation now governed applications for new mines, and companies were expected to show that their activities would benefit local communities.

The conflict between Impala and the Luka community was also an expression of simmering tension between local communities and the mining companies in the area (not just Impala but also the other two large platinum companies, Anglo Platinum and Lonmin, and other smaller platinum and chrome mining companies). This tension was in many ways an indictment of past approaches to CSR by these companies. The Luka villagers staunchly opposed Impala's proposed new mine on the grounds that the community had not benefited historically from the company's activities in the area and had not been adequately compensated for negative impacts, such as cracked houses and, allegedly, a degraded water supply. An overarching concern was the steady growth of informal settlements—or squatter camps—around Luka (and indeed the entire Rustenburg area), a growth that was linked at least in part to the mining companies' historical and, to a lesser extent, continuing labour recruitment and housing practices. Finally, much of the Luka residents' resentment was based on the belief that in the past Impala's communication with, and contributions to, the traditional authority—the Royal Bafokeng Nation—had not benefited the community.

In response to these concerns, Impala made efforts to communicate directly with community representatives on the local government ward committee. These efforts included constructing a small office building for community meetings and interaction with the company. However, the traditional authority felt threatened by the company's engagement with the local council and ordered the destruction of the building before it could be completed (on the grounds that it had not approved the plans as owner of the land). To make matters even more difficult for the company, a more radical faction emerged within the community, identifying the resistance of the villagers as an opportunity to make more far-reaching demands of the company and threatening to derail the negotiations and embark on protest action and sabotage.

On the one hand, Impala was arguably struggling with the legacy of irresponsible mining practices and community engagement in the past. On the other, the company found it difficult to respond systematically to one of the core concerns raised by the Luka community and others—the continued growth of informal settlements and the associated deteriorating socioeconomic conditions in the area. Very little could be done without some level of collaboration and coordination between the mining company, the local municipality, the traditional authority and the local communities—yet such collaboration seemed near impossible given the conflict between the groups and low levels of trust and communication. This case study analyses some of the developments that led to this intractable situation in the study area and some of the efforts the various stakeholders made to respond to it.

The historical and policy context

South Africa is endowed with the world's largest reserves of a number of minerals—such as gold, platinum and titanium—and hence the mining sector has been a crucial force in the country's industrialization and modernization process, including state development. Although mining contributed only about 12% of South Africa's gross domestic product (GDP) between 1950 and 1990, the country's economic dependence on the sector has been significant because of the large workforce employed on the mines, the sector's important contribution to exports, and the dominant role of a few large, diversified mining houses, including the predecessors of two of today's largest mining corporations, BHP Billiton and Anglo American.

The extent to which mining companies, and industry in general, colluded with or underpinned the apartheid state is still a matter of debate. Most commentators agree, however, that the mining houses' activities were inextricably linked with colonial and subsequently apartheid policies through the migrant labour system—the primary aim of which was to ensure the supply of low-cost labour to the mines. The final report of the Truth and Reconciliation Commission goes so far as to argue that: "The blueprint for 'grand apartheid' was provided by the mines and was not an Afrikaner State innovation."[2] The adverse social impacts of mining companies' practices, especially those related to the migrant labour system and the single-sex hostels, have long been documented.[3]

In the wake of the transition to democracy in the early 1990s, two kinds of institutional change took place that had implications for the evolving CSR debate in South Africa's mining industry. The first was market-related change. In the early 1990s, South Africa's capital markets were gradually re-integrated with international markets, and the mining houses came under increasing pressure to conform to international expectations. One result was organizational restructuring so as to focus on core competencies; another was that many of the large South African companies moved their primary or secondary listing to one of the main international stock exchanges, most commonly London. Market-based

2   Truth and Reconciliation Commission of South Africa (TRC) (2003) *Truth and Reconciliation Commission of South Africa Report, 21 March 2003* (Johannesburg: TRC; www.info.gov. za/otherdocs/2003/trc/rep.pdf, July 2005): 150.
3   L. Flynn (2002) *Studded with Diamonds and Paved with Gold: Miners, Mining Companies and Human Rights in Southern Africa* (London: Bloomsbury).

drivers of CSR have also gained prominence in South Africa with the publication of the King 2 code on corporate governance in 2002 and the launch of the Johannesburg Securities Exchange (JSE) Socially Responsible Investment Index.[4]

The second kind of change was driven by the state. One of the first acts passed by the new government was the Mines Health and Safety Act of 1996, targeted at the dismal safety record of South African mines. The ultimate aim of the new government, however, was to establish an entirely new mining dispensation, which culminated in a new law promulgated in 2002. This law proclaims state sovereignty over mineral resources (private ownership was common previously) and requires all companies to renew their prospecting or mining licences. This licensing process allows the government to support previously disadvantaged South Africans in the industry under the rubric of black economic empowerment (BEE). The most prominent aspect of BEE has been the government's insistence that blacks should own significant company shares, which prompted fears of value dilution in established companies. These fears became most acute when, in July 2002, a draft government proposal stipulated that 51% of the industry be owned by blacks within ten years, and led to a massive sell-off of shares.[5]

This intense reaction, especially by foreign investors, inspired a renewed commitment to negotiation and a search for compromises. The negotiations took place in the newly formed Sector Partnership Committee and resulted in the "broad-based socioeconomic empowerment charter for the South African mining industry".[6] The target that was agreed on for equity transfer was 26% within ten years, but, most importantly, this was placed within a broader set of requirements by which to judge mining companies' transformation efforts.

What is known as the BEE "scorecard" includes such important CSR-related items as community development, improved employee housing and affirmative procurement (see Exhibit 1). Companies are now assessed with respect to this scorecard in their quest for transforming their "old order rights" into "new order rights", and in competing for new exploration or mining licences.

4 Johannesburg Securities Exchange (JSE) (2003) *JSE SRI Index: Background and Selection Criteria* (Johannesburg: JSE).
5 Reportedly, over 52 billion rand (exchange rate R10.00 = $1.00) was lost from the market capitalization of South African listed mining companies within two days, with the JSE resource index falling 5% and the gold index 12% (interview with Roger Baxter).
6 www.dme.gov.za/minerals/mining_charter.htm, accessed July 2003.

EXHIBIT 1 Scorecard for the broad-based socioeconomic empowerment charter for the South African mining industry

Source: www.dme.gov.za/minerals/pdf/scorecard.pdf, accessed July 2003

Human resource development

- Has the company offered every employee the opportunity to be functionally literate and numerate by the year 2005 and are employees being trained?
- Has the company implemented career paths for HDSA [historically disadvantaged South African] employees including skills development plans?
- Has the company developed systems through which empowerment groups can be mentored?

Employment equity

- Has the company published its employment equity plan [in accordance with the Employment Equity Act] and reported on its annual progress in meeting that plan?
- Has the company established a plan to achieve a target for HDSA participation in management of 40% within five years and is implementing the plan?
- Has the company identified a talent pool and is it fast tracking it?
- Has the company established a plan to achieve the target for women participation in mining of 10% within the five years and is implementing the plan?

Migrant labour

- Has the company subscribed to government and industry agreements to ensure non-discrimination against foreign migrant labour?
- Mine community and rural development
- Has the company cooperated in the formulation of integrated development plans [as required in local government and planning legislation] and is the company cooperating with government in the implementation of these plans for communities where mining takes place and for major labour sending areas? Has there been effort on the side of the company to engage the local mine community and major labour sending area communities? (Companies will be required to cite a pattern of consultation, indicate money expenditures and show a plan.)

Housing and living conditions

- For company-provided housing has the mine, in consultation with stakeholders, established measures for improving the standard of housing, including the upgrading of the hostels, conversion of hostels to family units and promoted home ownership options for mine employees? (Companies will be required to indicate what they have done to improve housing and show a plan to progress the issue over time and is implementing the plan.)
- For company-provided nutrition, has the mine established measures for improving the nutrition of mine employees? (Companies will be required to indicate what they have done to improve nutrition and show a plan to progress the issue over time and is implementing the plan.)

Procurement

- Has the mining company given HDSAs preferred supplier status?
- Has the mining company identified current level of procurement from HDSA companies in terms of capital goods, consumables and services?

- Has the mining company indicated a commitment to a progression of procurement from HDSA companies over a 3–5 year timeframe in terms of capital goods,
consumables and services? And to what extent has the commitment been implemented?

Ownership and joint ventures

- Has the mining company achieved HDSA participation in terms of ownership for
equity or attributable units of production of 15% in HDSA hands within five years
and 26% in ten years?
- Beneficiation
- Has the mining company identified its current level of beneficiation?
- Has the mining company established its base line level of beneficiation and indicated the extent that this will have to be grown in order to qualify for an offset [of
equity transfer requirements]?

Reporting

- Has the company reported on an annual basis its progress towards achieving its
commitments in its annual report?

The case study area

The Bushveld Complex (see Exhibit 2) stretches across the North West and Lim-
popo Provinces in the north of South Africa and contains the world's largest
reserves of the platinum group of metals, as well as other metals and minerals,
including chrome. It has been described as "a geological feature unmatched anywhere on Earth, and the repository of unparalleled mineral wealth".[7]

By about 2000, South African mines accounted for 75% of the world's platinum
supply, almost all of which was produced by three companies. These were (in
order of size by revenue):

- Anglo Platinum—a Johannesburg-listed subsidiary of Anglo-American

- Impala—listed in Johannesburg

- Lonmin—listed in London

The case study area is the mining region surrounding the town of Rustenburg
in North West Province, where platinum mining first began in the late 1920s. It
includes the largest and oldest mines, Anglo Platinum, Impala and Lonmin (all of
which have been in production since at least the early 1980s), as well as Anglo
Platinum's smaller, relatively new mine called BRPM and a mine owned by the
Australian company, Aquarius Platinum (both of which have been in production
since 1999). Also in the area are the chrome mines of Samancor (a subsidiary of
BHP Billiton) and Xstrata (listed in London).

---

7   J. Reader (1998) *Africa: A Biography of a Continent* (London: Penguin): 13.

Exhibit 2 Map of South African platinum mining areas, showing the study area

Source: Johnson Matthey (2003) *The Expansion of Platinum Mining in South Africa* (www.johnsonmatthey.com, accessed October 2003)

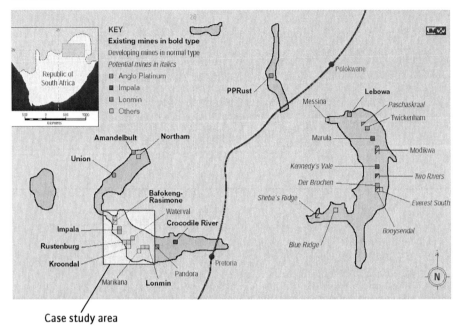

Case study area

Selected statistics for the various mines in the study area, in aggregate terms by company in 2002, are provided in Table 1. This table makes it clear that a large number of mineworkers are employed in the study area. Also evident is the significant income of the platinum mines, owing to the rise in platinum prices since the mid 1990s. In 2002 almost half of the total workforce in the area was employed in the mining sector.[8] The unemployment rate was estimated at 26% in the 1996 census and at 32% in the 2001 census. The latter puts unemployment in some of the informal settlements scattered around the mines at about 44%.[9]

The first platinum mine, Rustenburg Platinum Mines (now owned by Anglo Platinum), was established near the town of Rustenburg about 75 years ago, while Impala started its operations in the late 1960s. In line with dominant historical practice in the sector, mining companies in the region employed migrant labour (from areas such as the Eastern Cape, Lesotho and Mozambique), housed workers in large single-sex hostels, and relied on the apartheid state or the Bophuthatswana government (the nominally independent Bantustan

8 Bojanala Platinum District Municipality (BPDM) (2002) *Integrated Development Plan 2002* (Rustenburg: Bojanala Platinum District Municipality; prepared by Plan Associates, Pretoria).

9 Uncertainty about unemployment data is pervasive in South Africa. This is also due to disparate metrics, with the census counting as unemployed only those who are still actively looking for work.

TABLE 1 Estimated employee and production figures for mines in the study area in 2002, in aggregate terms for each case study company

Source: company annual reports, interviewees

	Anglo Platinum	Impala	Lonmin	Aquarius	Samancor	Xstrata
Workers	21,500	28,000	25,000	1,350	4,200	1,200
Platinum group metals production (ounces—thousands)	1,560	1,900	1,500	240	N/A	N/A
Operating income (rand—millions)	3,630	6,150	3,300	400	−14	Not given

Note: These are rough estimates only due to varying accounting systems and diverging definitions in use in 2002 (there has been a trend towards greater uniformity in recent years). In particular, Anglo Platinum's figures for workers exclude contract workers—a significant number—while other companies' figures include them. Aquarius employed only about 16 people directly in 2002, with most of the mining done by contractors. The exchange rate for much of 2002 was about $1.00 = R10.00.

homeland that included much of the study area prior to 1994) to prevent informal settlements and community or labour protest. So, for instance, in the late 1980s, Impala Platinum reportedly employed over 40,000 employees in the area (according to various interviewees), almost all of whom were migrant workers housed in four large hostels. Until the 1990s, the large mines were therefore like industrial islands in what was still a predominantly agricultural area.

The landscape became much more industrialized and populated during the late 1990s. As one interviewee noted, "in 1997, there was a sudden change; before, this was a quiet area, then it suddenly became industrialized". Table 2 provides population figures from 1980 to 2005.

TABLE 2 Census figures and projected population in the Rustenburg local municipality

Source: These figures are adapted from Bojanala Platinum District Municipality (BPDM), Integrated Development Plan 2002, which in turn relies on the 1996 census.

Year	1980	1985	1991	1996	1999	2005
					(Projections)	
Urban or peri-urban areas	103,200 (73%)	167,400 (83%)	198,600 (83%)	291,900 (91%)	335,700 (92%)	421,400 (93%)
Non-urban	37,400 (27%)	33,900 (17%)	41,000 (17%)	27,600 (9%)	30,400 (8%)	31,100 (7%)
Total	140,600	201,300	239,700	319,500	366,100	452,500

Note that the projections have proven to be roughly correct in comparison to more recent data; see Rustenburg Local Municipality's *Rustenburg Five-Year Integrated Development Plan, 2007–2012*.

The increase during the 1990s was especially due to the promise of employment on the mines, which grew in number and increasingly employed labour through local labour brokers, rather than directly from far-off labour-sending areas. Combined with less severe access and settlement control by the new government, the immigration led to the growth of informal settlements (also known as squatter camps), particularly around the mines' single-sex hostels. These settlements commonly do not have formal recognition from the landowners and do not receive basic municipal services (see Exhibit 3).

Exhibit 3 Growing informal settlements represent the area's most significant development challenge. These settlements are concentrated around the mine hostels—the one in the photograph being adjacent to an Anglo Platinum hostel

Source: Ralph Hamann

Informal settlements have been identified for some time as a key development challenge in the area. In an acknowledgement that local government, traditional authority and mining companies need to collaborate on the issue of informal settlements, a Housing Strategy Forum was established in 1999, comprising the local government, the Royal Bafokeng Nation and all the case study companies. It commissioned the preparation of a strategy for dealing with informal settlements in the area, and reported that:

> Informal settlement takes place at a rapid rate (estimated 24.2% per
> annum) in the Greater Rustenburg area and to the effect that there are
> currently an estimated 13,600 units in informal settlements accommo-
> dating about 34,000 people. This excludes the backyard dwellings in
> Thlabane and surrounding areas which totals an additional estimated
> 11,000 units. The [growth of] informal settlements . . . is mainly associ-
> ated with mining activities in the area. There is, however, no coordi-
> nated strategy in place to sufficiently manage the problem. In the past,
> initiatives launched by any of the role-players . . . were conducted on
> an ad hoc basis and usually with limited consultation with other par-
> ties. This resulted in uncoordinated development and unnecessary
> duplication of skills and facilities.[10]

The geographical spread of the informal settlements "broadly follows
the . . . curve created by the mineral belt". The report underlines the role of the
single-sex hostels in the growth of informal settlements.

> This option [single-sex hostels] caters for the bulk of the mineworkers
> but not for their families. This gives rise to informal settlements being
> established adjacent to the mining hostels. It is generally agreed that
> this is not a socially preferred option.[11]

There are a number of housing initiatives under way, but the Forum argues in
its report that, even if these were implemented according to plan, they would
not cover the backlog in all areas. Furthermore, the initiatives commonly rely
on government subsidies, which exclude many mineworkers. Further problems
identified include inappropriate planning, without sufficient consideration of
the socioeconomic needs of informal dwellers who come from different origins
and speak different languages.

The deteriorating conditions in many of the informal settlements, coupled
with a labour dispute between, in particular, Anglo Platinum and workers'
unions, contributed to violent unrest in the late 1990s that led to the deaths
of at least 60 people. In response, a Conflict Resolution Consortium (CRC) was
established which, among other things, conducted a survey of Anglo Platinum's
hostels to better understand the root causes of conflict. The findings are broadly
representative of conditions in the hostels at the time. The survey noted that
the large majority of hostel residents were immigrants to the area and that they
commonly had additional accommodation in the informal settlements outside
the hostels, in part because the conditions in the hostels were cramped and
dangerous. It argued that:

---

10 *Greater Rustenburg Informal Housing Strategy* (2001) (compiled for the Housing Strategy
   Forum by Plan Associates, Pretoria): 1.
11 Ibid.: 6.

> [S]ingle-sex hostel accommodation . . . creates an unnatural situation where a healthy community is difficult to foster. If nothing is done, informal settlements will continue to flourish.[12]

The CRC also conducted a survey of some of the informal settlements. It found that:

- Three-quarters of respondents were from outside the province

- Almost all the dwellings in informal settlements are made from corrugated iron, cardboard, plastic, etc. In the more formal villages, many residents make backyard shacks (called *mikuku*) available for rent to mineworkers or others

- Two-thirds of the respondents had been unemployed for more than three years, with hawking and farming being common survival strategies

- Though schools are on average only two to three kilometres from most informal settlements, they commonly use the Setswana language as the medium of instruction, thereby excluding other ethnic groups

- Water and sanitation services are unreliable or non-existent in informal settlements. The CRC said:

  > This poses a great health risk and danger to the people within and outside these communities. It was explained by the residents . . . that during the rainy season, it was common to see sewage from the bushes, including decomposed bodies from shallow graves, being swept into the water in the dams. Apart from the health risks, this produced a very unpleasant smell and polluted the water in the dam.[13]

- Existing services or development efforts conducted by provincial or local authorities were considered by respondents insufficient and unreliable. A crucial constraint was related to the tribal ownership of land: "The Royal Bafokeng Authority was against the District Council's provision of services to the residents of informal settlements including the erection of permanent infrastructures such as sewerage, as this would legalize their stay on the RBA land."[14]

- Leadership structures in the informal settlements lacked legitimacy, with the majority of respondents saying that these structures were "imposed" and ineffective

12   Conflict Resolution Consortium (CRC) (2001) *Rustenburg/Anglo Platinum Conflict Stabilization Project* (Rustenburg: CRC): 57.
13   Ibid.: 62.
14   Ibid.: 63.

The adverse living conditions experienced in the informal settlements were described by numerous interviewees. Susan Robinson, director of a local non-governmental organization (NGO), highlighted the vicious circle of unemployment, substance abuse, domestic violence and HIV/AIDS:

> The onset of industrialization and all the money [that the mines] brought to the area, brought many informal settlements around the mines, but the mines do not establish infrastructure in those settlements, there is no recreation ... Around the mines we have people from the Eastern Cape, from Mozambique, from Angola, from Swaziland, from Lesotho, and local Tswana people—there is such a mix, there is a lot of alienation; people cannot talk to other families; they are not part of an intact culture or established traditions ... In the *kampongs* [hostels] there are many males together, without wives; there is a very high consumption of alcohol, there's nothing to do ... So in the mining areas, people want to get drunk quick, to be knocked out. Here around the mines there's a big problem with homebrew, which is so toxic because they add battery acid and other chemicals to speed up fermentation. This kind of toxic homebrew acts as a hallucinogen and makes people extremely violent. The result is the complete disintegration of the family: violence against women and children, and a vicious cycle between poverty, alcohol abuse, and violence. Children in these areas ... become part of the adult drinking culture; they start drinking alcohol from a very young age, in order to deal with stress and frustration. This also increases the amount of risky sexual behaviour and the prevalence of HIV/AIDS.

The picture that emerges is of an area thrust into significant demographic, institutional and economic change. A key force here is the immigration of migrant workers and those seeking jobs in the mines or attendant industries or services. In the wake of institutional changes, especially at local government level after 1994, and changing employee housing practices on the mines in the 1990s, the informal settlements that have been forming around the mines have become the main nexus of social problems in the area. The role of CSR, in its varying guises, in preventing or mitigating these developments has been very limited.

CSR and its discontents

In line with general trends in South Africa, the companies in this study traditionally understood their social responsibility in terms of ad hoc charitable donations to good causes, motivated by a sense that it was "the right thing to do" (company interviewee). Apart from contributions to national business initiatives, these donations were generally for education or health initiatives in neighbouring communities, and were administered by mine managers or HR managers without dedicated policies, budgets or organizational structures. Significantly, there was no integration between this "corporate social investment" (CSI) and companies' business plans, as noted by one company employee:

> The view that CSR is primarily CSI is a result of how things were structured, in the sense that businesses thought that they needed to pay what some people referred to as blood money, but it never needed to be part of the business processes. So in order to operate, they needed to do some charity work or CSI, but it has never been key to their own business strategy.

After 1994, the new government's policies, as expressed in the Reconstruction and Development Programme (RDP), established a culture of expectation that companies would contribute more to social development around the mines, and this expectation became more pertinent with the growth of informal settlements there. The response, particularly in the large platinum companies, was to formalize CSI with a dedicated budget (commonly pegged at about 1.0% of pre-tax profit) and a management structure that administers the funds and supports the various projects, most of which focus on education and health services and, more recently, small business development in surrounding communities (see photographs of selected CSI projects in Exhibit 4).

Exhibit 4 Selected CSI activities by mining companies in the study area: (a) a mobile clinic supported by Anglo Platinum; (b) a school supported by Lonmin; and (c) a small agricultural enterprise supported by Impala

Source: Ralph Hamann

(a)

(b)

(c)

However, though these CSI efforts are welcome contributions to development, there are crucial limitations to this traditional interpretation of CSR as CSI. For a start, a simple reason why companies' CSI projects cannot make a significant dent in the development needs of the area is their general avoidance of informal settlements around the mines. As one mine's HR manager noted: "No one takes care of the squatter camps." According to most interviewees, this is due to the uncertain legal status of these settlements—the companies are unwilling to support the formalization of informal settlements until there is an agreement between the residents and the landowners (which, in large parts of the study area, is predominantly the Bafokeng traditional authority).

A more fundamental criticism of companies' CSI efforts is that they did not have any impact on core business practices, in particular the continued reliance on migrant labour and single-sex hostels. Indeed, most mining company inter-viewees accepted this link between their business practices and the informal settlements. As one company's corporate affairs director said:

> You don't have to be a genius to see what the real threats are [in the area]: unemployment, crime, the disrupted social fabric created by the migrant system, and the fact that you have a lot of single men living in hostels in proximity to your operations.

Here it is important to note that all the companies in the study have, since the mid 1990s, decreased their reliance on single-sex hostels. A mixture of inter-nal and external motivations (including the BEE scorecard in Exhibit 1) has led them to significantly reduce the numbers of workers living in these hostels.[15] However, this reduction has taken place as part of a modernization drive moti-vated by an emphasis on core competencies, in which employee housing was considered expendable. In many mines, workers were given a so-called "live-out allowance" so that they could arrange their own accommodation, but, because this amount was generally very low and because wages remained low for most employment categories, many workers preferred to live in shacks in the informal settlements. The social implications of these changes to corporate employee housing policies did not feature prominently in management discussions, much less were they part of a broader CSR strategy. Hence the way the mines have reduced their reliance on single-sex hostels has, paradoxically, been a further reason for the rapid growth of informal settlements in the area.

The challenge of collaboration

A further overarching reason why companies' past CSR activities have not been able to make a difference to the growing informal settlements is that they had not been part of, much less contributed to, a comprehensive coordinated and collaborative approach involving the other key role-players in the area, particu-larly the local government, traditional authority and local communities. This is not because of a lack of awareness, as illustrated by the establishment and the findings of the Housing Strategy Forum mentioned above. Companies have also

---

15 To illustrate, according to interviewees, in 2002 Anglo Platinum's mines in the province (including two mines outside the study area) reportedly had about 7,000 workers living in six hostels, out of a total of 24,000 employees, excluding contractors; this is a significant reduction from the initial situation, where most workers lived in hostels. Impala Platinum had about 10,000 hostel dwellers, out of 24,000 employees, whereas the majority of its ini-tial 50,000 employees in the late 1980s were in hostels. Lonmin's Eastern Platinum mine had brought down the number of hostel dwellers from 3,000 to 1,900 (out of 4,500 employees), while Samancor still had about half of its 1,300 workers staying in hostels. Xstrata's alloys division had no hostels.

neglected or been unable to contribute to the local municipality's Integrated Development Plan (IDP), a mechanism through which the municipality is meant to facilitate a participatory process to develop a spatial development framework and a municipal budget. One company manager noted that: "Companies must input into the IDP; but this didn't happen as well as it should have, it wasn't well managed."

The absence of regional development coordination is not only constraining the effectiveness of companies' CSR efforts; it is a fundamental impediment to an integrated response to the problem of the growing informal settlements. For a start, the companies' CSI activities are impeded by a lack of coordination, for instance when there is no land available for the construction of low-cost housing—a big concern for company representatives. More fundamentally, improved communication structures between companies, government and community groups would allow for a more efficient and context-dependent delimitation of development roles and responsibilities. The need for a stakeholder forum has also been raised in connection with the increasingly pressing need for bulk service provision—as one mining manager noted:

> In the past, it was the responsibility of government to provide services like water and electricity; but if we sit down and wait for local government, we will not be a profitable organization—that synergy in tri-sector partnerships is absolutely critical.

Finally, improved collaboration at the municipal level should do more to resolve or prevent conflicts between companies and local communities, such as that between Impala and the people of Luka.

Over and above isolated initiatives involving the major mining companies in some joint welfare and literary projects and a regional HIV/AIDS initiative, there have been a number of attempts to improve development coordination in the region. These have been initiated by local government or the traditional authority, as well as mining companies. For instance, between 2001 and 2003 there was an attempt by local government to convene a Joint Development Forum in order to coordinate planning for bulk infrastructure provision and local economic development. More recent attempts have centred on particular housing initiatives and the municipality's IDP, and there have been separate joint planning efforts by the Royal Bafokeng Nation. However, for the most part these initiatives have failed to bring the key role-players together for effective, collaborative plans and actions at the local level. There are three salient reasons for this.

The first is the difficulty in bringing about inter-company collaboration in circumstances where the various parties have for a long time acted unilaterally and with very little coordination. As one mining CSR manager said, "In Rustenburg policy implementation is more reactive, because mines have been established for a long time." Another noted that the linear dispersion of mines along the platinum reef (see Exhibit 1) contributed to this insular approach among the companies: "Rustenburg platinum occurs along a corridor and development occurs along the line of the shafts . . . each mine has its own area that it manages."

The second reason is the lack of capacity and clarity within local government, as a result of the uncertainties about how governance jurisdiction and responsibility are shared between the elected local government and the traditional authority.[16] Significantly, the Royal Bafokeng Nation plays an important quasi-governmental role in the area as the traditional authority of the Bafokeng community, which owns most of the land in the area. The Bafokeng also own a significant stake in Impala Platinum, which is one of the reasons they are colloquially referred to as "the richest tribe in Africa".[17] Despite high-level efforts to establish a working relationship between the municipality and the traditional authority (which at one stage even involved a visit by President Mbeki to the area), fundamental tensions continue to thwart coordination and collaboration between them.

Furthermore, the local government's policy framework has only recently been set up so as to play a facilitative role in regional coordination. Most interviewees agree that local government is the legitimate institution to play this central role, particularly through the statutory IDP process. However, there are widespread concerns that the municipality does not have the capacity to facilitate an inclusive participation process that involves all the key role-players, especially in the context of the continuing tensions between the municipality and the Royal Bafokeng Nation.

The third reason is the role of the mining companies and the absence of high-level commitment to effective cross-sectoral collaboration, at least until relatively recently. Indeed, some of the underlying motives for companies' CSR efforts are widely recognized to have militated against collaborative approaches. Thus a key motive for the above mentioned CSI projects has been to gain competitive advantage, particularly in terms of local and national reputation. As Impala's CSI manager said: "Every company wants to be seen to be doing much more than what the others are doing, so there is always that competition."[18]

More fundamentally, mining company leadership's commitment to cross-sector collaboration at the local level has been limited. Companies' social managers commented that there had been insufficient senior management buy-in into previous efforts at establishing a multi-stakeholder forum and this had

---

16 In this context, it should be noted that, in the wake of the transition to democracy in 1994, national policy on local government has been in a state of flux, with clear structures and processes emerging only fairly recently.

17 See, for instance, A. Manson and B. Mbenga (2003) " 'The Richest Tribe in Africa': Platinum-Mining and the Bafokeng in South Africa's North West Province, 1965–1999", *Journal of Southern African Studies* 29.1: 25-47.

18 However, this competitive streak seems to have diminished in recent years. One company's social manager argued that "now we have matured" and another argued that inter-company competition had decreased due to the high platinum price and companies' long-term supply contracts with customers.

resulted, for instance, in the job of company representative being delegated to low-ranking employees. According to other stakeholders, most notably some local government officials, the primary reason for this lack of commitment has been the reluctance of companies to take responsibility for social issues around the mines, especially the growth of informal settlements.

Indeed, there have been fundamental disagreements over this responsibility. For instance, at a focus group discussion facilitated for this case study research, the director for local economic development at the relevant municipality argued that the primary constraint to dealing with social problems in the area was not the lack of coordination, but rather the fact that:

> ... mining companies have not accepted their primary responsibility for being the root cause of the informal settlements [around the mines] . . . through the migrant system and the single-sex hostels.

Mining company representatives responded that mining companies are, indeed, accepting some of the responsibility for housing around the mines, as evidenced by the budgets that have been allocated and the houses that are currently being built (though there was some disagreement about the extent of this commitment). Crucially, however, it was argued that mining companies would never want to accept sole responsibility for informal settlements—after all, there are informal settlements elsewhere, too—and that the responsibility for dealing with these social issues needs to be shared between business and government. Anglo Platinum's CSI manager argued the companies' case thus:

> The municipality likes to blame the mines for the informal settlements. They say that 20 per cent [of residents] in the informal settlements are Anglo workers. But they [the informal settlements] are not only our responsibility . . . There are lots of reasons for them . . . It is very much a government responsibility as well . . . Ultimately we can't do anything without government—it's their terrain. They need to provide the land use planning and infrastructure.

More recently, some of the companies have seemed willing to accept a shared responsibility for the informal settlements, partly because of their growing understanding that informal settlements are a business risk and that there is a need to facilitate cross-sectoral collaboration to mitigate this risk. The most significant indication of this has been Anglo Platinum's commitment to establishing a tri-sector forum, premised on a step-by-step process starting with improved company internal coordination on CSR-related issues, as Anglo Platinum's local CSR manager explained in 2003:

> At the last [executive committee] meeting, we passed an agreement on [the establishment of a] tri-sector partnership in Rustenburg. We want to start with an internal company forum, including representatives from a number of company departments, where we discuss socioeconomic

issues, business issues, utilities, etc. . . . The second step is to have a forum of the major producers, Impala, Lonmin and us: the commercial forum. The objective is to get synergies on basic issues, like water, which is a major problem here in Rustenburg . . . The third step is the private–public forum, where we engage the Rustenburg municipality and the Bojanala district municipality . . . Almost parallel to that we would consolidate the social forum, where we bring in the communities, traditional leaders, NGOs, into one organized unit. Once they are organized, then we can bring business, government and civil society together. Our timing is to reach the Joint Development Forum, the tri-sector partnership, by June next year [2004]. We have exco approval; we have a memorandum . . . One of my key performance areas is to ensure that we have a tri-sector partnership by June next year.

Unfortunately, at the time of writing (2007) these targets remained unmet and indeed most of the challenges and difficulties discussed above also still remained. However, there have been slow but important changes in corporate perceptions and policies on these issues, especially with regard to the growing understanding of informal settlements as a business risk. This is also reflected to some extent in companies' public reports, though more so in Lonmin's (2006) and Anglo Platinum's (2006) than in Impala's (2006). There is also an increased awareness that improved cross-sector collaboration is required, with a central role for local government. For instance, the 2006 Anglo Platinum sustainability report states that:

> One of the most notable consequences of the rate of development [in the Rustenburg area] is the recent proliferation of informal settlements and structures within the municipality (both in free-standing individual settlements and backyards). In response to these challenges, the municipality, in partnership with Anglo Platinum, embarked on a process to prepare a five- to ten-year housing strategy . . . The project was funded by Anglo Platinum but under the leadership and ownership of the municipality. In addition, Anglo Platinum provided technical assistance.[19]

Hence the companies have identified local government capacity as a crucial prerequisite for successful collaboration, and their representatives have alluded to targeted support to this effect, particularly for councillors. The relationship between mining companies and local government is thus potentially progressing towards a situation where some companies are providing targeted support to local government, so that it can better fulfil its statutory responsibilities and facilitate improved regional coordination. This support includes, in particular, targeted human resource development, though this needs to be undertaken sen-

19 *Anglo Platinum Sustainability Report 2006* (Johannesburg: Anglo Platinum): 71.

sitively and transparently to prevent allegations of corruption or co-optation. In essence, companies must learn to "lead from behind" in facilitating more coordinated and effective responses to the development challenges in the area.

Conclusion

This case study of the Rustenburg area illustrates the crucial need in areas experiencing new mining developments for mining companies, the local municipality and other key role-players to negotiate and collaborate in the process of developing and implementing long-term, proactive and integrated development plans for the area. This has not been the case in the Rustenburg area, with the result that it is faced with deteriorating socioeconomic conditions, which also threaten the mining companies' strategic objectives. To illustrate, in mid 2007 Anglo Platinum's largest mine in Rustenburg was shut down for a week (costing the company close to 100 million rand) after 12 miners had died in that mine within the previous six months. Even more dramatically, the company's CEO, Ralph Havelstein, who had otherwise achieved notable successes with the company, resigned shortly afterwards with specific reference to safety—an unprecedented move in the South African mining industry. The relevance of this for the above discussion is that safety in the mines is, among other things, closely related to the socioeconomic conditions surrounding the mines. As a mining company manager said:

> . . . you cannot expect a worker living in a shack, without electricity or water, surrounded by shebeens and drinking, to enter the mine in the morning fit and refreshed for a long day's safe mining!

Yet, despite these increasingly important incentives, many of the challenges and difficulties constraining effective collaboration in the area remain; some of these are beyond the immediate influence of the mining companies. Most notably, the local government is the statutory authority responsible for upgrading the informal settlements and facilitating participatory, integrated development planning, but it is hampered by lack of capacity and ongoing conflicts with the influential and powerful traditional authority. Company managers are slowly learning that they need to do what they can to improve these broader local governance relationships, if they are to succeed in responding to the severe social problems around the mines.

Editors' reflections and questions

This case study emphasizes the challenges of facilitating cross-sector collaboration in the complex, strained socioeconomic context of a particular area in South Africa—though similar challenges exist elsewhere in South Africa and indeed in many other African countries. In the language of negotiation theory, it illustrates how difficult it can be for conflicting parties to move from an emphasis on their bargaining positions to their underlying interests, especially in the context of historical injustices, continued distrust and significantly diverging interests. It shows how necessary it is for key stakeholders to "step back" from particular instances of disagreement—such as the conflict between Impala and the Luka community—and to identify more systemic governance problems in the area and negotiate means of responding to them. Some of the questions worth pondering are as follows:

- For a long time, collaboration was impeded by disagreement about who was responsible for the informal settlements and the related social problems. More recently, these challenges are commonly being referred to as a shared responsibility, but this may deteriorate into glib rhetoric unless it is translated into tangible measures. How might shared responsibility manifest itself in an area such as Rustenburg?

- How significant are the changing incentives and pressures faced by mining companies to take greater responsibility for social problems around the mines? To what extent are they particular to the national and local context?

- Improved collaboration between the mining companies themselves and between the companies, local government, traditional authority and civil society groups was identified by various local role-players as a prerequisite for responding to the sustainable development challenges in the area, yet this collaboration remained elusive despite various attempts to achieve it. What are the key causes of these failures and how common do you expect these challenges to be in other contexts? What are possible responses to these challenges?

- This case study identifies limited local government capacity as a significant constraint and it also suggests that the private sector may be able to play a role in improving this capacity. How could this be achieved in an effective, unobtrusive way?

> Teaching notes for this case are available from Greenleaf Publishing. These are free of charge and available only to teaching staff. They can be requested by going to:
> **www.greenleaf-publishing.com/darkside_notes**

Part 3
Creating (or managing) crises

3.1
The Westray mine explosion

Caroline J. O'Connell and Albert J. Mills

On May 9, 1992, the Westray mine in Pictou County, Nova Scotia, Canada, blew up, killing 26 miners working at the time. Shortly thereafter, the premier of the province appointed Justice Peter Richard to sit as a Commission of Inquiry empowered by broad terms of reference to look into the causes of the explosion. Former miners, safety experts, engineers, Westray supervisors, union representatives, members of provincial and federal government, and two former Westray senior managers all testified at the Inquiry. Justice Richard's report, released in 1996, described a workplace characterized by unsafe practices and an overriding concern for productivity. He did not spare Curragh Resources, Westray's parent company, its executives, and managers in his assessment. He cited the company's tough negotiating stance to secure government backing, its autocratic style of management, management's contempt for miners who complained about safety, and both tacit and overt encouragement of unsafe practices in the interest of production. Justice Richard was equally condemnatory of provincial mine inspectors who disregarded the complaints of miners and operated in a bureaucratic system unable to follow up, manage or enforce its own regulations.

The case provides introductory material on the social, economic, and political contexts of Nova Scotia and Pictou County intended to situate the analysis within a framework that may not be familiar to many students. Pictou's long history of mining, its disproportionately high unemployment rates, and its lack of alternative job opportunities provide a partial explanation as to why miners continued to work in conditions that many recognized to be unsafe. (Most behavioral analysis and virtually all writing on the mine attempt to answer this question.) In addition, the case explicates a complex series of political relationships among the company, the provincial government, and the federal government. Zealous intervention by elected politicians led to controversial decisions by the province to invest $12 million in equity and to buy coal from the company for the provincial electrical utility, and by the federal government to guarantee a $100 million loan.[1]

The case tells the story in the words of many of the key players, primarily through their inquiry testimony and interviews conducted by a number of researchers subsequent to the explosion. The case also describes the interplay of these and other key players through the negotiations to establish the mine, its brief period of operation, the mine's explosion, and rescue and recovery efforts. The case concludes with commentary on the findings of the Commission of Inquiry and its fallout.

Introduction

It was February 6, 1996, and Carl Guptill sat at his kitchen table nursing a cup of coffee. He was a beefy man with long hair, often tucked through the back of a baseball cap. The next day he would testify at the Commission of Inquiry into the Westray mine explosion and friends had been phoning to offer their support. One caller, a geologist from nearby Antigonish, hadn't been in touch since working with Guptill at a mine in Guysborough County more than five years ago; but he wanted Carl to know he was thinking of him.

Carl Guptill's thoughts drifted back to another kitchen table—Roy Feltmate's. Feltmate, a longtime friend, had worked on B crew at the Westray mine. In April 1992, three months after he had left his job at Westray, Guptill met up with Feltmate and four other members of B crew at Feltmate's home. Talk quickly turned to safety at the mine. Conditions had continued to deteriorate and the men believed that an explosion or a cave-in was inevitable. They calculated their odds of being the crew underground when it happened at 25%. The men made Guptill promise that if they died in the mine, he would "go public" and tell the world what he knew. Mike MacKay implored him to "do it for our widows."

On May 9, 1992, a few short weeks after that kitchen meeting, the odds caught up with Roy·Feltmate, Mike MacKay, Randy House, Robbie Fraser, and 22 other members of B crew. At 5.20 am an explosion ripped through the Westray mine. All 26 miners underground died. Fifteen bodies were recovered, but 11 bodies, including Roy Feltmate's and Mike MacKay's, remained in the mine. Guptill would keep his promise to them.

---

1 In this chapter, all dollars are Canadian.

One miner's tale

Carl Guptill had worked in hard rock mines in Nova Scotia prior to being hired on at Westray. At the Gay's River Mine, he had chaired the health and safety committee, and at the Forest Hill Mine he'd been a shift supervisor to a crew of 35 or more men. He had completed an advanced management course at Henson College, the continuing education arm of Halifax's Dalhousie University. He was mine rescue certified and had been captain of a mine rescue team. As both a miner and a supervisor, he'd enjoyed a good working relationship with Albert McLean, the provincial mine inspector. Guptill had ended up working at Westray more by happenstance than by design. He had offered to drive his buddy to the mine site to fill out an application and had ended up being hired on himself. Guptill put safety first and believed he'd made that clear to Roger Parry, underground manager at Westray, when Parry interviewed him for a job. He demonstrated that commitment by joining the safety committee.

After only a few shifts, Guptill began to question safety practices at Westray. On his very first day, Bill MacCullogh, the mine's training officer, wasn't able to answer some of his questions. He noticed that farm tractors, which shouldn't even be used underground, were loaded beyond their capacity. Combustible coal dust was allowed to build up underground and the rock dust that should be spread to neutralize it wasn't anywhere to be found. Levels of explosive methane gas were too high and the methanometers that detected the gas were rigged to circumvent their intended purpose of warning miners when gas levels were dangerous. In addition, miners worked 12-hour shifts, often without breaks. The batteries for miners' headlamps could not sustain their charge and were often dim or out by the end of a shift. There were no underground toilets and miners relieved themselves in unused corners of the mine.

Complaints fell on deaf ears. One supervisor answered Guptill's concerns by saying "they got a few thousand applications up on top, men willing to come down here and take your place." On only his thirteenth shift, Guptill's supervisor ordered him to continue working after his lamp had dimmed. In the dark, Guptill stumbled and a steel beam he was attempting to move landed on him and injured him. After three days in hospital he called Roger Parry. The conversation quickly turned into a shouting match. Guptill then contacted Claude White, the provincial director of mine safety. White, in turn, sent him to mine inspector Albert McLean. Shortly thereafter Guptill met with McLean, John Smith, the man responsible for inspection of electrical and mechanical equipment in mines, and Fred Doucette, in charge of mine rescue. In this meeting Carl Guptill spoke of his accident and of the many safety violations he had observed in his short time working at Westray. Guptill expected that his report would result in a shutdown of the mine and a complete investigation. Weeks later, having heard nothing, he again called inspector Albert McLean. The two met once more, this time in a local motel room instead of the offices of the Department of Labour. McLean kept the television on high volume throughout the meeting. Puzzled, Guptill later concluded that McLean was fearful he would tape the meeting. McLean told Guptill that the other men had not backed up his complaints and he could do little. He did offer to "put in a good word" for Guptill with management if he wanted to return to work. This was the story Carl Guptill told the Commission of Inquiry.

A snapshot of mining in Pictou County

The four communities of Trenton, New Glasgow, Westville, and Stellarton run into each other to make up Pictou County, Nova Scotia. All told, 25,000 people live there, descendants of Scots that landed with the ship *Hector* along with immigrants from the other British Isles and Europe that followed Britain's General Mining Association overseas in the early 19th century. Hardy stock, they had mined the county's 25 seams of coal for generations. One historian estimates that nearly 600 residents lost their lives in coal mines—as many as had been killed in both world wars. Although full of coal, the seams were considered among the most dangerous in the world; the beds were uneven and the ash content was high. The mines were subject to rock falls and flooding. Most significant were the high levels of explosive methane gas.

At its peak in 1875, Pictou coal mines produced 250,000 tonnes of coal a year and employed over 1,600 men and boys. The last mine operating in Pictou was the small, privately operated Drummond Mine that closed in 1984. By the mid 1980s, the only coal mines left in Nova Scotia were operating under heavy federal subsidy in Cape Breton—an economically depressed area in the northern-most part of the province.

Cape Breton mines might have met the same fate as those in Pictou had they not been in the territory of a powerful federal Member of Parliament as the oil crisis in the Middle East dominated headlines and economies in the 1970s. Under the Organization of the Petroleum Exporting Companies (OPEC), oil from the Middle East was subject both to price hikes and embargoes. This rejuvenated the dying Cape Breton coal industry and coal rebounded as a source of energy in Nova Scotia.

In the late 1980s and early 1990s, a similar opportunity presented itself to the industry in Pictou. An evolving environmental agenda was driving power generation. The provincial electrical utility, Nova Scotia Power Corporation, was seeking to lower its sulphur dioxide emissions. It needed an alternative to high-sulphur Cape Breton coal. Enter Clifford Frame.

Politics and big guns

Clifford Frame, a big man who drove big cars, raised cattle and smoked expensive cigars, was a self-made tycoon in the style of a previous era. In his youth he turned down a chance to play for the New York Rangers farm team. Instead he got a degree in mine engineering and worked his way from the pit to the corner office. After rising to the post of president of Denison Mines, he'd been fired in 1985 after a very public project failure in British Columbia. He formed Curragh Resources in 1985 and had early success reviving a lead–zinc mine in the Yukon. In 1987 the industry publication *Northern Miner* named him "Mining Man of the Year." That same year he incorporated Westray Coal and a year later, in 1988, he bought out Suncor's coal rights in Pictou County.

In his time at Denison, Frame had come to know key political players in Ottawa. Through these connections he was introduced to Elmer MacKay, then federal representative for Pictou and Minister of Public Works. Frame aggressively sought federal and provincial support for his operation. Pictou County was burdened by a 20% unemployment rate and Frame promised that his mine would employ at least 250 people in jobs paying $35,000–60,000 annually for 15 years. Economic spin-off in neighbouring communities would total in the millions of dollars.

Politicians, including the then premier John Buchanan, supported Frame. Perhaps the project's greatest advocate was local provincial MLA (Member of the Legislative Assembly), Donald Cameron, who became Minister of Economic Development as the project evolved and ultimately was elected premier (his position at the time of the explosion).

Frame successfully negotiated a $12 million equity loan with the provincial government, as well as an $8 million interim loan when federal negotiations lagged. He also struck a so-called "take or pay" agreement that guaranteed a market for Westray coal. Under this contract, the Nova Scotia government would buy 275,000 tonnes of coal if other buyers did not materialize. Westray would pay back any revenues from this agreement without interest at the end of 15 years.

The federal government proved a tougher sell and discussions dragged out over three years. Ultimately, the federal government came through with a loan guarantee of $85 million and an interest buy-down of nearly $27 million. This was much less than the amount originally sought by Frame and much more than the government's policies usually allowed for such projects. Harry Rogers, a federal deputy minister, was involved in the negotiations and would later describe Clifford Frame as:

> personally abrasive and abusive . . . Probably the most offensive person I have met in business or in government.

However, a deal was struck, and in September 1991 at Westray's official opening, politicians at both levels lined up to congratulate each other. Nor did they hesitate to parlay their support into jobs for constituents. One phone call from a politician's assistant could result in the hiring of an inexperienced young man with the right family connections. Indeed, Bill MacCullogh had been able to jump from the development agency, where his job included lobbying government to support the mine's development, directly onto Westray's payroll. In August 1991 he became the company's training officer.

Rules of the game

Mining is dangerous work. The first regulations to protect the safety of miners date back to 1873 and provided for the inspection of mines. In 1881, legislation allowed for the certification of miners and mine officials. The new rules also called for gas testing and banned smoking underground. This legislation followed a disaster in which 60 miners died and, according to one mining historian, made Nova Scotia mines the safest in the world. In 1923, the age limit for working underground was raised from 12 to 16. (It would not be raised to age 18 until 1951.) By 1927, the maximum allowable level of methane in a mine was 2.5%. At the time of the Westray explosion, a methane reading of 2.5% required the removal of all workers from the site, while a reading of 1.25% mandated the shutdown of electricity that could spark an explosion.

At the time the Westray mine exploded, the regulation of coal mining in Nova Scotia fell primarily under the Coal Mines Regulation Act, a 160-page piece of legislation considered 30 years out of date. An example of its anachronisms could be found in section 94, which outlined the duties of stablemen who tended the horses underground. A further indication of just how out of date the legislation was, and how limited was its power to deter unsafe behaviours, was the fine schedule: the maximum fine that could be levied under the Act was $200. It also regulated the qualifications required for various levels of mining competency, including miners, managers, owners, and inspectors. Most significantly for Westray, the legislation regulated maximum allowable levels of methane. It also stipulated the removal of highly combustible coal dust and the spreading of limestone dust to neutralize its effects. The Act included provisions for roof supports and the prohibition of tobacco products and matches underground; it permitted worker inspections of the mines and limited shift duration to eight hours. All would become issues for public scrutiny after the explosion.

Operating in parallel was the provincial Occupational Health and Safety Act enacted in 1986. It imposed on employers the obligation to ensure workplace safety and to provide appropriate training, equipment, facilities, and supervision. This legislation also required employees to take safety precautions, to wear appropriate clothing or equipment, and to cooperate with employers, regulators, and other employees in these goals. The Act also mandated joint occupational health and safety committees for workplaces with designated numbers of employees. These committees were made up of both employer and worker representatives and were charged with educating on safety issues, maintaining records, inspecting the workplace and responding to complaints. A key element of this legislation was a worker's right to refuse to do unsafe work and not be discriminated against or punished for doing so. The Act also provided that the legislation itself must be available for inspection by workers so that they could be aware of their rights. It also required employers to report to the regulators any accident resulting in an injury.

When the occupational health and safety legislation was passed, responsibility for enforcement was transferred from the provincial Department of Mines and Energy to the Department of Labour. Inspectors also retained jurisdiction over the Coal Mines Regulation Act. Both acts authorized inspectors to order a work stoppage and the Coal Mines Regulation Act, under section 64, specifically empowered an inspector to order a dangerous mine closed.

Training at Westray

William (Bill) MacCulloch began his job as the training officer at Westray on August 1, 1991, just over a month before the official opening of the mine. He had been on the job nine months when the mine blew up. Previously he had worked as an economic development officer with the local municipality, providing information and support to the business community. In particular, he helped companies from outside the area that were considering investing in Pictou County. In this capacity he had brokered relations between Curragh executives and local contacts, lobbied government for funding and promoted the project prior to the mine's opening. His connections in the community were extensive. Earlier in his career he'd worked both as a bank teller and radio personality. He had a high school diploma and a certificate in economic development acquired through part-time studies at the University of Waterloo. He had no mining experience.

In his time at Westray, MacCulloch attempted to create a comprehensive training package that included certification in underground skills and equipment operation, mine rescue, health and safety, first aid, and the handling of hazardous materials. Much of the training protocol was already enshrined in legislation. This was reflected, for example, in the employee manual that included, among other provisions the following:

Health & Safety Philosophy

It is the personal responsibility of each member of the management team to ensure that the necessary education and training to equip all employees, to encourage a zero accident rate while reducing possible threats to good health and safety is provided . . . It is the personal responsibility of each supervisor to ensure that employees receive

adequate training in work procedures so maximum productivity can
be achieved within a safe work environment.

MacCulloch understood his job to be that of administrator of the program,
ensuring schedules and facilities as well as sourcing materials and expertise.

Of particular importance at Westray was the training of inexperienced miners. Legislation stipulated a 12-month progression under a "black tag" (certified)
miner. In this time a miner would begin with basic labour and would gradually
be introduced to and trained in the safe operation of the bolter, the continuous
miner, and other equipment. This period could be shortened to six months if
systematic training took place at a work face in the mine designated as a training
area.

MacCulloch developed a three-day orientation program building on a handbook already in existence when he began the job. He envisioned classroom
modules on gas levels and safe ventilation, and practical demonstrations with
equipment like the self-rescuer. His plan was forwarded to the provincial Department of Labour as required.

The union drive

Bob Burchell had been a miner and mine inspector for almost a decade. In
his current role with the United Mine Workers of America he organized union
drives, lobbied for political and social reform, negotiated on behalf of miners,
and advocated for safe mining practices. He had trained at the Mine Safety and
Health Administration (MSHA) Academy, and returned annually to maintain and
upgrade his credentials. He was unabashedly zealous in his work and could, on
occasion, be loud, aggressive, and profane.

Burchell had been on what he termed a "scouting" mission at Westray over
the summer months of 1991. Some of his contacts had passed on word that
conditions underground were not optimal. Burchell positioned himself near the
mine's entrance, hoping to catch miners coming or going. Early response was
less than encouraging. He had to jump out of the way of the miners' cars as
they raced on or off the property. "They knew who I was," he said. It wasn't long
before management also delivered a message. Having refused Burchell access to
the men at shift change, they sent a police officer to remove him. When Burchell
persisted, management drove down the access road, parked nearby and either
watched him silently or engaged him directly in conversation. One day, Gerald
Phillips even sent his wife down to chat. To the miners, management presence
at the entrance was a clear message.

Undaunted and continuing to hear rumours of unsafe practices, Burchell established a base in nearby New Glasgow. A few emboldened miners stopped by one
day and talked to him. They told him about the use of farm equipment under-

ground. They expressed concern for their safety, but were pessimistic about the union's potential for a successful certification drive. They told Burchell that many miners had moved to take jobs at Westray and would have to repay their relocation expenses if they stayed less than a year. Despite the miners' fears of repercussions, the union drive progressed slowly and under a cloak of secrecy. The men asked Burchell not to take notes at their meetings. A local woman, who owned the restaurant where Burchell often met the men, told him that she'd received a call from Bill MacCulloch at Westray. He had asked her, "as a long-time friend," to "keep tabs" on who was coming and going at the restaurant and to report back to him. Offended, she refused.

Burchell received permission from his Washington superiors to send union cards out in the mail instead of delivering them in person. Miners could sign them in the privacy of their homes and return them by mail. Meanwhile, information continued to accumulate, painting a picture of ill-trained miners working without adequate safety knowledge. In one meeting, Burchell listened as one young man, a new miner, described his high-quality, stainless steel first-aid kit, issued to him with the words, "Here, this is in case of an emergency." Burchell realized the young man was unwittingly referring to his self-rescuer—the only thing between the miner and death in the event of a cave-in. "It blew my mind," said Burchell.

Ultimately, the union lost the certification drive by 20 votes.

A day in the life[2]

The continuous miner roared, cutting coal from the face of the mine and loading it into shuttle cars for transport to a conveyor belt. A huge machine, it allowed previously unheard-of quantities of coal to be mined in a day. Pictou miners knew it was a far cry from the pick and shovels of their grandfathers' mines and the explosives of their fathers' mines.

The men at work that day were the usual mixed bag of experienced miners and untried "greenhorns." Like most days at Westray, even those with underground experience had gained it in hard rock mines, not coal mines. There were simply not enough certified coal miners in the area to fill the jobs. Claude White had granted the company an exemption under the Coal Mines Regulation Act to use hard rock miners in their place.

Lenny Bonner and Shaun Comish were old friends and veterans of hard rock mining. They had been hired together and their pit talk this morning centred

---

2 All events described in this section are based on the sworn testimony of miners and other witnesses to the Commission of Inquiry. They are told here as if they happened on one workday. Except for this change in chronology, they are an accurate depiction of work underground at Westray as described by the parties.

on a recent accident in the mine. A young kid, Matthew Sears, had had his leg crushed when he tried to replace a roller on the conveyor belt. As he stood on the belt, it started up without the usual warning and his leg was jammed in a large roller. The men in the mine at the time had reported that Ralph Melanson kept pulling the safety cable to stop the belt, but it kept restarting. Sears had been through five surgeries since the accident and would be months off work. "Poor kid," said one to the other, "he told me that his first day on the job he didn't even know how to turn his lamp on." Roger Parry had sent him down alone to meet his crew and he'd stood there, shocked by how dark it was.

Both Bonner and Comish recalled their first day at Westray. Without any orientation, they'd been issued with their self-rescuers and sent underground. At the time they had laughed because neither of them understood most of what Roger Parry said to them. Between his British accent and his wad of chewing tobacco, they were lucky to catch half of what he said. Both men had progressed quickly underground from installing arches on the roadway and roof supports in the rooms being mined to operating equipment—drills, the bolter, the shuttle car. Neither had received any specific instruction. As Comish put it, "I got on it and [he] showed me what levers to move and what was your brake and what was your throttle and away you go." He recalled with some nostalgia the mine in Ontario where he had learned to drive a scoop tram in a designated training area away from production. Both men knew that, at Westray, the more equipment a miner could operate, the higher his pay.

The continuous miner had come to a stop. This meant the methanometer, or "sniffer," had detected too much gas. Comish pressed the reset button a few times to no effect. Bonner was running the shuttle car and waited. Comish overpowered the trip switch and kept filling the shuttle car. He disliked overriding a safety measure that was really for his own protection, but he'd been shown how to do it and he understood what was expected. The mine's bonus system was simple: more coal meant more money.

As he did every four days when he was back underground, Comish thought about quitting. But, instead, he thought about the roof over his family's heads and the food on their plates, sighed, and got back to work. Some days there was no need to override the sniffer. Comish recalled working in the southwest section of the mine one shift when the methanometer wasn't working. Comish had turned to Donnie Dooley and joked, "If we get killed, I'll never speak to you again." Despite the jokes and the camaraderie, Comish couldn't escape the feeling that things weren't quite right. He decided that this day he just didn't want to be in the mine. He planned to tell his supervisor that he had to leave at five to get his car fixed—a harmless white lie.

Some of the men underground that day wondered when Eugene Johnson would be back from Montreal. His name had been selected from a draw to go to a ceremony where the industry association would give out the John T. Ryan Award honouring Westray as the safest coal mine in Canada. The award was based on reported accident statistics. The men had laughed about the award since they knew management had "jigged" the accident stats to ensure a good record. Nonetheless, they didn't begrudge their co-worker and friend a trip to the big city. Johnson and his wife were scheduled to see a game by the Toronto Maple Leafs, one of Canada's most popular teams in the National Hockey League. They were having a big night out with Clifford Frame and his wife. The men were sure Eugene would have some good stories from his trip.

Bonner asked Comish if Wayne Cheverie was underground that day. Neither could recall seeing him at the beginning of the shift. With no tag system in the deployment area, at any given time there was no way of knowing who or how many people were underground. Lenny Bonner thought back to his time at the Gay's River Mine. The tag system there had been stringently enforced. One day, he'd forgotten to tag out, meaning that his tag was on the board and therefore he was officially still underground. Although his shift boss had watched him leave the property, he could not remove a miner's tag from the board. Instead, Bonner had driven back, tagged out and his shift boss had been required to wait since he could not leave until all men under his charge were accounted for.

The men were interested in Wayne Cheverie because he was making a lot of noise about safety lately. Even back in September at the official opening of the mine, he had buttonholed Albert McLean after the ceremonies. Cheverie reported that he had told McLean many of his concerns about roof conditions and the lack of stone dust, and asked him point blank if he had the power to shut the mine down. McLean told him no. Cheverie knew the outcome for other miners who had complained—harassment and intimidation. However, it was well known among the men that Cheverie was coming to the end of his rope. He was not only talking about complaining to the Department of Labour, but he was also threatening to go to the media. Recently, after refusing work, Cheverie had been told by Arnie Smith, his direct supervisor, that if he left the mine he'd be fired. His response: "fired or dead, Arnie, that's not much of a choice, is it?"

Bonner understood how Cheverie felt. A chunk of the mine's roof had fallen on his head one day. Bonner had gone home with a sore leg and back and an egg on his head. He'd had to fight with management to get paid for the day. Roger Parry had said, "we don't pay people for going home sick." Bonner had replied, "you call the roof coming in and chunks of coal hitting you on the head and the back and almost killing you 'going home sick!'" Eventually he had been paid for the shift. He reflected that at least he was better off than that poor kid Todd MacDonald. On MacDonald's first day of work, there'd been a roof fall and the kid had been buried up to his waist. He was flat on his back, facing the roof, as if he'd watched it fall instead of running the hell out of there.

Bonner and Comish and a few of the other men stopped work for a quick and belated break. They often didn't get to their lunches until after their shifts. Bonner sat down with his lunch pail but jumped up again quickly. He had picked a spot too close to a pile of human waste, but in the dark he hadn't noticed it until the stink hit him. Back when he'd first started work at the mine, Bonner had spoken to mine manager, Gerald Phillips, about installing underground toilets. Phillips had told him that he was considering a number of different models. In the meantime, Bonner felt demeaned, like an animal forced to crouch on the ground. As it turned out, their lunch break was short-lived anyway. Shaun Comish had warned the others that he saw a light approaching and the men had scattered like rats, fearing that Roger Parry was on his way down. With his usual profanities he would send them back to work. End of shift couldn't come soon enough.

Disaster and after

Within minutes of the explosion, neighbours and family members began to gather at the mine site. Within hours, local, national, and international media had set up equipment and reporters in the community centre that served as their hub. Family members, in an arena directly across from the centre where they awaited news of their loved ones, resented the prying cameras and intrusive questions. For six days they waited, they cried, they drank coffee, they smoked cigarettes, and comforted their children and each other with hopes for a triumphant rescue. Each silently held close the tale of the Springhill mine disaster of 1958. After eight days, the last men there were taken alive out of the mine after the explosion or "bump." Their story remains that of the longest that men underground have ever survived in a mine disaster, and the lore of their dramatic rescue resonated with fearful families.

Family and community, producers, and reporters, along with viewers everywhere grew to know Colin Benner as the "face of Westray." He had been appointed to the position of president of operations in April and had been responsible for the Westray mine less than one month when it blew up. He had just barely begun the processes that he hoped would help dig Westray out of its financial hole. Production was short, with the mine failing to provide the 60,000 tonnes a month to Nova Scotia Power for which it had contracted. Sales in the previous six months had reached $7.3 million, but costs had exceeded $13 million. Benner had also heard rumblings about safety, discontent among the miners, and the heavy-handed techniques of Gerald Phillips and Roger Parry.

All this, however, was put aside as he dealt with the crisis. He served as media liaison, updating on the progress of the rescue efforts. By the sixth day he was showing the strain—his tie off, his sleeves rolled, his shirt wrinkled with sweat and wear as his hands raked through his hair. It was with obvious sorrow on May 14 that he announced the search was being called off as there was no hope that anyone could have survived the blast. It was simply too dangerous for the rescue crews to continue.

The search for truth

On May 15, just one day after Colin Benner had announced that the search for the miners had been suspended, Premier Donald Cameron appointed Justice Peter Richard to lead a Commission of Inquiry into the explosion. His terms of reference were broad and mandated him to look into all aspects of the establishment, management, and regulation of the Westray mine. They specifically empowered the Inquiry to determine if any "neglect had caused or contributed to the occurrence" and if the events could have been prevented.

A tangled web of legal proceedings held up the Inquiry for more than three years. In that time, both provincial health and safety charges and federal criminal charges were laid, then withdrawn, against the company and its managers. The Inquiry heard its first testimony on November 6, 1995.

Justice Richard also undertook a substantial study on coal mining and mine safety to prepare for the task. He visited mines in Canada and the United States, and consulted with experts in South Africa, Great Britain, and Australia. He commissioned technical reports from six experts in subjects that included mining ventilation and geotechnology. He commissioned academic studies in history, economics, psychology, and political science. These reports provided him with insight into the history of mining in Pictou, the multiplier effect of large-scale employment on the communities, the impact of production bonuses on miners' behaviour, and the role of ministerial responsibility in the public sector.

The Inquiry heard 71 witnesses in 76 days of testimony and produced 16,815 pages of transcripts; it entered 1,579 exhibits into evidence after examining 800 boxes of documents. The total cost of the Inquiry was nearly $5 million.

More than 20 miners testified before the Inquiry. All told similar tales of life underground with little training and less respect. They told of accidents never documented and management promises never kept. They told of conversations with Inspector Albert McLean that he testified never happened. The Inquiry questioned McLean about his response to Carl Guptill's complaints. McLean authenticated a memorandum to his director in which he stated, "in conclusion, I find no flagrant violation of regulation in this case." In a dramatic moment of testimony, shown repeatedly on television news, McLean admitted that he did not know what the word "flagrant" meant. Bill Burchell of the United Mine Workers testified that prior to Westray he had felt great respect for Albert McLean, calling him responsible and efficient—"one of the best inspectors I've ever worked with." He said that his response to McLean's inaction was similar to the betrayal felt by a cuckolded spouse. Another pivotal moment in the Inquiry was the examination of the premier at the time of the disaster, Donald Cameron, who blamed the accident on miners who smoked underground. Bill MacCulloch, Westray's training officer, acknowledged that he could produce no records of completed training and that he had assumed that the required supervised progression underground had occurred. He also testified that he had misrepresented to the board of mine examiners the hours of classroom training miners had received.

The Inquiry also felt the presence of a group that came to be known as "The Westray Families Group." Legal counsel represented the group and had standing to question all Inquiry witnesses. The group exerted its influence to ensure that the testimonies of the miners would be heard "at home" in Pictou County, but lost an application to have the entire Inquiry take place there rather than Halifax, the provincial capital and seat of government. Media coverage of the proceedings often focused on their taut faces and passionate pleas.

Justice Richard's findings are contained in a three-volume, 750-page report entitled, *The Westray Story: A Predictable Path to Disaster*. He released his report on December 1, 1997. His key conclusion was that the explosion was both predictable and preventable. He acknowledged the 20/20 vision that accompanies hindsight but in specific, detailed, and readable prose he isolated the many factors that contributed to an explosion that cost 26 men their lives, left over 20 women widows and over 40 children fatherless. He set the tone of his report by quoting the French sociologist and inspector general of mines, Frederic Le Play (1806–1882), who said, "The most important thing to come out of a mine is the miner."

In dedicating the report to the memory of the lost miners, Justice Richard, in the preface, stated:

> The *Westray Story* is a complex mosaic of actions, omissions, mistakes, incompetence, apathy, cynicism, stupidity, and neglect.

He noted with some dismay the overzealous political sponsorship of Westray's start-up, but he clearly implicated management as the entity most responsible through its arrogance, its lack of training, its tacit and overt support of unsafe practices, and its production bonus system.

Only Colin Benner and Graham Clow, an engineering consultant to Westray, were singled out for praise. Each had attended the Inquiry without subpoena and at his own expense. They were the only Curragh executives to testify after numerous attempts to subpoena Clifford Frame, Gerald Phillips and Roger Parry failed. Benner in particular offered key testimony on his plans for the mine. He had struck a Mine Planning Task Force to address the safety and production problems in the mine. His goal had been to design a safe and achievable mine plan that incorporated human relations and mutual respect among workers and managers. His plans had been cut short by the explosion.

Justice Richard also noted the many failures of the provincial inspectorate, describing it as "markedly derelict." He singled out inspector Albert McLean for his incompetence and lack of diligence, but did not spare McLean's supervisors to whom McLean's failings should have been obvious. Finally, he vindicated Carl Guptill. He concluded that McLean's treatment of him was a "disservice to a miner with legitimate complaints."

Epilogue

In 1993, a review of Nova Scotia's Labour Department's management and practices recommended sweeping changes that included staff training, development and performance reviews.

In 1995, all criminal charges against Westray and mine officials were stayed for procedural reasons.

In 1997, a revised Occupational Health and Safety Act became law.

In 1998, in an embarrassed response to the findings of the Commission of Inquiry, the Canadian Institute of Mining, Metallurgy and Petroleum (CIM) rescinded the John T. Ryan Award for safety that had been presented to the late Eugene Johnson on behalf of Westray on the eve of the explosion.

In 1999, Alexa McDonough, the federal leader of the NDP, an opposition party in the federal parliament, introduced a private member's bill in the House of Commons to amend the Criminal Code to hold corporations, executives, and directors liable for workplace deaths. The bill died on the order paper after an election call.

In 2001, the Nova Scotia Court of Appeal denied the Westray Families Group the right to sue the provincial government, concluding that such a lawsuit contravened provincial workers' compensation legislation. The Supreme Court of Canada upheld this decision in 2002. In May 2002, ten years after the explosion, and despite all lobbying and legislative efforts, parliament was still considering the issue of corporate criminal liability.

Albert McLean and others were fired from their positions in the Department of Labour. Donald Cameron won a provincial election in 1993, but was defeated in 1998. Shortly thereafter he accepted a posting in Boston as Consul General to the United States. It was reported that Gerald Phillips had been charged with attempted homicide in Honduras as a result of an injury to a young man caught up in a protest to prevent a mine operation that threatened his village. A Vancouver-based mining company subsequently hired Phillips in 1998. Although Curragh Resources dissolved into bankruptcy as a result of the explosion, Clifford Frame continued to attract investors and at last report was still developing mines. Roger Parry was last known to be driving a bus in Alberta. Many miners left Pictou County and looked for work in western and northern Canada. Carl Guptill operates an aquaculture business on Nova Scotia's eastern shore. Some of the "Westray widows" have moved, remarried, and rebuilt their lives, while others remain frozen in loss. The bodies of 11 miners remain underground.

Discussion questions

I. Learning

1. How did Westray management select, orient, and train miners? Propose an outline for an orientation/training program that links learning theory to organizational outcomes at Westray.

2. Give examples of both explicit and tacit knowledge communicated at Westray.

3. Consider the relationship between behaviour and consequences to explain miners' actions.

4. What are the characteristics of effective feedback? What role did feedback play in Westray's operations?

II. Motivation, applied motivation, outcomes, and stress management

1. How might either a content theory or process theory of motivation help to explain miners' decisions at Westray?

2. Propose a reward structure for Westray that you believe might have prevented the disaster.

3. Consider the role stress played in the Westray explosion. Which stressors might have been minimized at Westray? Is it possible or desirable to eliminate stress?

4. What role, if any, did job satisfaction and organizational commitment play at Westray?

III. Team processes: power and politics, conflict and negotiation

1. Why did the first union drive at Westray fail?

2. Consider the five sources of power. For each source, identify a "player" in the Westray drama that exhibited the capacity to influence others through the power source.

3. Contingencies of power may limit the ability to exercise power. Use two of the contingencies to argue that Westray's miners lacked power.

IV. Decision-making, employee involvement, leadership, and ethics

1. How would you characterize leadership at Westray and what impact did it have on the eventual disaster?

2. After the explosion, many expressed moral outrage at management practices at Westray. The report of the Commission of Inquiry adopted a similar tone. Use the ethical principles of utilitarianism, individual rights, and distributive justice to provide alternative evaluations of the organization.

V. Organizational structure, culture, and change

1. Describe the main features of the structure at Westray and discuss how this may have contributed to the disaster.

2. Identify cultural artefacts that characterized the organization.

3. Discuss the role socialization played in the communication of organizational culture at Westray.

4. Contrast espoused and enacted values at Westray. Support your analysis with specific examples.

5. In his testimony to the Westray Inquiry, Colin Benner implied that, had he been given the opportunity, he had intended to be an agent of change at Westray. Using Lewin's framework and other OB theories and concepts, write a memorandum to Benner proposing a plan for effective change.

Teaching notes for this case are available from Greenleaf Publishing. These are free of charge and available only to teaching staff. They can be requested by going to:
www.greenleaf-publishing.com/darkside_notes

The story behind the water in Walkerton, Ontario

Elizabeth A. McLeod and Jean Helms Mills

In May 2000, seven people lost their lives and over 2,300 became ill after drinking water contaminated with *Escherichia coli* O157:H7 and *Campylobacter jejuni* bacteria from manure spread on a farm near Well 5 in Walkerton, Ontario. Schools, daycare centres and businesses were shut down. The sports arena was converted into a depot where volunteers handed out bottled water and bleach, which it was necessary for them to add to the water in Walkerton before using it to wash their hands. Helicopters flew overhead transporting sick patients in air ambulances from local hospitals to a specialized hospital in London, Ontario.

Justice Dennis O'Connor concluded: "The most serious case of water contamination in Canadian history could have been prevented by proper chlorination of drinking water, according to a judicial inquiry report about Walkerton, Ontario's fatal *E. coli* outbreak". His report also "points to the region's public utilities managers and Ontario government cutbacks as contributors to the tragedy".

The pedagogical note presents options for discussing the case in the classroom. Accompanying the case are questions and answers, and links to audios and videos available online which include interviews with:

- Stan Koebel, manager of the Public Utility Commission (PUC) at the time of the tragedy in May 2000
- Frank Koebel, water foreman
- Dr Murray McQuigge, Medical Officer of Health for the Grey Bruce region of Ontario

Subject area

To illustrate and provoke discussion about topics taught in undergraduate or MBA management courses, including organizational behaviour, organizational theory, and business ethics.

Key issues

- To teach critical thinking skills

- To enhance problem-solving skills

- To demonstrate the applicability of management concepts, such as decision-making, power, politics, communications, organizational culture and structure to aid our understanding of how organizational disasters occur

- To make students aware of the link between business ethics and corporate social responsibility and the actions of organizational members

Case description

In May 2000 seven people lost their lives and over 2,300 became sick from drinking water contaminated with *Escherichia coli* O157:H7 and *Campylobacter jejuni* bacteria from manure spread on a farm near Well 5 in Walkerton, Ontario.[1] Schools, daycares and businesses were shut down. The sports arena was converted into a depot where volunteers handed out bottled water and bleach, which was necessary to add to the water in Walkerton before using it to wash their hands. Helicopters flew overhead transporting sick patients in air ambulances from local hospitals to a specialized hospital in London, Ontario.

According to a judicial inquiry report about Walkerton, Ontario's fatal *E. coli* outbreak by Justice Dennis O'Connor:

> The most serious case of water contamination in Canadian history could have been prevented by proper chlorination of drinking water.[2]

---

1 "Walkerton report highlights," *CBC News Online*, January 2002 (www.cbc.ca/news/background/walkerton/walkerton_report.html, 23 October 2006)
2 Ibid.

Justice O'Connor's report also "points to the region's public utilities managers and Ontario government cutbacks as contributors to the tragedy."[3]

Accompanying the case are a timeline of the Walkerton tragedy and a comprehensive bibliography that includes links to audios and videos of broadcasts by the Canadian Broadcasting Corporation (CBC). These include interviews with:

- Stan Koebel, manager of the Public Utility Commission (PUC) at the time of the tragedy in May 2000

- Frank Koebel, water foreman

- Dr. Murray McQuigge, Medical Officer of Health for Grey-Bruce

Introduction

It was 3 May 2000 and Stan Koebel, the manager of the Public Utility Commission in Walkerton, was preparing to leave for a conference in Windsor, Ontario.

Little did the residents of the small farming community know that, over the next few days, a series of faulty decisions that had been made by Stan and his brother over a long period of time would culminate in the death of seven people, including a two-year-old child, and that nearly half of Walkerton's population of 4,800 would become sick from *E. coli*.

The subsequent inquiry into the worst case of contaminated drinking water in North America would reveal that, although officials knew Walkerton's water system had been foul from 1995 to 1998, warnings from the Ministry of Environment to the PUC were largely ignored by Stan Koebel, records of water testing had been continually falsified by both brothers over a long period of time, and important information was being withheld.

How could this happen in Canada—a country that participates in the development of World Health Organization (WHO) guidelines for drinking water? What factors contributed to the final tragic outcome and why wasn't something done sooner? The simple answer might be to lay the blame solely on the Koebel brothers, but others have suggested that the cause is much more complex and involves a sequence and change of events that culminated in the disastrous outcome.

---

3 Ibid.

The Public Utilities Commission and the Koebel brothers

Stan Koebel put his feet up on the desk and closed his eyes for a few minutes while he waited for his brother Frank to show up. Frank was the water foreman for the PUC and would be in charge of the water utility while Stan was away at the conference. The previous day there had been a problem with one of the three wells that supplied water to the town and Stan needed to tell Frank what had to be done.

As the rain beat hard against the window, Stan reflected on how different this job was now from when he and Frank had started with the PUC in the early 1970s. Jobs in this small town were scarce and both brothers considered themselves lucky to get jobs with the water utility. Their father, Frank Sr., was already working there as a foreman, so he was able to keep his eye on both boys. Stan, in particular, had done well for himself, despite not having taken any courses or written the exams for certification in water management. Yes, it was a long way from his first job as a general labourer, and luckily for Stan, a voluntary "grand-parenting" scheme, which was not uncommon for long-term utility employees, meant that he received certification based on his on-the-job experience. Now, at the age of 47, Stan was the manager of the PUC in Walkerton and his brother Frank, who hadn't done badly either, was the water foreman.

As he looked down at the mess of papers and files on his desk, Stan remembered that there had been a time when the job had been much simpler. Now, not only was he responsible for the water utility, but for all utilities and projects that the PUC managed. This meant that he was spending less time looking after the water utility and more time trying to stay on top of the management of other projects, something he found increasingly difficult. In fact, lately he felt he was only giving about 5% of his time to the water utility, while he was struggling to keep abreast with all the projects that he was now in charge of managing.

Stan couldn't help but think that, since the Conservative government had come to power in Ontario in 1995, the PUC he now worked for had changed dramatically from the company he had known in the 1970s. At first the change was imperceptible, but when the town of Walkerton was amalgamated with two other municipalities, not only did Stan's workload and responsibilities increase but, because there were so many new employees, the Walkerton PUC no longer had the same feel of family.

If that hadn't been bad enough, when the budget for the Ministry of the Environment was cut by almost half during the first three years of Premier Harris' term, the way things were down at the water utility really started to change. First, the staff responsible for safe drinking water was cut from 161 to 43, which led to a decrease in the number of tests in water, including testing for *E. coli* in water plants like Walkerton. Furthermore, in an attempt to find new ways to generate funds, the government had decided to charge municipalities a fee for water tests that had previously been done for free. This resulted in municipalities switching to less expensive private labs and the eventual closure altogether of the ministry labs. At this stage, Stan recalled, even Walkerton had no choice but to hire a laboratory called GAP EnviroMicrobial to conduct its water tests.

A knock on the door awakened Stan from his daydreaming. As Frank settled into the chair across from him, Stan wasted no time in filling Frank in on a problem they were having with Well 7, which was currently the primary source of water for the town. Although there were other wells supplying the area, only three (Wells 5, 6, and 7) remained in use but, because Wells 5 and 6 were much shallower, Well 7 was the preferred source. Even though Well 7 had been activated the previous day, the chlorinator, which dispersed the chlorine needed to purify the water, was not being added to Well 7. Although Stan and Frank were both of the opinion that non-chlorinated water tasted better, a new chlorinator had been ordered and Stan wanted Frank to install it when it arrived. Assuring him that he would look after things, Stan went home confident that he would have one less thing to worry about.

A tragic chain of events

As he was driving along the highway on the outskirts of Walkerton, Frank wondered if the rain was ever going to end. It was Tuesday and it seemed like it had been raining forever. Stan had been away for three days and Frank still hadn't gotten around to installing the new chlorinator for Well 7. Instead, he had decided to deactivate Well 7 as the water source and was just coming from activating Well 5, a shallower well but one with a working chlorinator, as the primary source, which he knew wouldn't be a problem, given the heavy rains.

As Frank passed by David Biesentha's farm, about a half a kilometre from Well 5, he could smell the cattle manure David Biesentha had spread over the field of his Stonegate farm. Dave had owned the farm since 1969 and he did what he could to protect the environment and his cattle, including fencing the waterways on his property to keep his cattle out. To prevent runoff, he put eaves troughs on his barn to direct the rainwater away from the manure pile, which was stored on a cement pad. So when he had spread 70 tonnes of cattle manure on his field in April, he was careful to follow proper practices but there was no disguising the stench of the manure.

On Saturday, Frank set out to perform a routine check of the operating wells. Turning on the radio, he was just in time to hear a report that the previous day's rainfall had been 69.85 mm (2.75 inches) and that, from May 8 to May 15, a record of 133.35 mm (5.25 inches) had fallen! Although this made for lots of mud and flooding, it also meant that the wells would be full. Driving along Frank was thinking how nice it would be to get home, sit down and have a beer or two, especially now that the weather had improved. Although he knew he had a battle with the bottle, it had been a long week, so what harm could there be in a couple of drinks on a Saturday afternoon? He thought about stopping at Well 5 but why bother? Nobody ever really checked these things. Besides, he had been falsifying the records for years and nothing bad had every happened. All he had to do was fill up the sample bottle with tap water, record an acceptable status for the chlorination in the logbook and nobody would be the wiser and he could go home and enjoy the rest of the day.

By Monday, Stan was back from the conference and had met briefly with Frank, who gave him an update of the events of the previous week, including the information that Well 5 had been the primary source of water for Walkerton since the previous Tuesday. After Frank left his office, Stan decided that, even though Well 7 was still without a chlorinator, he would reactivate it, switch the supply back to Well 7 and shut down Well 5. He also had to make sure that water samples were collected from the wells, so they could be sent off for routine tests the next day to A&L Canada Laboratories, the firm that had taken over Walkerton's water testing when GAP dropped the contract.

Thinking nothing more of it, Stan was not totally surprised to receive a telephone call from A&L Laboratories on Wednesday morning informing him that the water sample that they tested was contaminated. This wasn't the first time there had been problems with the water system in Walkerton. A Ministry of Environment inspector had discovered that Walkerton had tainted water between 1995 and 1998, and had made recommendations to test more frequently and to increase the chlorine levels in the water supply. Although Stan had vowed to comply with the recommendations, he hadn't done anything. Why bother to make more work for himself? Besides, the water tasted better without chlorine.

Nothing happened before, so it was unlikely that this situation was any more serious. Stan knew that the reporting guidelines, which had been changed in 1997, meant that the results wouldn't go any further unless he chose to reveal them. In the old days, the Ministry of Health would have to have been informed of any irregularities, but, with new privacy rules, the results of the water were sent directly to the customer, in this case the PUC, and could only be passed on to the Medical Officer if the customer gave permission. So Stan decided to do nothing, despite a follow-up fax on Thursday by A&L Laboratories emphasizing that Walkerton's entire system was contaminated with *E. coli*.

Serious medical impact

Suddenly during the third week of May the residents of Walkerton, especially children, seemed to be getting more ill than normal. On Friday May 19, Dr. Murray McQuigge, Medical Officer of Health for Grey-Bruce, was working at his desk at home when he received a call from Dr. Kristen Hallett, a pediatrician from Owen Sound. She wanted to report two suspicious cases that she had referred to her from the Walkerton area. One was a seven-year-old girl with bloody diarrhea, and the second was an eleven-year-old boy with abdominal pain and a fever who developed bloody diarrhea later that evening. Dr. Hallett was concerned because she felt that things weren't right, that "there must be something going on."

Dr. McQuigge sprang into action and immediately contacted Stan Koebel at the PUC about any irregularities in testing. Reassured by Stan that the water was perfectly safe to drink and was frequently tested, Dr. McQuigge decided to look at food poisoning as a possible cause of the illnesses.

It was pretty clear that this was a problem that wasn't going away. By Saturday over 40 people had been admitted to the local hospital with bloody diarrhea and excruciating stomach cramps, head-fogging nausea, fever and chills. and sweats, and many other Walkerton residents and visitors were beginning to suffer similar but less severe symptoms. Whatever the source, the symptoms of these illnesses looked like the result of *E. coli*, a type of bacteria commonly found in the intestines of animals and humans and generated from human and animal waste. Although *E. coli* can be washed into creeks, rivers, streams, lakes, or groundwater during precipitation and end up in drinking water that is inadequately treated (which was why Dr. McQuigge at first suspected the water supply), it could also turn up in poorly prepared food. Worried about the effects on the young, Dr. McQuigge asked his staff to personally contact the parents of children under five and give them instructions for purifying water.

The whisteblower

On Saturday evening Bob McKay was feeling tense. He decided he could stand it no longer. His neighbours on both sides had come down with the mysterious illness and who knew when it would end? As a long-time employee at the PUC, Bob knew that what he was about to do would most likely jeopardize his career but what choice did he have? He had seen the fax from A&L Laboratories that had arrived at the PUC the previous Thursday and now he knew he had to do something.

Picking up the phone, Bob slowly dialed the number for the Environmental Emergency Centre. When the operator answered, he told her that he wanted to remain anonymous but he had information on the cause of the sicknesses that were spreading through the community. Bob them proceeded to tell them that the PUC had received a fax from A&L Laboratories on May 18 warning it that the water samples contained the deadly *E. coli* bacteria.

The operator immediately notified Dr. McQuigge, who was upset with the PUC's slow response because it had wasted valuable time as medical officials continued to look for food sources for the outbreak of *E. coli*. He decided to call Stan Koebel, the manager in charge of the water utility at the PUC. But, first, he contacted his secretary to issue an immediate "boil water advisory."

The PUC cover-up

Over at the PUC, Stan was working late, even though it was a Sunday night. He had just gotten off the phone with the Health Unit and they were asking awkward questions. They had received an anonymous tip about the fax from A&L Laboratories and Stan suspected it was one of his employees. Stan thought he had stalled them by misleading them about the sources of the positive samples, but he knew that they would be back and wanting to see the records of chlorination and water sampling. Stan called Frank and told him he needed to see him right away.

When Frank arrived, Stan closed the door to his office and told him what was happening. Even though neither brother believed that tainted water was the source of the illnesses, they both knew that if the Health Unit started to poke around the files they would show that the chlorinator had not been replaced in Well 7. Not only was Stan taking the heat for delaying the report from the lab, but when he had met the Environmental Ministry the month before, he had promised to be more vigilant over the water sampling and chlorination. They all knew that it was likely that the Health Unit would want to see evidence of chlorine levels, especially in Wells 5 and 7.

Concerned, Stan asked Frank to change the logbook to conceal these facts on Well 7. He was also worried about the water sample entries for chlorine levels, especially since two of the shallower wells (5 and 6) were located very close to agricultural lands and heavy rains might have allowed surface water to seep into the water supply. Trouble in the past with non-compliance with Ministry of Environment directives for more frequent testing and increased chlorination made Stan wary that they would be particularly on the lookout for accurate and up-to-date records.

Frank said he would change the logbook entry for Well 7's chlorinator and told Stan that there was also no need to worry about the water samples from the wells because, while Stan had been away, Frank had taken care of it by filling in some blanks on the testing sheet, indicating chlorine residual levels, even though the chlorinator was broken at Well 7 and there wasn't any chlorine in the water to record. He then forged Stan's signature, so everything would match up. Stan was relieved that his brother had had the foresight to take care of this. It was one less thing to worry about at a time when they needed to make sure all the details matched. Both Stan and Frank went home, thinking the worst was over.

The epidemic

Stan slept well Sunday night, believing that he and Frank had the situation under control. But, when he awoke Monday morning and turned the radio on, the news wasn't good. The death of Lenore Al was being reported and the cause was blamed on contaminated water. The second bit of bad news for Stan was that the Ministry of Environment was opening an investigation into the town's water problems. On Tuesday, when the Medical Health Office finally had confirmation that the water supply was contaminated, Stan realized that he had to confess to receiving the fax and also that the chlorinator in Well 7 had not been working and had not been replaced.

By Thursday there had been two more deaths. On Friday, when it was announced that a criminal investigation was being launched by the Ontario Provincial Police, Stan and Frank both knew it was only a matter of time before their falsification of records was discovered. The only question now was when.

Even though the source of the outbreak was beginning to be under control, the Emergency Health Unit was trying to stem the spread of the contamination by handing out bottled water and bleach from the sports arena, which had been turned into a temporary depot. More than 40% of Walkerton's population had been affected by the bacteria and the very ill patients were being airlifted to a specialized unit in the bigger hospital in London, Ontario, because the local hospitals were being stretched beyond their capacity.

The final count would be that at least 2,300 people became ill. The final death toll included seven people who died directly from *E. coli,* while complications from *E. coli* were given as the cause of death for another 14 elderly people.

The Walkerton inquiry

A public inquiry led by the Honourable Dennis O'Connor was established by the Ontario government after the tragedy. It lasted nine months and heard the testimony of over 114 witnesses.

Evidence revealed that there were "more than 20 years of lies, cover-ups, and deception," as Stan Koebel testified that he had falsified water samples, faked chlorine records, and, after heavy flooding the previous May, had run one of the town wells without a chlorinator. When his lawyer asked if he should have been the manager of the PUC, Stan Koebel replied, "Looking back on it now, no. I didn't have enough educational background or experience." In a report put out by the Canadian Broadcasting Corporation (CBC), Stan blamed his previous boss at the PUC for his actions. Stan said that he learned how to fake tests and disregard government regulations from his supervisor, and that these were normal practices at the PUC because of complacency. When he became the manager he also encouraged those under him to do the same thing.

The cause of the contamination of the well water was straightforward. The unusually heavy rains created an overflow of surplus water, which drained from the manure treated fields into the shallow unchlorinated wells. Despite the precautions David Biesentha took to maintain environmental standards, his cattle were, at the time, carriers of *E. coli* and their manure carried the deadly bacteria straight into the untreated water supply.

The Inquiry found that illnesses could have been prevented if Stan Koebel had monitored chlorine levels in the drinking water and installed a chlorinator. But it also blamed deregulation of water testing and cuts to the Environment Ministry by the Ontario government as contributing factors to the tragedy. The bigger question is how was this able to happen?

Epilogue

On March 25, 2003, Stan and Frank Koebel were "charged with public nuisance, uttering and forgery and breach of public duty." The brothers pleaded guilty on November 30, 2004, and were sentenced to imprisonment; Stan was sentenced to one year in jail and Frank was sentenced to nine months house arrest. Stan Koebel was released after serving only four months.

Timeline of the Walkerton tragedy

1995: The Ontario government closes down all four publicly run water-testing laboratories.

1997: Walkerton—always responsible for its own water—has no set methods for certifying laboratories, or a legal requirement to test water or report results.

June 18, 1998: Walkerton Town Council complains to Ontario's conservative government about cutbacks and the closing of labs, calling on the Ministry of Energy and the Environment to ensure basic, healthy water standards for all Ontarians.

1999: Walkerton and two other local municipalities were amalgamated into Brockton.

April 22, 2000: Dave Biesentha follows proper practices and spreads 70 tonnes of cattle manure over the field of his Stonegate farm, close to Walkerton's Well 5.

May 2, 2000: Activated Well 7 without installed operating chlorinator.

May 3, 2000: Stan Koebel instructs Frank Koebel to install the new chlorinator while he is away.

May 5, 2000: Stan Koebel leaves for a water conference in Windsor, Ontario.

May 8–15, 2000: Heavy rains, totaling 133 mm (5.25 inches).

Tuesday, May 9, 2000: Deactivated Well 7.

May 9–15: Well 5, a very shallow well, was the primary source of water for Walkerton.

Friday, May 12, 2000: Excessive rainfall swept southern Ontario, 70 mm (2.75 inches).

May 12, 2000 or shortly after: *E. coli* O157:H7 and *Campylobacter jejuni* contaminants enter the Walkerton system through Well 5.

Within a week: Walkerton residents and visitors begin to suffer symptoms of bloody diarrhea and excruciating stomach cramps, head-fogging nausea, fever and chills, and sweats. Doctors advise patients to drink lots of water.

Saturday, May 13, 2000: Frank Koebel does not check chlorine residual at Well 5 during routine check, falsifies the readings.

Sunday, May 14, 2000: Stan Koebel returns from conference to find that brother Frank has falsified records on status of Well 5.

Monday, May 15, 2000: Stan Koebel turns Well 7 on without chlorination at 1.15 pm.

Tuesday, May 16, 2000: Water samples received by A&L Canada Laboratories.

Wednesday, May 17, 2000: Patients start being treated for symptoms of cramps, fever, bloody diarrhea, and vomiting. A&L Laboratories telephone Stan Koebel to inform him that the water is contaminated.

Thursday, May 18, 2000: Stan Koebel receives a fax from A&L water testing lab stating that the entire system was contaminated with *E. coli*. Koebel does not report the findings and tells the mayor that the problem is not serious.

Friday, May 19, 2000: Dr. McQuigge, Medical Officer of Health at the Bruce-Grey-Owen Sound Public Health Unit, is notified by Dr. Kristen Hallett, a pediatrician, of two cases of bloody diarrhea referred from the Walkerton Hospital to Owen Sound Hospital.

May 19, 2000: Stan Koebel assures the Public Health Unit that the water is fine. The Public Health Unit starts looking for a possible food source to explain the documented illnesses. New chlorinator is installed on Well 7 and Stan begins flushing and superchlorinating the system.

Saturday, May 20, 2000: The Health Unit's Environmental Emergency Center, Spills Action Centre (SAC), is informed of failed lab test results in the Walkerton water system taken from a construction site by an anonymous call placed by Robert (Bob) McKay, an employee of the PUC.

May 20, 2000: Forty more people report to hospital with bloody diarrhea and test positive for *E. coli* 0157:H7.

May 20, 2000: PUC reassures the Public Health Unit that Walkerton's water supply is safe.

Sunday, May 21, 2000: The Health Unit contacts Stan Koebel who assures them that the positive samples were only from the construction site. Nonetheless, Dr. McQuigge decides to issue a "boil water advisory" to the people of Walkerton telling them not to drink the water.

Monday, May 22, 2000: John Earle, a Senior Environmental Officer with the Ministry of the Environment, Owen Sound District, is assigned to investigate the water problems in Walkerton.

May 22, 2000: Lenore Al, 66, is the first person to die from the contaminated water.

Tuesday, May 23, 2000: The Medical Health Office (MHO) laboratory confirms positive test results for *E. coli* in the water. Stan Koebel finally tells MHO about the fax on May 18 and admits that the machine that puts the chlorine in the town's drinking water supply did not work for some time. Stan instructs Frank to clean up the operating log sheets for May 2000.

May 23, 2000: Edith Pearson, 83, and Mary Rose Raymond, 2, die.

Wednesday, May 24, 2000: Vera Coe, 75, dies.

Thursday, May 25, 2000: Drinking water system taken over by Ontario's Clean Water Agency.

Friday, May 26, 2000: Ontario Provincial Police launch a criminal investigation in Walkerton.

Monday, May 29, 2000: Laura Rowe, 84, dies.

Tuesday, May 30, 2000: Betty Trushinski, 56, dies.

Wednesday, May 31, 2000: Conservative Premier, Mike Harris, reverses his earlier position and calls a public inquiry. James Bolden, former mayor of Walkerton, visits local hospital with symptoms. He reports that "while crowded, everything is running efficiently, including flights to London Health Sciences Centre, which now holds 11 patients (ten of them children)."

By June 1, 2000: Death toll has reached 11 with a further 784 treated for symptoms, including 90 who were hospitalized.

June 9, 2000: Ministry of Environment issues an Order requiring that Well 5 remain closed and disconnected.

June 15, 2000: Death toll upgraded to 14. Seven more cases investigated by the coroner. There are estimates that half of the population of Walkerton had got sick from the water contamination.

July 25, 2000: Evelyn Hussey, 84, dies of kidney failure as a result of the *E. coli* poisoning.

December 5, 2000: Boil order lifted.

December 20, 2004: Stan Koebel sentenced to one year in jail. Frank Koebel sentenced to nine months of house arrest.

April 2005: Stan Koebel granted parole and released from prison after serving less than four months of his sentence.

Bibliography

Canadian Broadcasting Corporation (CBC) news archives

CBC (2000a) "Words cannot begin to express how sorry I am" (CBC Digital Archives, broadcast 19 December 2000; archives.cbc.ca/IDC-1-70-1672-11521/disasters_tragedies/walkerton/clip1, 26 October 2006).

CBC (2000b) "London hospitals treat Walkerton citizens" (CBC Digital Archives, broadcast 24 May 2000; archives.cbc.ca/IDC-1-70-1672-11533/disasters_tragedies/walkerton/clip1, 23 October 2006).

CBC (2000c) "The hunt for *E. coli* O157:H7" (CBC Digital Archives, broadcast 2 June 2000; archives.cbc.ca/IDC-1-70-1672-11517/disasters_tragedies/walkerton/clip1, 29 October 2006).

CBC (2000d) "Town epidemic" (CBC Digital Archives, broadcast 2 June 2000; archives.cbc.ca/IDC-1-70-1672-11515/disasters_tragedies/walkerton/clip1, 26 October 2006).

CBC (2000e) "What is *E. coli* O157:H7?" (CBC Digital Archives, broadcast 27 May 2000; archives.cbc.ca/IDC-1-70-1672-11519/disasters_tragedies/walkerton/clip1, 11 September 2006).

CBC (2000f) "Deadly water: the lessons of Walkerton. A Tragic Flaw?" (News in Review, September 2000; www.cbc.ca/newsinreview/Sep2000/walkerton/tragic.htm, 12 August 2006).

CBC (2001) "Walkerton was a wake-up call for all of us" (CBC Digital Archives, broadcast 29 June 2001; archives.cbc.ca/IDC-1-70-1672-11541/disasters_tragedies/walkerton/clip1, 26 October 2006).

CBC (2002a) "Is Canada's drinking water safer?" (CBC Digital Archives, broadcast 18 January 2002; archives.cbc.ca/IDC-1-70-1672-11530/disasters_tragedies/walkerton/clip1, 26 October 2006).

CBC (2002b) "Indepth: Inside Walkerton. Key figures in Walkerton's water crisis" (*CBC News Online*, January 2002; www.cbc.ca/news/background/walkerton/players.html, 26 October 2006).

CBC (2002c) "Indepth: Inside Walkerton. Walkerton report highlights" (*CBC News Online*, January 2002; www.cbc.ca/news/background/walkerton/walkerton_report.html, 23 October 2006).

CBC (2003) "A nightmare that won't end" (CBC Digital Archives, broadcast 26 May 2000; archives. cbc.ca/IDC-1-70-1672-11531/disasters_tragedies/walkerton/clip1, 27 October 2006).

CBC (2004a) "Sentencing the Koebels" (CBC Digital Archives, broadcast 17 December 2004; archives.cbc.ca/IDC-1-70-1672-11529/disasters_tragedies/walkerton/clip1, 27 October 2006).

CBC (2004b) "Indepth: Health. *E. coli.* FAQs" (*CBC News Online*, 23 June 2004; www.cbc.ca/ news/background/health/ecoli.html, 26 October 2006).

CBC (2004c) "Indictment in the Superior Court of Justice: Her Majesty the Queen against Stan Koebel and Frank Koebel" (*CBC News Online*, November 2004; www.cbc.ca/news/ background/walkerton/gfx/koebel.pdf, 24 October 2006).

CBC (2004d) "Indepth: Inside Walkerton. Canada's worst ever *E. coli* contamination" (*CBC News Online*, 20 December 2004; www.cbc.ca/news/background/walkerton, 23 October 2006).

CBC (2004e) "Indepth: Inside Walkerton. Timeline" (*CBC News Online*, 20 December 2004; www. cbc.ca/news/background/walkerton/timeline.html, 26 October 2006).

CBC (2005a) "Fake records, forged signatures, disastrous cover-up" (CBC Digital Archives, broadcast 7 December 2000; archives.cbc.ca/environment/pollution/topics/1672-11537, 12 September 2006).

CBC (2006) "Indepth: Health Timeline: *E. coli* contamination in Canada" (*CBC News Online*, 26 September 2006; www.cbc.ca/news/background/health/ecoli-timeline.html, 26 October 2006).

Official sources

Health Canada (2006) "Drinking Water. Environmental & Workplace Health" (www.hc-sc.gc.ca/ ewh-semt/water-eau/drink-potab/index_e.html, 23 October 2006).

Health Canada (2008) *Guidelines for Canadian Drinking Water Quality—Summary Table* (Ottawa: Health Canada; www.hc-sc.gc.ca/ewh-semt/alt_formats/hecs-sesc/pdf/pubs/water-eau/ sum_guide-res_recom/summary-sommaire-eng.pdf, 21 August 2008).

O'Connor, D.R. (2002a) *Part One: A Summary. Report of the Walkerton Commission of Inquiry: The Events of May 2000 and Related Issues* (Ottawa: Ontario Ministry of the Attorney General; www.attorneygeneral.jus.gov.on.ca/english/about/pubs/walkerton/part1/WI_Summary.pdf, 29 October 2006).

O'Connor, D.R. (2002b) *Part Two: Report of the Walkerton Inquiry: A Strategy for Safe Drinking Water* (Ottawa: Ontario Ministry of the Attorney General; www.attorneygeneral.jus.gov. on.ca/english/about/pubs/walkerton/part2/Front_material_web.pdf, 30 October 2006).

Ontario Ministry of the Attorney General (2002) "Report of the Walkerton Inquiry" (www. attorneygeneral.jus.gov.on.ca/english/about/pubs/walkerton, 29 October 2006)

Ontario Ministry of the Environment (2006) "Frequently asked questions about water and its usage" (www.ene.gov.on.ca/envision/water/waterFAQ.htm, 11 September 2006).

Regional Niagara (2002) "Water and Land Use Planning. Walkerton Inquiry Report. Planning Act and Official Plans" (DPD 118–2002; Regional Municipality of Niagara; www.regional.niagara. on.ca/news/publications/pdf/DPD%20118-2002.pdf, accessed 22 October 2006).

Books and journal articles

Jones, G., A.J. Mills, T.G. Weatherbee, and J. Helms Mills (2006) *Organizational Theory, Design, and Change* (Toronto: Pearson; Canadian edn).

Lee Burke, B. (2001) *Don't Drink the Water: The Walkerton Tragedy* (Victoria, BC: Trafford).

Mullen, J., N. Vladie and A.J. Mills (2006) "Making Sense of the Walkerton Crisis," *Culture and Organization* 12.3: 207-20.

Pelley, J. (2000) "Deadly *E. coli* outbreak focuses Canadian privatization debate," *Environmental Science and Technology* 34.15: A336.

Schreier, H., and L.M. Lavkulich (2002) "Safe Drinking Water—a Local Example of a Global Challenge," *Journal of Business Administration and Policy Analysis* 30.31: 265.

Other sources

"Case Study: The Walkerton Experience, The Events of May 2000" (Microsoft® PowerPoint® presentation; www.glrcap.org/image_upload/File/Walkerton%20case%20study%20ppt%20J MV.ppt, 13 September 2006).

Cheng, T.Y. (2002) "What Happened In Walkerton? A Tragedy Made Sense", honours' thesis, Mount Allison University, Sackville, New Brunswick.

"Enteropathogenic *Escherichia coli* in Walkerton, Ontario" (wvlc.uwaterloo.ca/biology447/modules/module4/enteropathogenic.htm, 30 December 2006).

Walkerton and District Chamber of Commerce (2006) "Map of Walkerton, Brockton, Bruce County, Midwestern Ontario and Ontario" (town.walkerton.on.ca/Chamber/Maps.html, 29 October 2006).

"Walkerton Tragedy" (Wikipedia; en.wikipedia.org/wiki/Walkerton_Tragedy, 26 October 2006).

Discussion questions

1. What role did stress play in contributing to Stan Koebel's actions? Discuss the types of stressors that affected him.

2. What communication tactics did Stan and Frank use to delay the flow of information and what effects did they have?

3. Describe the organizational culture at the Public Utility Commission (PUC). How did the culture influence Stan and Frank Koebel's actions?

4. Using the decision-making model as a guide, explain why you think Stan made the decision to hide the fax from the Health Unit doctor.

5. Using the principles of bureaucracy describe how the PUC failed the municipality.

6. What effects did the government cutback have on the restructuring of the PUC and how did these changes contribute to the tainted water?

7. Was there any attempt at ethical behaviour by the PUC? Describe Stan and Frank Koebel's actions from an ethical perspective; and Bob McKay's actions as a whistleblower.

8. Discuss power and politics as they relates to this case.

9. Using Expectancy Theory, discuss how Stan Koebel's job was not motivating and what could be done to ensure that his successor doesn't take the same shortcuts.

10. Could this disaster have been prevented? How can OB/OT help us understand why this was allowed to happen and what could have been done differently?

Teaching notes for this case are available from Greenleaf Publishing. These are free of charge and available only to teaching staff. They can be requested by going to:
www.greenleaf-publishing.com/darkside_notes

Dark territory
The Graniteville chlorine spill

Jill A. Brown and Ann K. Buchholtz

Avondale Mills began 2005 with hope for a bright future. Even though the textile industry faced fierce foreign competition, the company seemed financially sound and poised to reap the benefits of investments in new machinery and efficiency improvements. Then on January 6, a Norfolk Southern freight train, traveling at 45 miles per hour, struck a parked train. Fourteen cars derailed and a tanker containing 131 tons of chlorine immediately released 90 tons of chlorine gas in toxic clouds that travelled to the Avondale Mills plants. Nine people, including six Avondale workers, were killed and 5,400 people were evacuated from the local area. The company spent $140 million to clean up the chlorine, but it was to no avail. A $215 million insurance settlement was not enough to cover the true costs of the derailment. Computer drives were destroyed and production was stopped for nearly six months. Over 5,000 workers across several Avondale plants, most of whom did not have a high school education, lost their jobs. The small mill town community of Graniteville (population 1,158) was decimated, real estate prices tumbled, and the state spent nearly half a million dollars on health screenings for toxic gas exposure.

This case is based on secondary sources as well as interviews with former executives of Avondale Mills. No elements of this case are disguised—the incident is a matter of public record. Avondale Mills Chief Operating Officer, Keith Hull, has read and endorsed the case. The introduction of the case is written as seen through his eyes.

This case would be appropriate for an undergraduate or graduate course in the following areas:

- Business ethics
- Environmental ethics
- Social issues in management

- Issues management
- Crisis management

It could also be used to stimulate class discussion in more general management classes such as principles of management, strategy, or leadership.

Teaching and learning objectives
This case covers a broad territory and so individual instructors may choose to use it for innumerable purposes. At the very least, students should undertake a critical examination of the systemic factors that allowed the spill to happen and a managerial examination of how the key decision-makers could lessen the likelihood of such an incident occurring as well as respond effectively if it does. Instructors can gear the discussion and expectations to the level of cognitive learning appropriate for the class and the nature of the course in which it is given.

   Students should be able to apply the knowledge they learn in the classroom to this real incident faced by corporate managers. Ideally, they will be able to analyze the event and synthesize the various elements to further develop their moral awareness and critically examine a system that carries with it such great risk. Astute students will have the opportunity to evaluate the systemic factors that led to the tragedy, as well as the actions and responses of the managers involved.

Introduction

On January 6, 2005, Avondale Mills Chief Operating Officer Keith Hull received a call at about 4.00 am from the local plant in Graniteville, South Carolina, that there had been an accident on the railroad tracks. As he scrambled to focus, Keith had a hard time processing the information. Chemical spill? What could have happened? Avondale was a textile manufacturer that produced yarn and dyed and undyed fabric. What chemicals could possibly be involved? What did Avondale have to do with the railroad? All Keith could think about was the status of the third shift workers. How many were working at the time? He quickly calculated that there were at least several hundred workers completing an order for a large denim distributor. He immediately went on his way to the plant to investigate. Getting into his car, he shook his head. Just when he thought the company had succeeded in another competitive year . . .

Avondale Mills

Avondale Mills, Inc. is a manufacturer of yarn and dyed and undyed fabric, which was acquired by a privately held company, Walton Monroe Mills, Inc., located in Monroe, Georgia. As is the case for many textile companies, Walton Monroe Mills began in 1895 as a family-owned and -operated business started by George W. Felker Jr.

The business performed well through the 1950s, when George groomed his son, George W. Felker III, to take over the family business. George W. Felker III graduated from Georgia Tech with a degree in textile engineering and served in the Army in World War II. After working for several textile firms, he took over as head of the family business in 1962. Under his guidance, despite fierce foreign competition and changing technology, the company grew through a series of acquisitions, purchasing Dakotah Mills in 1984 and Avondale Mills in 1986 to become the 325th largest U.S. private company by 1993, with mills located in the Carolinas and in Georgia. By FYE August 27, 2004, sales were $564 million, with assets of $325.9 million and about 5,000 employees. In addition to manufacturing yarn and undyed fabric, Avondale was also involved with the design, manufacturing, and marketing of a broad line of indigo-dyed denim for both branded and private-label apparel producers of denim jeans, slacks, shorts, skirts, and jackets. Avondale also designed and manufactured an extensive line of piece-dyed sportswear.

The Avondale Mills purchase in 1986 was a particularly risky one for Walton Monroe. The decision to buy Avondale Mills was spearheaded by George Felker's son, Stephen, who became president of Walton Monroe in 1980. During his first three years as CEO, Walton Monroe sales dropped from $30 million to $25 million, largely because of a host of imports that began to push many American mills out of business. In a daring move to rejuvenate the company, Stephen invested over $18 million in new, efficient machines and set sights on growing Monroe by acquisitions. After purchasing Dakotah Mills in North Carolina for $5.5 million, Stephen boldly decided to buy Avondale Mills, a publicly held company three times the sales size of the privately owned Walton Monroe. Avondale sales had begun to decline from a high of $300 million in 1982 to $240 million in 1986, and the owners were looking to sell. Stephen felt comfortable with the company, especially since he had worked there immediately after college as a management trainee at Avondale's yarn and denim weaving plant in Sylacauga, Alabama. The majority owners of Avondale felt comfortable with Stephen as well, and when a bidding war began between Walton Monroe and two other textile manufacturers, Stephen was able to purchase 39% of Avondale stock from a descendant of the mill's founder, former Alabama governor B.B. Comer. With this stock and the help of some creative mezzanine financing by Atlanta investment bankers, Felker acquired Avondale and began to go to work—looking for efficiencies, and pumping over $40 million into new machinery. He hired Keith Hull to be his Director of Marketing, and moved him to the Graniteville, South

Carolina Avondale Mills plant to oversee production. Stephen promoted Keith to Chief Operating Officer in 2004.

The textile industry

The textile industry has been a beleaguered industry for decades. Some cite the General Agreement on Tariffs and Trade (GATT; 1947), the North American Free Trade Agreement (NAFTA; 1994) and the Dominican Republic Central America Free Trade Agreement (DR-CAFTA; 2005) as international trade agreements that have contributed to the decline of American textile manufacturers. All of the agreements served to phase out tariffs and quotas on textiles, perhaps inhibiting the ability of U.S. manufacturers to compete on price. Under GATT, textile manufacturers endure global product quotas under the Multi-Fiber Arrangement (MFA) that provide a means to control imports. Under NAFTA, the establishment of a free trade zone between Canada, the United States and Mexico, manufacturers offered the opportunity for businesses to "follow the cheaper wages out of the country"[1] by relocating facilities and businesses outside of the boundaries of the U.S. and by allowing import options for raw cotton and limiting cotton export opportunities. The Dominican Republic Central Free Trade Agreement is a trade agreement that includes the United States, El Salvador, Nicaragua, Guatemala, Honduras, Costa Rica, and the Dominican Republic, establishing bilateral trade agreements similar to NAFTA. In this agreement, the national assemblies of the participating countries met and approved the reduction of remaining quotas to allow Asian textiles to be brought through Central America without paying duties.

A surge in imported cotton products along with an availability of cheap labor overseas has devastated U.S. textile mills. From a high U.S. cotton mill production of 16.53 million bales in 1999, the U.S. textile industry has continued to contract, with current U.S. cotton mill production below 6 million bales.[2] This has occurred despite new technological innovations that make the industry very efficient, with the use of computer-aided design, high-tech imagery for shaping color and streamlined just-in-time delivery programs. As an indication of this efficiency, and despite the decline of active "spinning positions" (a measure of cotton production), the pounds of cotton used per position have increased sevenfold from 200 pounds per position in 1980 to 1,400 pounds per position in

---

1 C. Norwood (2006) "NAFTA cited by many officials as factor in Avondale Mill's closing," *Daily Home Online*, May 24, 2006; www.dailyhome.com/news/2006/dh-localnews-0534-cnorwood-6e24m0244.htm.

2 This is US textile mill cotton production as of August 2006: National Cotton Council of America (www.cotton.org/econ/textile-crisis.cfm).

2000.[3] However, these efficiencies cannot seem to combat the market forces that continue to plague the textile industry. The overall decline in U.S. mill demand affects the prices that U.S. cotton growers might charge. This decline, combined with the difficulties of variable annual export volumes and the resultant fall in the U.S. futures market, has caused prices for cotton growers to go well below the U.S. Department of Agriculture's estimated cost of production.

Beyond the debate over the impact of free trade agreements on the textile industry, there is growing concern over the violations of past trade agreements by China. Because of the growing U.S. trade deficit with China, numerous proposals have been put in place to restrict imports from China. The competitiveness of Chinese exports has been enhanced by the value of its currency, the yuan, which does not float freely with market forces, but rather is determined by the Chinese government's policy of pegging its currency to the dollar. Industry groups such as the National Council of Textile Organizations, and the National Cotton Council, to name a few, have been actively working with the World Trade Organization (WTO) under litigation to require China to allow the value of its currency to be determined by market forces. China is subject to additional "safeguard quotas" as a result of the U.S. government following the petitions of these industry groups to limit import growth by product category.

Despite the nature of the textile industry and pressures from foreign competition, Avondale executives always cited the positives of free trade. CEO Felker stated in the 2004 annual report that:

> The [NAFTA] agreement contains safeguards sought by the U.S. textile industry, including a rule of origin requirement that products be processed in one of the three countries in order to benefit from NAFTA. In addition, NAFTA requires, with limited exception, merchandise to be made from yarns and fabrics originating in North America in order to avoid trade restrictions . . . Based on experience to date, NAFTA has had a favorable impact on [Avondale's] business.[4]

Felker goes on to cite the advantages of other trade agreements including the Andean Trade Preference Act (ATPA), the United States–Caribbean Basin Trade Partnership Act (CBI), and the Africa Growth and Opportunity Act (AGOA), all of which, according to Felker, make the U.S. a more attractive location for textile sourcing.

3 National Cotton Council of America (2005) "US cotton industry faces challenging economic climate," January 29, 2005; www.cotton.org/news/releases/2005/econoutlook. cfm?renderforprint=1&.
4 Avondale, Inc. 10-K file with the U.S. Securities and Exchange Commission (SEC) on 11/12/04 for FYE 8/26/04. SEC File # 33-68412.

Avondale, Inc.

At the beginning of the calendar year 2005, Avondale was as well positioned as a textile company could be in the global competitive environment. Assets were stable, at approximately $326 million, first quarter sales were up from the previous year, and cash flow was positive at $2.1 million.[5] The denim business was in an upswing as blue jeans became a fashion rage once more. The company expected a positive cash flow FYE 2005 as the technological efficiencies from the late 1990s were beginning to pay off with substantial operating margin improvements. In fact, COO Keith Hull anticipated a profit for FYE 2005, because of these efficiencies, in addition to the retirement of some more debt, and some additional denim business from one of their largest customers, Levi Strauss, who was experiencing its own financial resurgence.

The chlorine spill

On January 6, 2005, at approximately 2.45 am, a Norfolk Southern freight train traveling from Macon, Georgia, to Columbia, South Carolina, struck a parked train in Graniteville, SC, just 15 miles north of Augusta, GA. The train was traveling at 45 miles per hour and 14 cars derailed. The train had three chlorine gas cars, one liquid sodium hydroxide car and one liquid creosol car. A tanker containing 131 tons of chlorine immediately released 90 tons of chlorine gas in toxic clouds that traveled to the nearby Avondale Mills Textile Valley.

Witnesses at the scene saw a plume of yellow/green smoke that engulfed the area that immediately caused their throats to burn and their eyes water. Nine people died and more than 554 residents were injured after the train derailment. Over the next 24 hours, 5,400 people were evacuated from the local area, as they waited for the chlorine toxins to subside. Over 500 workers were on duty on the night shift at Avondale Mills, and many of them gathered in the back room of the plant until the gas smell got too strong, when they eventually left. Six of these workers died as they tried to leave the property.[6]

The collision occurred in an area known as "dark territory" where electronic control and track signals are not used.[7] A subsequent investigation found the

---

5 Avondale, Inc. 10-Q file with SEC on 1/5/05 for 1st Quarter 11/28/04. SEC File #33-68412.

6 Jerry T. Mitchell, Andrew S. Edmonds, Susan L. Cutter, Mathew Schmidtlein, Reggie McCarn, Michael E. Hodgson, and Sonya Duhé (2005) "Evacuation Behavior in Response to the Graniteville, South Carolina, Chlorine Spill" (Quick Response Research Report, 178; Boulder, CO: Natural Hazards Center, University of Colorado; www.colorado.edu/hazards/qr/qr178/qr178.html).

7 J. Nesbitt (2005) "Fatigue, 'dark territory' can cause accidents", *Augusta Chronicle*, January 12, 2005; chronicle.augusta.com/stories/011205/met_3066593.shtml.

cause of the wreck to be operator error, as tired Norfolk Southern rail operators from the night before had left a switch to park locomotives open when
they checked into a local motel to get some rest. The open switch enabled the
oncoming freight train to steer onto a sidetrack and collide with the parked train.
Immediate responders to the crisis included the Aiken County Sheriff's Office,
the South Carolina Department of Health and Environmental Control (DHEC),
Emergency Management Services (EMS) from public and private sectors, the
U.S. Environmental Protection Agency (USEPA) and the U.S. Coast Guard, who
took air samples from the surrounding area.

In a case eerily similar to the infamous *Exxon Valdez* and *Hurricane Katrina*
scandals, the response to the spill was slow, ineffective, and hampered by bureaucracy. The Federal Emergency Management Agency (FEMA) rejected Governor
Mark Sanford's request for federal disaster relief as it determined that the Graniteville derailment and chemical spill did not warrant an emergency declaration.
The safety of emergency response workers was compromised when firefighters
rushed to the scene before taking appropriate protection. Fish and wildlife in
over 1,700 yards of adjacent creeks died slowly as local officials waited for the
results of federal testing. Additionally, Norfolk Southern Railroad did not make
the call to the National Response Center until over an hour after the release of
the chlorine, in violation of USEPA rules, and hampering the coordination of
communication between the various responders.[8]

Avondale closes

On January 24, 2005, Governor Sanford rescinded the state of emergency for
Aiken County as displaced residents returned home. The transfer of chlorine
from the derailed cars had taken approximately two weeks, but the after-effects
continued well on through 2006.

Avondale Mills, the textile company that was adjacent to the tracks and not
associated with the chlorine delivery, suffered irrevocable damage that caused
the company to close its doors in July 2006. Over 5,000 workers lost their jobs.
This occurred after the company spent $140 million to clean up the chlorine
damage, to no avail as equipment rusted before their eyes. According to CEO
Felker, the $215 million settlement with Avondale's insurance company for dam-
ages caused by derailment was:

> . . . not nearly enough to cover the full value of losses incurred as a
> result of the derailment.[9]

8   Mitchell *et al.*, op. cit.
9   A. Thompson, (2006) "Local Avondale plant closing," *Tifton Gazette,* May 24, 2006: 1.

Keith Hull remained employed at Avondale for 18 months after the chlorine spill. Within the first months of the cleanup, Keith knew the damage was substantial and probably irreversible: "I began to think that I could see the equipment rusting in front of my eyes." Computer hard drives were lost forever, and production was stopped for almost six months.

The time delay for start-up, combined with the huge capital needed to bring the plants back to being fully operational eventually led to Felker's decision to close down Avondale, despite help from fellow industry competitors who volunteered to fill production orders under contract with Avondale at the time of the crash. Keith lost his job, his health insurance, and the business that he had nurtured for almost 30 years. Stephen Felker continues to liquidate the assets of the company. All Avondale operations had ceased by July 2006.

Graniteville suffers

The community of Graniteville is a small community of 1,158; a small mill town of 90 homes, boarding houses, two churches, and a school. In addition to Avondale Mills, it houses a Bridgestone/Firestone Tire and Rubber plant. Because of the chlorine spill, real estate prices began to tumble as ongoing public health concerns continue to foster.

In 2006, the Department of Labor announced that it would give $280,000 to local economic leaders to try to foster redevelopment in Aiken and the surrounding communities like Graniteville, in part to combat any lost revenue from the accident.

The South Carolina Department of Health and Environmental Controls continues to provide free health screenings, totaling approximately $450,000 in 2006, to people who were exposed to the toxic gas.

The South Carolina Department of Education provided a $100,000 grant in 2006 to Graniteville-area workers who lost their jobs when Avondale Mills went out of business. Approximately 60% of those workers do not even have a high school education, so grant money will be issued for English literacy and high school education.

Norfolk Southern flourishes

Rail shipments of hazardous materials take place every day. In the past ten years, rail transportation of hazardous materials led to 864 serious incidents, with 17 fatalities and $138,287,161 in damages.[10]

---

10 Hazardous Materials Information System, U.S. Department of Transportation (hazmat.dot. gov/pubs/inc/data/10yearfrm.htm); data as of February 1, 2008.

Norfolk Southern Corporation is one of the nation's largest transportation companies with its Norfolk Southern Railway operating over 21,000 route miles in 22 states. It is the largest carrier of metals and automotive parts, coal, chemicals, agriculture, and paper and, as such, is responsible for a significant proportion of hazardous material rail shipments.

In one year from March 2006 to March 2007, over ten Norfolk Southern derailments occurred in Illinois, Ohio, Pennsylvania, Tennessee, West Virginia, Virginia, New York, and Indiana. Several of these derailments involved hazardous materials that leaked, including spilled lye, hazardous molten sulfur, and STP auto fluids; however, these were minor leaks compared to the Graniteville crash. Table 1 details the accident statistics for Class 1 railroads in 2004 as reported by the US Department of Transportation's Federal Railroad Administration (FRA). Class 1 railroads are the largest railroads as determined by operating revenues.

TABLE 1 Class 1 railroad accident statistics

Source: Federal Railroad Administration (2005) *Railroad Safety Statistics: 2004 Annual Report* (Washington, DC: FRA)

Class 1 railroads	1	2	3	4	5	6	7	8	9	10
Amtrak	19.32	2.83	4.35	3.72	15.99	2.62	5.15	1.37	19.22	1.91
Burlington Northern Santa Fe	7.62	3.49	1.64	2.39	3.48	0.78			27.63	1.58
CSX Transportation	10.76	4.78	2.29	4.57	4.71	1.30			25.83	2.20
Grand Trunk Western RR	11.20	2.55	3.36	4.26	7.30	1.06			5.00	1.89
Illinois Central	12.82	3.53	2.60	8.98	5.70	0.29			7.44	2.19
Kansas City Southern	23.76	14.81	3.28	13.51	7.25	1.90			61.28	7.30
Norfolk Southern Corp.	9.06	3.25	1.19	5.90	3.37	1.02			13.53	1.67
Soo Line	7.61	1.93	2.25	2.79	4.79	0.54			3.64	1.49
Union Pacific	9.15	4.86	1.99	2.78	4.03	1.25			37.96	1.93

1. (Total accident/incident rate of all reported events × 1,000,000)/(train miles + hours)
2. (Train accidents × 1,000,000)/total train miles
3. (Employee deaths, injuries, illnesses × 200,000)/total hours worked
4. (Highway rail incidents × 1,000,000)/total train miles
5. [Other events (not train accidents or crossing incidents) × 1,000,000] /(train miles + hours)
6. (Trespassing deaths and injuries × 1,000,000)/total train miles
7. (Passenger on train deaths and injuries × 100,000,000)/total passenger miles
8. (Passenger train accidents × 1,000,000)/passenger train miles
9. (Accidents on yard track × 1,000,000)/yard switching train miles
10. (Accidents on other than yard track × 1,000,0000)/(total train miles – yard switching)

As Avondale was closing its doors in 2006, Norfolk Southern announced its "third consecutive record year" for safety, revenue, volume, income, and earnings per share.[11] Revenues grew to $11.96 billion from $10.644 in 2005. Net income was $1.4 billion, up from $1.2 billion in 2005 and $772 million in 2004. Total assets were $26 billion, and earnings per share jumped from $3.17 to $3.63. The stock price was at a four-year high of $50.29.

In a 2005 note to investors, the company announced that it anticipated $30–$50 million in settlement over the Graniteville derailment. It also announced its efforts to help Katrina victims in post-hurricane cleanup. In announcing its 2006 successes, CEO Wick Moorman stated:

> This annual report tells the story of how we were able to achieve our 2006 results, and how we're planning for the future. The central theme is "Thoroughbred Success through Service," because quality service has been and will be the key to our long-term success.[12]

---

11 Norfolk Southern News Release, AP Norfolk, VA, March 16, 2007.
12 Ibid.

Discussion questions

1. How would you assess Norfolk Southern's safety performance from Table 1?

2. Which stakeholders are primary and which are secondary?

3. Which stakeholders are core, strategic, and environmental?

4. What is the nature of the various stakeholders' stakes?

    a. Do they have an interest?

    b. Do they have a right?

    c. Do they have ownership?

5. How salient are the various stakeholders on that map (before and after the derailment)?

6. How did the salience of various stakeholders shift?

7. Can a company like Norfolk Southern legitimately claim "Thoroughbred Success through Service" after such an incident?

Teaching notes for this case are available from Greenleaf Publishing. These are free of charge and available only to teaching staff. They can be requested by going to:
www.greenleaf-publishing.com/darkside_notes

Part 4
Gray areas in the global context

4.1

The dark side of water
A struggle for access and control

Latha Poonamallee and Anita Howard

This case has been designed for use in multiple teaching contexts, including classes in business, business and society, strategy, critical studies in management, human resources management, organizational behaviour, and organization and the natural environment. It is designed to allow teachers to fit it into their own literature, discourse, and course design.

The primary objectives of this real-life case are to provide the students with an opportunity to:

- Understand the complex world that we live in, systemically
- Appreciate multiple perspectives and realities
- Reflect about their own role and responsibility in the whole system
- Consider approaches/pathways to action, tied to what they want to achieve and how they want to achieve it in light of their own value system

---

PART I

Case overview

Water is a life-sustaining resource that many global citizens take for granted. But for the citizens of Chennai[1] in India, access to water cannot be automatically assumed. This case presents a contemporary story on the struggle for access

---

1 Formally known as Madras.

to and control of water, a scarce resource in Chennai, the state capital of Tamil Nadu.

Chennai's struggle for water deeply impacts not only Kuthambakkam, a village on the outskirts of Chennai where the water supply is relatively plentiful, but also other rural areas and the entire state. Open access to water, and the desire to protect and control that access, compels the interest of many stakeholders in this story. The key players in this case are outlined in Table 1.

TABLE 1 Key players and core concerns

1	**The City of Chennai**	
	Key players	Urban population of Chennai, regardless of their class and party affiliation
	Core concern	Supply of water for all basic needs
2	**Government entities**	
	Key players	State officials and City officials
	Core concern	Oversight of government processes and policies for water allocation
3	**Business and management**	
	Key players	Coca-Cola managers and managers of the bottled water companies
	Core concern	Unrestricted access to water
4	**Villagers and village activity**	
	Key players	Pro-water–sharing villagers, anti-water–sharing villagers, village change leaders
	Core concern	Securing the livelihood and lifestyle of villagers

Chennai: its predicament and politics

Chennai is a southern metropolis situated on the coast of the Bay of Bengal and, paradoxically, water-starved. A sprawling city with a population of over six million, it is growing by the day. Like almost every city in a "developing nation," it is a city of contrasts.

Almost every leading software organization in India has a "development centre" here, every leading multinational bank operating in the country has its back-end operations in the city, and it is also the hub of automobile and automotive industry in the country. It has Pizza Huts, air-conditioned shopping arcades, and new and trendy bars and discotheques catering to the yuppie crowd. Alongside posh apartment complexes, it also has slums that supply the city's domestic labour, plumbers, and electricians, as well as its prostitutes, pushers, and gamblers. It also has a sizeable population of families who have been living on the city's sidewalks for generations. It is also a city whose roads can never be in really good shape because it has around 5,000 tankers fetching and spilling water to this parched city. Over the last 15 years, this search for water has spread wider and wider because of the falling water table around the city.

Chennai, though now perennially thirsty, was not always this way. Historically, the city's water security was ensured by a network of tanks that stored rainwater and recharged the groundwater aquifers that serve as the primary sources of water for the city's population. This network has long since fallen into decay. Most of the watersheds and water bodies have been built upon. What remains have been turned into cesspools of garbage, sewage and plastic wastes. According to the Central Ground Water Authority, more than 80% of the city's groundwater resources are already being tapped. The water scarcity in the metropolis reaches crisis proportions every summer.

The role of state government in the provision of water

State government is responsible for managing water and irrigation, and while almost the entire state is water-starved during drought summers, Chennai is a focal area. Being the state capital whose population is a large vote bank can be quite influential in the determination of power configurations. During the year of this case study, the water scarcity has commenced around February instead of due to a drought around May (the case most years). This year, the lack of water has become even more acute for multiple reasons.

- While water has been pumped for many years from villages on the East Coast Road on the outskirts of Chennai, this year most of the wells on the East Coast Road have dried up and hence the government had to begin to look for alternative sources of water. Similarly, Neyveli, a coal-mining township around 250 km from Chennai that supplied water for years, is also drying up as well as causing some major damage to the mines due to such an inordinate drop in the water table

- Some of the villages have organized a protest movement against this indiscriminate pumping of water to supply the city. People in a cluster of villages around Madhurantakam Lake that used to be cooperative are now refusing to allow access to their water

- Most importantly, however, is the fact that the central (federal) elections are due in a couple of months, where the state ruling party with its alliance partners is standing for re-election. Even though water is a state control issue and not directly pertinent to the central elections, the present ruling party coalition cannot afford to antagonize the urban population, considering the number of votes in question. They know that they have no party allegiance from the urban poor, who wouldn't hesitate to put them out of power. Neither can they afford to antagonize the middle and upper classes who, unlike the urban poor who must depend on government water allocation, are able to pay for their water. Nor does the coalition want to alienate the private water suppliers who are used to making a lot of money from this water-starved region, especially not when the wheels of the political and bureaucratic machinery are already so well greased. This summer, therefore, groundwater is being pumped from areas around Kuthambakkam—a village about 40 km from Chennai.

The village picture

Kuthambakkam is a group of hamlets or colonies covering an area of about 36 km^2 with a population of around 5,000. It has been a long-lived habitat for over a thousand years, a delightful village with numerous ancient temples. A vast lake irrigates around 1,400 acres while another 700 acres are rain-fed.

Seventy-five per cent of the inhabitants are dalits (the lower caste) who own only around 2% of the land. The inhabitants of this village district come in multiple colours and hues, and are not necessarily a completely homogenous population. There are many caste divisions, though the major division is between those of the upper castes and scheduled tribes, who form the lower-caste Hindus. The literacy rate for this village is around 85%, but the difference in levels of education among different castes is quite high. The upper-caste Hindus own almost 85% of the cultivable land in the village, while most of the lower-caste Hindus have traditionally worked as labourers on these farms. Almost all the villagers share a reliance on water for their livelihood, even though a few of the landowners are educated and have other sources of revenue.

Usually, even in the midst of rampant caste politics, anti-social activities like brewing illicit liquor, and lack of amenities and hygiene, this village has been prosperous due to its longstanding and highly effective rainwater harvesting practices. Rainwater harvesting has been an extremely important practice in the history of irrigation in India because most of the country is dependent on monsoons for its water. It is important not only for people to save water when they can, but also to ensure continuous renewal of the underground water aquifers as they provide the water supply for the rest of the year and the future.

The traditional rainwater harvesting structures (ponds, tanks, lakes, and small earthen check dams) not only serve as catchment areas for rainwater during the monsoon season, but also continually renew the underground water resources. They are also eco- and human-friendly because they do not cause damage like flooding and the displacement of villages that often results around bigger dams. These structures are built around the needs of each village and are their "commons." The state of Tamil Nadu is especially well known for its historic tank irrigation system.

These practices in Kuthambakkam allowed the village farmers to grow three crops a year, which meant that most of the population had a steady income and therefore did not go hungry—even in the midst of severe drought. But more recently this has been changing with the depletion of water resources by multiple parties. As mentioned before, one such offender is the Tamil Nadu state government along with the private contractors who have been using deep wells to pump water from the villages to supply the city. Apollo, Happy, and Hello are just three of the many companies that package water from the village to be sold in the city as "pure water."

The market for water

While the depletion of water reserves spells a potential disaster for the citizens of Tamil Nadu and their ecology, the pumping of water has created a multi-million-dollar packaged water industry. Over the last several years, water-starved Chennaiites have paid nearly $10 million (Rs 500 million) to private water companies for 3.7 billion litres of potable water each month to augment the inadequate supply delivered by the state-run Metro Water. Table 2 gives statistics on Chennai's water market.

TABLE 2 Chennai's water market

Source: South Indian Packaged Drinking Water Manufacturers Association

5 million quarter-litre packets at 2 cents (Rs 1) each
75,000 1-litre bottles at 20–25 cents (Rs 10–12) each
100,000 12-litre cans at 38–63 cents (Rs 18–30) each
25,000 20–25 litre bubble-top containers from 80 cents (Rs 38) upwards
10,000 water tankers carrying 12 000 litres each at $15–19 (Rs 700–900) per tanker

According to the South Indian Packaged Drinking Water Manufacturers Association (SIPDWMA), more than 200 legal and 400 illegal water-packaging units operate in the city and its surroundings. By sinking deep bore wells and running powerful pumps in their small plots of land, water-packaging companies have privatized entire aquifers of common groundwater resources.

The all-India market for packaged water is $145–210 million (Rs 8–10 billion) and is growing at the rate of nearly 40% per annum. Even though it accounts for only 5% of the total beverage market in India, branded bottled water is the fastest-growing industry in the beverage sector.

While the single largest share in the mineral water market might still belong to an Indian brand—Parle's Bisleri brand has a 40% share—multinational corporations are not far behind. Nestlé and Danone are vying to purchase Bisleri, and Pepsi's Aquafina and Coke's Kinley brands have been extremely successful in edging out many of the small and medium-sized players with buyouts and exclusive licensing deals. In less than two years since its launch, Aquafina has cornered 11% of the market and Kinley has almost a third of the market (Table 3). News reports indicate that other multinationals, like Unilever and Nestlé, are also eying the market. Currently, Kinley is being manufactured in 15 bottling plants across the country, and according to Coca-Cola India President and CEO Alex von Behr, Coke had invested Rs 4,000 crore[2] in India between entering the market in 1993 and December 2001.

TABLE 3 Market share in Indian branded water market

Source: "Boomtime ahead for bottled water market in India," *Food and Beverage News*; www.fnbnews.com/article/print. asp?articleid=22233

Brand	Percentage
Parle's Bisleri	40
Coke's Kinley	25
Pepsi's Aquafina	10
Others	25

The three water bottling concerns in Kuthambakkam village are proprietary companies owned by individuals who had the forethought to buy about half an acre of land each and put in a deep-well motor system to pump the water. Their capital investment is limited to the bottles, transportation, and labour for those who bottle and seal the water. All these companies use a similar modus operandi. They hire about five to eight women from the local villages and a couple of men to do the heavy lifting, and invest in a van to transport these employees to work and back home. The women simply fill the tanks and seal them, and the men put them away for transportation to the city's hundreds of retail outlets that distribute the water cans to offices and households. It is a smart business decision assuring an attractive return on investment. Almost a little cartel operating in this area, the owners of these companies are in regular touch and on quite friendly terms.

Coca–Cola in crisis

Additionally, on the outskirts of the village there is a Coca-Cola bottling plant set in about 25 acres, equipped with tens of sunken bore wells up to 3,000 feet to pump water for bottling operations. The plant uses up to 132,000 litres a day. This plant is a reasonably new arrival to the village, starting its operations less than a decade ago. The present team of managers have taken up their jobs in the last five years, and, as per the practice of most multinational companies, the initial green-field team was disbanded once the plant was up and running.

---

2 An Indian crore is equal to 10 million.

Their mandate is to make the plant profitable and therefore, according to them, the ongoing pumping and deepening of wells for the bottling operations is an inevitable business decision.

Coca-Cola has had a disastrous financial year worldwide and recent reports have announced that the company is in a slump, primarily because its markets in the U.S. and Europe are rapidly eroding as consumers get health-conscious and obesity becomes an epidemic. Now, Neville Isdell, the new CEO, has announced that it will be focusing its efforts on growing markets in India, China, Brazil, and Russia.

Coke's company-owned bottling operations in India (27 in total) are some of the largest in the world. So are the losses of over $476 million (Rs 2,000 crores). Isdell, a Coke veteran of 35 years with huge interest in bottling operations, may split Coca-Cola India into two clear divisions: concentrate and bottling. Whether Coca-Cola India will have two CEOs is still uncertain. Isdell has created a new post called president of bottling investments to directly look after bottling operations in countries where the company either owns bottling or has equity in it. The new structure will result in a totally new model for consolidated bottling investments by creating what is essentially an internal bottler that will interact with the company's concentrate business in the same way as independent bottlers. So, as sources point out, India can no longer remain in tier three of Coke's global system. Isdell will soon be expecting growth from India where $750 million has already been sunk into buying bottlers and establishing the business.

Coke has also spoken about a long-term strategy of moving into healthier products like water and therefore is attempting to buy out several water-bottling companies all over the world. Coke's fledgling water network has come together with little fanfare and still resembles more of a patchwork than a formal strategy. But observers think Coke is aiming at getting a bigger and bigger handle on the world's water market. "They've been aggressive in buying brands," said John Faucher, an analyst with JP Morgan. "From an acquisition standpoint, water has been a big focus for them" (*Atlanta-Journal-Constitution* 2003).

For all of Coke's global activities, water remains a small part of the company's business. Coke still gets 85% of its business from soft drinks. But, in 2002, Coca-Cola's global water business grew by 68%. Coke spokesperson Kelly Brooks said the company's three-year compounded growth rate for water was 59% (*Atlanta-Journal-Constitution* 2003). The once humble commodity has become more important for major Coke bottlers, too.

Precious water wasted

Independent observers say that the permit system in India for licensing commercial activities involving extraction of water is fundamentally flawed because no means exists to independently verify the quantity of water drawn by companies. In the absence of accurate data as to who is drawing how much, it is virtually impossible to ensure efficient usage of water and minimize wastage.

Engineers from the Tamil Nadu Pollution Control Board concede that, under the circumstances, figures reported by the industry are likely to be gross under-estimates. Even the conservative figures declared by the industry indicate that packaged water units waste anywhere between 15% and 35% of the water they draw from the ground.

This rampant depletion of groundwater resources has led to a major water crisis in the village of Kuthambakkam, in turn leading to loss of livelihood for the large section of the population dependent on agriculture. Today, the village is in the throes of a drought. Almost 80% of the population has suffered the loss of their livelihoods and are looking for any kind of work that might come their way to make sure that their children eat at least once a day. Neighbours and family members share the available jobs, so everyone can have a chance to make ends meet. Communities that were until recently self-sufficient for water are now on the edge of desperation as their water security is being compromised to serve the interests of the consumers in cities like Chennai.

The mood of the villagers

On the subject of water sharing, the Kuthambakkam villagers are split into two groups. One is a group that wants to rally support to protest against the rampant pumping and transportation of water from their village. They feel betrayed and let down by all the powers that be and would like to restore their own rights over their natural resources. Some of them were employed by the soft drink company when the plant started running and then let go. The second group of villagers is pro water sharing, partly because they are generous and are willing to share, but partly because they don't believe they have the power to question or stop this exploitation. Also of concern is their belief that the community will lose even the few jobs that the water-bottling plants offer. Like the first group, they draw their conclusions from their experience this year as well as their experience with the bottling companies over the last few years. A third group falls in between the first two groups and can be swayed by either.

Village change leaders

Kuthambakkam is not only known for its water and poverty, but also for its unique efforts at enhancing the effectiveness of their panchayat (village government) system. Elango, the president of the panchayat board, a dynamic 45-year-old man, was one of the handful of fortunate men from this village who had access to an engineering education that took him away from the village for around 15 years. After his education, he decided to come back and work for his homeland's welfare. While many such men usually work through non-governmental organizations (NGOs), Elango chose a completely different route. While most of the educated middle class of the country choose to stay away from politics, he jumped into the fray and became the president of the village government. Along with his colleagues on the governing system, he is trying to build what he calls a "network economy" among a few neighbouring villages. This is a system in which the local economy builds, sustains, and nurtures itself without dependence on the mainstream global economy but while not completely divorcing itself from it either.

Elango's ambition is to demonstrate this idea through a working model on which other local economies can follow. He has also founded a Trust for Village Self-Governance through which he imparts these ideas to village leaders from other parts of the state and country. Kuthambakkam is on its way to becoming the first hutless village in the country. New dwellings are being built using indigenous materials, technology, and labour. Furthermore, the government resources are being augmented by the villagers themselves and by funds raised personally by Elango through his connection agencies and well-wishers.

LABS: a bridge between urban and rural contexts

Livelihood Advancement Business Academy (LABS) is a corporate consortium that trains underprivileged youths in vulnerable age groups for livelihood in the new economy. It also places them in mainstream career tracks in many corporations across the city. The young people are trained in a variety of skills, ranging from automobile maintenance, photography, animation, medical transcription, home nursing care, hospitality, retail sales, marketing and sales, and computer skills—addressing requirements of both traditional and new economies. They are socialized to adopt the mainstream professional work ethic, trained in conversational English, and put through intensive goal-setting and planning exercises. LABS claims that it is not just preparing the youth for livelihood and opening up their access to multiple opportunity structures, but ultimately preparing them to become contributing members of the community. LABS is now looking to expand its catchment areas for recruitment of underprivileged youth by including rural areas, and the village of Kuthambakkam offers good potential.

LABS Chennai centre, though only a couple of years old, has already provided this service for hundreds of teenagers, thus opening doors that never existed before by providing access to opportunity structures that attempt to integrate this youth population in the new economy. The key corporates in LABS Chennai are:

- Murugappa Group—a large South Indian business conglomerate with interests in many sectors including farm inputs, financial services, engineering, transportation, and travel

- Rane Group—an engineering company focusing on the automobile industry

- PepsiCo—a multinational soft drink manufacturer

- Khivraj Automobiles—a company that has generously offered up some of its prime commercial real estate space for this venture

Not only do these organizations offer financial support for this initiative, several managers from various levels in these companies participate in different capacities. Junior- and middle-level managers act as visiting faculty, hosts for the students' industry visits, mentors to the students, as well as offering support in operational issues. Senior managers are members of LABS steering committee, addressing strategic issues; they also review/monitor progress and support LABS in networking with other potential employers in the region.

Though LABS is a non-profit entity, it has well-qualified management professionals at the helm and a well-established career track for the trainers (who are called facilitators), who can go on to become coordinators for the centre and region. This organization also has a well-defined and -monitored performance management system that tracks the performance of the employees across multiple parameters. It additionally rewards initiative by allowing employees to move up to head centres if they can start and run viable new centres for training. The responsibilities of the employees include recruitment, selection, training, and placement of the target population, and therefore are not solely limited to curriculum delivery. Each employee is responsible for a particular stream of training, which they call an academy.

Rajesh, a key figure from LABS involved in creating a new centre, is looking to expand the pool from which the target population would be drawn. Kuthambakkam appears to be a possibility considering its current lack of employment and its proximity to Chennai, which might even allow the students to commute everyday.

Rajesh visits the village to talk to Elango, the panchayat leader. Although Elango can appreciate the value of such a program for the youth of his village, he is also concerned about creating local, sustainable livelihood to avoid potential migration of educated youth out of the village. He wants the village youth to take up roles of leadership and responsibility to implement and spread the message of "network economy." Elango also believes that, on completion of his second term as the panchayat president in 2006, he should move out so the work that he started can be carried on by the next generation. He also wants to begin focusing on spreading the message to other parts of the country through the Trust for Village Self-Governance he founded and runs.

Bibliography

Newspaper articles

Presented in chronological order.

"Villagers blame Coca-Cola for water woes in Thane," *Times News Network,* June 5, 2003.

"Growing resistance against Coke and Pepsi," *Frontline,* June 7, 2003.

"Coca-Cola's grip on water," *The Atlanta-Journal-Constitution,* June 11, 2003.

"Coke's water world," *The Atlanta-Journal-Constitution,* June 11, 2003.

"Kerala village plans unique protest against Coke," *Rediff.com,* January 20, 2004.

Parikh, R. (2004) "Soft drink, hard realities," *Combat Law* 3.2 (June–July 2004; www. indiatogether.org/combatlaw/vol3/issue2/softdrink.htm, March 16, 2009).

"Coca-Cola plant may be forced to close in Kerala," *Associated Press,* June 23, 2004.

"Why is Coke's Isdell visiting India?" *Times News Network,* June 24, 2004.

"Harvard study links coca-cola to diabetes, weight gain," *Boston Herald,* August 25, 2004.

"Minister for Water Resources admits excessive groundwater use by Coca-Cola," *Business Standard*, September 2, 2004.

"Coca-Cola awarded prize for contaminating water," *Daily Telegraph,* October 1, 2004.

"Coke moves public relations head to India," *Financial Express,* October 13, 2004.

"Coke to increase marketing in India, Brazil, China, Russia," *Adweek,* November 11, 2004.

"Coca-Cola reduces profit targets," *The Guardian,* November 12, 2004.

"High Court rules 'commercial interests are subservient to fundamental rights' in Coca-Cola appeal," *Daily Telegraph,* November 4, 2004.

"Supreme Court orders thorough examination of soft drink contents," *Financial Express,* January 4, 2005.

"Stir before Coke plant enters 1000th day," *The Hindu,* January 16, 2005.

"Parched village sues to shut tap at Coke: drought-hit Indians say plant draining groundwater," *SF Chronicle,* March 6, 2005.

India Resource Center documents

All available from www.indiaresource.org/campaigns/coke (presented in chronological order)

"Coca-Cola bends its rules in India," May 13, 2002.

"No Water? Drink Coke!" CorpWatch India, May 28, 2002.

"Coke: arrogance of the multinational," July 20, 2002.

"Coke and Pepsi vandalize the Himalayas," December 1, 2002.

"Communities protest Coca-Cola in Tamil Nadu," June 20, 2003.

"How Coke arm-twisted the Indian Government," June 21, 2003.

"Coke in Varanasi: facing local ire," July 10, 2003.

"Coke with yet another new twist: toxic Cola," January 31, 2004.

"Coke vs people: the heat is on in Pachimada," April 14, 2004.

"Coca-Cola: continuing battle in Kerala," July 10, 2004.

"Rising struggles, falling water: anti-Coca-Cola agitation picks up in Kaladera, Rajasthan," September 24, 2004.

"Coca-Cola lacks fizz for farmers," October 23, 2004.

"Campaign to hold Coca-Cola accountable," November 14, 2004.

"Coca-Cola spins out of control in India," November 15, 2004.

"Fax action: Coca-Cola: STOP destroying lives, livelihoods, and communities in India," December 21, 2004.

"Coca-Cola greeted with protest in New Year: we will come with our mouths shut and hands tied and still show our strength," January 4, 2005.

"Second massive protest against Coca-Cola in India in New Year: community commemorates thousand day anniversary of vigil against Coca-Cola in Kerala," January 13, 2005.

India Resource Center Issues: Water (www.indiaresource.org/issues/water/index.html).

Discussion questions

Based on what you presently know about this case, produce a systemic analysis of it by answering the following questions:

Players

1. Who are the players?

2. What are their interests? What are their values?

Alignments

1. Whose interests are aligned?

2. What impact does this alignment have on the players' access to resources, opportunity structures, and power centres?

Conflicts of interest

1. Whose interests are in conflict? Are there points of alignment even among those who are in conflict?

2. Are there any other key elements or factors in this case? Create a visual that captures your analysis.

3. If you were these players, how would your stakeholder group deal with this scenario? In anticipation of what you think will happen next, how will you plan your strategic moves (e.g. during and after the elections)?

4. What is your prediction for the future? What do you think will happen to the various players in the immediate, medium-term and long-term future?

PART II

Case update

Read the following update on what happened next in this case. Based on the information given here, revise your systemic analysis done for Part I by answering the questions that are found at the end.

Coca-Cola crisis

There is an ongoing fight against soft drink manufacturing companies in India and a number of grassroots resistance movements have sprung up across the country focusing on the issue of water exploitation. In fact, many non-governmental organizations have refused to accept funding for tsunami relief and reconstruction efforts from Coke.

The following is a list of facts that have emerged about Coca-Cola's practices in India:

- Communities across India living around Coca-Cola's bottling plants are experiencing severe water shortages, directly resulting from Coca-Cola's massive extraction of water from the common groundwater resources. The wells have run dry and the hand water pumps do not work any more. Various studies, including one by the Central Ground Water Board in India, have confirmed the significant depletion of the water table

- When the water is extracted from the common groundwater resource by digging deeper, the water smells and tastes strange. Coca-Cola has been indiscriminately discharging its wastewater into the fields around its plant and sometimes into rivers, including the Ganges. The result has been that the groundwater has been polluted as well as the soil. Public health authorities have posted signs around wells and hand pumps advising the community that the water is unfit for human consumption

- In two communities, Pachimada[3] and Mehdiganj,[4] Coca-Cola was distributing its solid waste to farmers in the area as "fertilizer." Tests conducted by the BBC found cadmium and lead in the waste, effectively making the waste toxic. Coca-Cola stopped the practice of distributing its toxic waste only when ordered to do so by the state government

---

3 Surendranath, C. (2004) "Coke vs people: the heat is on in Plachimada" (April 14, 2004; www.indiaresource.org/campaigns/coke/2004/heatison.html, March 16, 2009).
4 Adve, N. (2004) "Coke lacks fizz for farmers in Mehdigani" (October 23, 2004; www.indiaresource.org/campaigns/coke/2004/cokemehdiganj.html, March 16, 2009.

- Tests conducted by a variety of agencies, including the government of India, confirmed that Coca-Cola products contained high levels of pesticides, and, as a result, the Parliament of India has banned the sale of Coca-Cola in its cafeteria. However, Coca-Cola not only continues to sell drinks laced with poisons in India (that could never be sold in North America or Europe), it is also introducing new products in the Indian market

Coke's strategy

Soft drink major manufacturer Coca-Cola, which has been drawing considerable flak on allegations of groundwater exploitation by environmental activists in India, brought in its Asia group communications head David Cox, possibly for damage control or an image makeover. He remained in India for about two months, travelling across the country to familiarize himself with and understand in greater detail how the Indian media works. Based in Hong Kong, Cox has been in India several times before, even when the company was battling the pesticide issues. "It's difficult for him to have a perspective on what is happening in India while sitting there in Hong Kong. It's important for him to understand how things are," the company source said.[5]

Industry sources, however, say that there could be more to the visit of Cox than this. According to them, an intense anti-Coke movement is gaining ground in the country on account of allegations of depletion of groundwater levels, and that may well have prompted Coke to call in its Asia group communications head for damage control. Coca-Cola has also just announced plans to significantly increase the marketing budget in India for next year.

Neville Isdell, Coca-Cola's CEO since April 2004, chose India as the first country to visit after assuming office. However, it was a "stealth" visit and was discovered by Indian journalists only when they pried. Isdell was rightly concerned that a public announcement of Coca-Cola's top man in India would be met with a sizeable protest.

The Indian government's response

According to P.R. Dasmunsi, minister for water resources, soft drink manufacturers like Coca-Cola and PepsiCo will have to work with the Ministry of Water Resources to replenish the groundwater they use to produce the branded beverages. Dasmunsi made this statement at a seminar on rainwater harvesting and groundwater recharge organized jointly by the Federation of Indian Chambers of Commerce and Industry (FICCI) and the Bharat Chamber of Commerce

---

5 "Coke brings in official for damage control," *Financial Express*, October 13, 2004.

(BCC).[6] The Ministry would seek corporate sector participation for preserving and recharging the groundwater resources, said Dasmunsi, who pointed out that voluntary participation of soft drink manufacturers, corporate bodies, and other private players is the only way to successfully complete the project. Excessive water usage by this industry—along with power-generating companies and other water-intensive industry—is a credible threat to the country's groundwater resources. Issues like contamination, lowering groundwater levels, and water wastage in some regions of the country are concerning because they might convert water into a "commodity" with a high price, fears the minister. Presently, 8% of the country is experiencing a decline in groundwater levels of more than 20 cm per year. If it continues like this, then the issue would become "critical, difficult, and perhaps impossible to control," said the minister.[7]

In order to bring some "regulation" on water usage, the Ministry of Water Resources has asked the state government for its opinion. After receiving these views, the Ministry intends to consult the Ministry of Environment and Forests about final action. The minister said the government would form a Rainwater Harvesting Council with FICCI, the Confederation of Indian Industry (CII), and corporate bodies for implementing a rain-harvesting project at the national level. The Central Ground Water Board has come up with a master plan for recharging groundwater at a national level. Participation of village-level governing bodies like panchayats and zilla parishads are essential for overall success.[8]

An update on Kthambakkam

Elango refused the offer of LABS to train the youth of his village in livelihoods for the new economy because he felt that this move would undermine his plan to build a sustainable village economy based on the principles of network economics. In the meantime, the acreage under cultivation is shrinking as lack of water continues to remain a colossal problem with no solution in sight. While the village still continues its quest for creating sustainable livelihood locally, the loss through migration is shrinking the economy, both in terms of producers as well as consumers.

Meanwhile, the city of Chennai is bursting at its seams with its unmanageably growing underbelly, which is only worsening the city's battle for providing its residents with basic amenities, including water. It is still continuing to search for places that could supply water to its thirsty residents. Part of the plan is to found satellite/suburban settlements around the city; one such possibility on its list of prospects is Kuthambakkam. The Tamil Nadu state government is

6 "Minister for Water Resources admits excessive groundwater use by Coca-Cola," *Business Standard*, September 2, 2004 (www.indiaresource.org/news/2004/1028.html, March 16, 2009).
7 Adve, N. (2004) "Coke lacks fizz for farmers in Mehdigani" (October 23, 2004; www.indiaresource.org/campaigns/coke/2004/cokemehdiganj.html, March 16, 2009.
8 Ibid.

considering conversion of the fallow land in this village into a housing colony. The villagers who continue to live in Kuthambakkam are concerned that this will affect them quite negatively, because whatever few jobs they could get through farming would be lost. Furthermore, they will never be able to afford the apartments being planned and they would most likely end up as domestic help for these new entrants to their region. This vicious cycle of mindless exploitation of the natural resources and the resultant isomorphic reproduction of the nightmarish living conditions in the suburban villages continues.

Discussion questions

1. Which of the developments mentioned in this section did you anticipate?

2. Among all the information provided in this section, what surprised you the most, and why?

3. Think about the interests, alignments, access to resources, opportunity structures, and power centres described in the case update. What is the same? What has changed? Ultimately, whose interests and objectives were served?

4. If you were charged with a mandate to find a way to break this vicious cycle, what would your strategy look like?

5. What implications does this case have for management theory and practice?

Teaching notes for this case are available from Greenleaf Publishing. These are free of charge and available only to teaching staff. They can be requested by going to:
www.greenleaf-publishing.com/darkside_notes

4.2

Mattel, Inc.
Lead-tainted toys

Adenekan (Nick) Dedeke and Martin Calkins

Thomas Debrowski, Executive Vice President for Worldwide Operations at Mattel, Inc., is in a quandary about what to do after hearing of two product failures attributed to paint suppliers in China. Although he understands the steps he must take to ensure public safety regarding a recent release of tainted toys, he does not know how to handle the quality and safety issues that continue to emanate from suppliers in less developed countries. Quality and safety problems persist even though Mattel has instituted some of the most detailed and comprehensive manufacturing standards in the consumer products industry, sought outside professional help, and looked to other industries for guidance. Debrowski must now make a recommendation to Mattel's Chief Executive Officer, Robert Eckert, about improvements to Mattel's social responsibility programs.

   This chapter focuses on the problems global companies can face as they attempt to manufacture consumer products in developing countries. It shows how problems often arise due to a lack of consumer protection oversight mechanisms by foreign governments and by an inability to monitor every facet of the supply chain. It also highlights Mattel's corporate social responsibility initiatives, especially its Global Manufacturing Principles (GMP).

It was a lovely day in El Segundo, California, in the last week of June 2006, but not within the walls of Mattel's headquarters. Thomas Debrowski, executive vice president for worldwide operations, was leading a tough early morning telephone conference with Mattel's executives in Hong Kong. A few days earlier, a quality lab had discovered excessive levels of lead in toy shipment that had been allocated to a large retailer in France. Debrowski had arranged a conference call to determine the cause of the lead contamination. However, while he was on the conference call, a telephone rang in the Hong Kong office. David Lewis, senior vice president for Asian operations, excused himself to take the call. A few minutes later David rejoined the teleconference. "I've got bad news," David Lewis said. "We've had another failure."[1] The call that Lewis had taken was from one of Mattel's safety labs in Shenzhen, China. The lab was responsible for testing toys that were made by independent vendors. The Sarge car sample that failed the lead test was sent to the lab by Hon Li Da Plastic Cement Co., Limited, Shenzhen, China, a major vendor for Mattel.

Until the new sample of lead-tainted toys was discovered, Debrowski had assumed that the tainted-lead toys issue was an isolated case. However, the discovery of traces of lead, in a sample of Sarge toys that was produced in 2005, and that had allegedly passed prior lead tests, was particularly alarming. The second discovery raised a red flag that Mattel may have a systemic problem plaguing its operations and the quality verification activities in China.

As the days progressed, Mattel's situation grew worse and, ultimately, Mattel had to recall 1.4 million toys suspected of being lead-tainted. Debrowski was responsible for ensuring the recall was handled properly and charged with managing Mattel's public pronouncements. In the midst of the challenges, he struggled with the recommendation he knew he had to make to Robert Eckert, Chief Executive Officer of Mattel. Since 1998, Mattel had developed and invested heavily in the implementation of its Global Manufacturing Principles (GMP). These were initiated in an effort to improve human rights, worker rights, and environmental protection in Mattel's global operations. The implementation of the GMP had been successful and praised widely within the toy industry. In 2000, however, the GMP was updated and issues of product safety and quality were eliminated. Now, these very issues seemed to be a problem for Mattel.

Thomas Debrowski wondered if he should recommend that product safety and quality be added back as a GMP audit component? Or if he should support the existing policy that exempted product safety and quality from the GMP audits? He was also wondered how Mattel might tighten its product safety and quality procedures to prevent a reoccurrence of the lead-tainted toys problem.

Background: Mattel, Inc.

Mattel, Inc. is a leader in the design, manufacture, and marketing of toys and family products. Its products include Barbie®, the most popular fashion doll ever introduced, Hot Wheels®, Matchbox®, American Girl®, Radica® and Tyco® R/C, as well as Fisher-Price® brands including Little People®, Power Wheels®, and entertainment-inspired toy lines. As a global corporation, Mattel is headquar-

---

1 Story, L. (2007) "After stumbling, Mattel cracks down in China," *New York Times,* August 29, 2007.

tered in El Segundo, California, and currently employs more than 30,000 people in 43 countries and territories, and sells products in more than 150 nations.[2] Its annual corporate results for 2003–2005 are summarized in Exhibit 3.

Mattel has been recognized as one of the 100 Most Trustworthy U.S. Companies by *Forbes* magazine and ranked among the 100 Best Corporate Citizens by *CRO* magazine. In 2006, it was listed on the FTSE4Good and Domini 400 Socially Responsible Investment Indices and, since 1978, been active in philanthropic ventures targeting children. It prides itself on its ethical manufacturing practices, having celebrated in 2007 the tenth anniversary of its Global Manufacturing Principles.[3]

Founded in 1945 by Ruth and Elliot Handler and Harold "Matt" Matson out of a garage workshop in southern California, Mattel grew into a global company that had employees in 43 countries and sold products in 150 countries. The first products of the company included picture frames and dollhouse furniture, which were made from picture frame scraps. Harold Matson soon sold his share in the business to his partners. The Handlers turned the company's emphasis to toys. In 1948, the Handlers incorporated the company with headquarters in Hawthorne, California.

In 1959, Inspired by her daughter's fascination with cutout paper dolls, Ruth Handler suggested the introduction of a three-dimensional doll that would enable little girls to play out their dreams. She named the doll "Barbie," after her daughter Barbara's nickname, and it quickly propelled the company into the forefront of the toy industry. By 2005, the Barbie line was responsible for more than 80% of Mattel's profits.

In 1960, the company went public and, in 1968, it expanded significantly with the introduction of a campaign called "World of the Young." This venture led to the acquisition of several companies including:

- Barnum & Bailey Circus

- Circus World—a theme park

- Western Publishing Company

- Radnitz/Mattel Productions—a motion picture production company

In 1977, Mattel acquired companies in the rapidly growing electronics game field, and, two years later, entered the Intellivision home video entertainment business.

Mattel then hit rough times. In 1983 it reported a loss of $394 million. This caused Mattel to re-evaluate its acquisitions of non-toy businesses and to eventually sell these ventures. Back on firm financial ground, the company went on

---

2   Mattel, Inc. (2008) "Investors and media. Mattel, Inc.," February 15, 2008 (www.shareholder.com/mattel/default.cfm, February 16, 2008).

3   Mattel, Inc. (2008) "2007 Global Citizenship Report" (www.mattel.com/about_us/Corp_Responsibility/cr_csreport.asp, February 16, 2008).

in the 1990s to acquire a number of toy companies, including Fisher-Price, which produced the wildly popular Tickle Me Elmo toy in 1996. Mattel earned $300 million in sales from this toy in the first two years of its production.

By 2002, Mattel had become one of the largest toy makers in the world by sales volume, with annual sales close to $6 billion that year. Mattel manufactured approximately 800 million products per year and about half of its toys were made in its own plants. It had company-owned or -controlled facilities in places as far-flung as China, India, Indonesia, Malaysia, Mexico, and Thailand. These facilities accounted for over 70% of the company's total output.

Throughout, Mattel maintained a laudable reputation for social responsibility with a strong focus on corporate accountability. As CEO Robert Eckert noted in the company's 2002 annual report:

> I strongly believe that the only way to operate, in life and in business, is with unwavering integrity. There is simply no room for compromise. In light of the public's diminished trust in corporate America, I'd like to emphasize the importance of our values at Mattel, from our consumers—inspiring kids' imaginations, and our work—striving for excellence and creativity in everything we do, to our partners—sharing success with customers, vendors, shareholders and communities, and even ourselves—taking ownership of all that passes in front of us and being accountable for the results of the business and the development of our fellow employees.[4]

Thomas Debrowski

Thomas Debrowski came to Mattel with a wealth of operations experience in a wide range of corporate cultures. He spent 20 years at Kraft Foods Global, Inc., where he rose to the position of vice president and director of grocery operations for Kraft USA. During his tenure there, he lived and worked overseas for seven years and was responsible for regional operations in both Europe and Asia-Pacific. In 1991, he went to work for The Pillsbury Company as vice president of operations for the baked goods division. Less than a year later, he was promoted to senior vice president of operations for Pillsbury Worldwide. In this new position, he was responsible for worldwide purchasing, manufacturing, quality, engineering, environmental affairs, logistics, and operations strategy.

Robert Eckert hired Debrowski for the position of vice president of worldwide manufacturing, distribution activities, and vendor operations. This meant that Debrowski was responsible for the entire supply chain, including oversight of the operations and distribution departments, which covers quality and operational technology, product integrity, and operational planning functions.

---

4   Mattel's Annual Report 2002: 8.

After he was hired, Debrowski explained his reasons for joining Mattel as follows:

> Since Bob has made better management of the supply chain a top priority for the company, it makes joining Mattel all the more exciting. I look forward to the challenges that lie ahead in improving customer service and lowering costs, as well as capitalizing on an already strong and dedicated worldwide team.[5]

Mattel's global supply chain

Mattel's successes were tied to its overseas ventures. As early as 1959, Mattel used Asian contract manufacturers to make toys for the company. In the 1980s, however, Mattel executives became concerned that outsourcing toy manufacture to vendors might put the company's trademarks at risk. In particular they feared disreputable vendors might produce counterfeit toys and undersell Mattel products. Furthermore, Mattel executives were convinced that they could manage plant efficiency better than foreign suppliers. Hence, the firm decided to build, own, and operate factories overseas. The firm expanded aggressively in China and Hong Kong. Mattel continued its practice of outsourcing primarily for non-core parts.

By 2006, Mattel owned or controlled 11 manufacturing and tooling facilities in China, Indonesia, Malaysia, Thailand, and Mexico. These so-called Tier I plants manufactured half of all Mattel's annual production and all core products, such as Barbie dolls and Hot Wheels. The remaining production was done by Tier II contract factories that Mattel did not own, operate, or manage directly. Most of these contract factories were in China, with a few others in India and Brazil. Typically, Tier II vendors allocated a portion of their production capacity to Mattel's products. The range of such vendor allocation ranged from high 90% to a low of around 30% of a vendor's annual production. In 2006, Mattel had around 75 Tier II plants. Each Tier I and Tier II factory employed between 5,000 and 15,000 workers. In addition, Mattel contracted with about 1,000 so-called Tier III manufacturers, which were licensees authorized to use Mattel's logos and characters on products such as clothing, electronics, sporting goods, and room decorations. These licensees independently manufactured Mattel products in about 3,000 factories around the world.[6] Exhibit 5 shows a list of selected Mattel toys as well as the plants around the world where they were manufactured.

---

5 Mattel, Inc. press release, November 1, 2000 (www.shareholder.com/mattel/news/20001101-43129.cfm, February 16, 2008).
6 Mattel, Inc. (2008) "2007 Global Citizenship Report" (www.mattel.com/about_us/Corp_Responsibility/cr_csreport.asp, February 16, 2008).

This was Mattel's "supply chain" and it was global in its reach. A supply chain is considered global when multiple partners located in different continents are involved in coordinated activities. In toy manufacture, the coordination involves product design, product development, purchasing, inventory management, manufacturing, assembly, quality management, shipping, and quality control.

In Mattel's case, the supply chain operated in the following manner. First, a new product was designed in-house by Mattel engineers or licensed to third-party designer firms. Then, Mattel worked with one of its company-owned or -controlled plants or contracted manufacturers to develop manufacturing processes for mass toy production. The developer then acted as the primary producer of the new product and was considered central to the global supply chain. The developer was responsible for coordinating subcontractors and assembling the components of the toy. They therefore sometimes had to deal with hundreds of subcontractors on a single project. After developing the product, the primary producer took over. Following Mattel's guidelines and standards, the producer inspected the product in one of its own labs or in approved third-party labs. These third-party labs were typically independent inspection agencies often contracted with major retailers such as Wal-Mart or Target. Having passed inspection, products were then shipped to export/import services for consolidation for shipment to retailers. The consolidators' responsibilities were to receive, aggregate, and ship the inspected products. Once the products arrived at the destination port, products went through another round of inspections by customs and excise agents before being cleared for entry. Finally, the toys were moved by local importers to warehouses or retail outlets for sale to customers.[7]

Understanding the context of China

Beginning in the 1990s, China emerged as an important player in the toy manufacturing industry. In 2006, Americans spent $22.3 billion on toys and sporting goods and China accounted for 86% of the toys imported into the U.S. From 2000 onwards, Chinese manufacturing ranked fourth behind the U.S., Japan, and Germany.

A number of factors propelled China to dominance in the global economy.[8] First, China's highly disciplined and non-union workforce allowed it to offer

7 Holstein, W., B. Palmer, S. Ur-Rehman and T. Ito (1996) "Santa's Sweatshop: in a global economy, it's hard to know who made your gift—and under what conditions," *U.S. News & World Report*, December 8, 1996 (www.usnews.com/usnews/biztech/articles/961216/archive_035166_8.htm, February 8, 2008)

8 Protecting Children from Lead Tainted Imports: testimony by M. Teagarden to the U.S. Congress, Energy and Commerce Committee, August 2007 (energycommerce.house.gov/images/stories/Documents/Hearings/PDF/110-ctcp-hrg.092007.Teagarden-testimony.pdf).

global companies low-cost labor that set China at an advantage compared with other countries. The cost difference was significant. Production cost differences between China and the U.S. was estimated to be as much as 30–50%. China's workers were key to the country's success, but they generally worked without benefits such as health insurance, unemployment benefits, and retirement savings accounts. Second, compared with Western countries, China had fewer regulations, minimal policing, and limited enforcement mechanisms to limit the activities of producers. China's industrial areas, for example, confronted serious environmental pollution challenges.

Third, China's weak enforcement mechanisms seemed to embolden product counterfeiting. The production of reverse-engineered products and outright copies of proprietary materials occurred virtually unchallenged. Counterfeiting of products in China had moved beyond selling "Lorex" watches to producing knockoffs of pharmaceuticals, such as Viagra, auto parts, and, of course, software. Fourth, China also had a fixed and low currency exchange rate that worked to its advantage. The low exchange rate resulted in undervalued exports and overvalued Foreign Direct Investment (FDI) inflows. China's fixed undervalued currency encouraged global companies to move operations to China and out of developed countries, thereby exacerbating unemployment and underemployment in traditional manufacturing locations such as the U.S., Western Europe, and Japan.

Finally, China's economic strategies are not entirely the result of market forces, but rather part of the country's economic plans. China's was run as a command economy, which meant that the Chinese government controlled most of the key aspects of the economy. The concentration of industries in certain regions, for example, was the result of government plans and policies to subsidize targeted (mostly heavy) industries. These industries were then concentrated in efficient "clustered" networks in particular locations in China and funded by state-sponsored banks that lack transparency. To support government policy, state-controlled banks sometimes loaned funds to companies at a loss to pursue the market segments targeted by the Chinese government.[9]

How global firms wielded influence in China

The result of China's economic strategies is that global companies have had strong incentives to relocate to China. Once immersed in China, companies find they are not only privy to low-cost production, but also to increased economic and political influence.

---

9 Navarro, P. (2007) *The Coming China Wars: Where they will be fought and how they can be won* (Upper Saddle River, NJ: FT Press).

Specifically, when a large retailer or producer moved significant proportions of its production into a region in China, it experienced a strengthening of its influence. Due to the abundance of vendors in the country that were competing for orders from global companies, such companies wielded control over their manufacturing partners. As the contribution of a global company in a region in terms of jobs and taxes grew, its representatives were able to lobby for preferences with governmental agencies and politicians, who had self-interest in retaining the global manufacturing orders within their regions.

Global companies quickly realized that a strong bargaining chip that they had was the threat of exit from a country. That is, they could threaten to leave China for other less developed countries should Chinese production become too costly or restrictive. Thus began the so-called "race to the bottom," where competition among nations for manufacturers' sites results in ever more harsh contractor demands and reduction of worker protection. With exit as an option, global companies were able to make all sorts of demands. They could require vendors to cut costs repeatedly without consideration of the impact of such demands. Vendors, in turn, then had to pressure subcontractors to do the same and a downward spiral of heightened expectations and harsh conditions ensued. Under these conditions, issues of worker rights and environmental conservation were neglected. Local government agencies were caught up in the race to retain the operation of global companies and to keep tens of thousands of people employed. They began to ease worker regulations and environmental restrictions to accommodate the needs of global companies. These strategies often led to more abuse of worker rights and more severe environmental pollution.[10]

Despite these strategies, costs continued to rise in several industries. As toy manufacturers concentrated in specific regions, the production volumes rose and vendors increasingly competed against each other in terms of cost. Sometimes, the contractor that lowered its price the furthest or fastest made a profit from its work with a global companies. Thomas Debrowski was quoted as admitting that between 2002 and 2007 "the labor prices in China doubled and the raw material prices doubled or tripled."[11]

Costs played a key role in the relationship between Chinese vendors and global firms such as Mattel. Initially, low costs attracted global companies to China. However, the survival of family-owned and privately controlled Chinese vendors that partner with global companies depended on their ability to cut costs continuously. To keep their factories working, many vendors comply with the demands of their global partners to cut costs. The impact on their businesses included razor-thin margins, inability to hire more workers, and lack of

10 Sethi, P. (2007) "Buying Responsibly from Chinese Supply Chains," Ethical Corporation, December 2007: 60-63.

11 Story, L. (2007) "After stumbling, Mattel cracks down in China," *New York Times*, August 29, 2007 (www.nytimes.com/2007/08/29/business/worldbusiness/29mattel.html?_r=2&ref=business&oref=slogin&oref=slogin, February 16, 2008).

funding to renew or upgrade their equipment or buildings. Older equipment requires frequent maintenance and high repair costs. Some vendors are not merely pressured to achieve lower costs, they also have to commit to produce higher volumes of product. Traditionally, vendors passed the sacrificed costs onto their workers by paying the minimum wage, cheating on overtime pay and mandating them to work longer hours. Under such conditions, worker turnover was generally high, and internal quality and worker training costs rose rapidly. High turnover in turn created a shortage of workers, which increased pressures to make employees work longer. In this context of extreme pressures and cut-throat competition, vendors made whatever decision was necessary to earn a profit on large orders from global players.[12]

Chinese government enact rules to protect worker rights

Under pressure from international organizations to curb worker abuses and stabilize the work environment in China, the Chinese government, in 2002, established rules and regulations that were intended to improve worker rights. The regulations set the minimum standards for operating in China. They established a minimum wage that varied from region to region. Wages could now be anywhere between 50–60 cents per hour in places with a heavy global contractor presence. The regulations also set 40 hours per week as a normal work week and established the notion of overtime pay. This meant that employees who worked more than 40 hours a week were legally entitled to overtime pay ranging from 80 cents to $1 an hour. In addition, the Chinese rules established a mandatory national social security program that gave workers access to health insurance.

Even so, American labor union representatives and others continued to complain about work conditions in China. They pointed out that the Chinese social security program did not include benefits such as affordable healthcare, paid holidays and vacations, sick days, maternity leave, or severance pay. Much to their displeasure, it disallowed the formation of independent unions.[13]

However, these positive steps were unable to eliminate worker rights abuses in global companies and in the companies of their vendors. Despite the legislation of "tougher" rules on length or work week, pay, and overtime, individual global companies were able to secure special waivers from the regional Chinese government that enabled them to deviate from the maximum length of the work-

---

12 Sethi, P. (2007) "Buying Responsibly from Chinese Supply Chains," Ethical Corporation, December 2007: 60-63.
13 Testimony by Charles Kernaghan before the U.S. Senate Committee on Commerce, Science & Transport, October 25, 2007.

ing week and overtime limits and the regulated minimum wages established by Chinese law.

Furthermore, investigative newspaper reports in 2004 revealed that the realization of worker rights still faced stiff challenges. *Los Angeles Times* reporters interviewed workers in 13 factories in southern China, Indonesia, and Mexico, including those that made Mattel products. Mattel even arranged five plant tours for the investigators. Many of the workers interviewed said they were worried about retaliation from supervisors. Some expressed concern that, if Mattel knew about the (real) conditions in their plants, the company would cancel its contracts, casting the workers onto the streets. As one Shenzhen factory worker said, "It's good that they monitor, but not if it costs our jobs." The investigators found workers who testified that they routinely worked 11 hours a day and six days a week. A worker claimed that, at a Mattel plant, prior to the arrival of internal inspectors twice in a year, managers promised to pay workers money if they repeated the vendor's company line to the inspectors.[14]

The need for corporate social responsibility

The Chinese experience of the inability of laws to regulate fully business behavior illustrates the need for corporate social responsibility policies. Broadly defined, corporate social responsibility (CSR) refers to the obligations and expectations of corporations, which are special sorts of businesses. In America and many other places, the corporation is a legal entity comprised of many people united into singular, artificial body and given society's approval to act (in most cases) as an individual person. The social responsibilities of these artificial persons encompass a wide range of obligations that go beyond mere legal compliance.

CSR extends from the notion of a social contract, which is simply an agreement between business and society. These relatively tacit contracts began to emerge about 30 years ago in the wake of a number of product liability cases. The fact that they were largely unstated meant that CSR came to mean something different depending on the situation. Some, for example, thought CSR was agreement among global companies and host countries that obligated companies to operate according to the expectations and requirements of stakeholders of host locations. Others thought it included the companies' contractual and legal obligations as well as additional social expectations not mandated by law. In either case, there was little agreement about whether CSR should be voluntary or codified. Some called for business codes of conduct, or sets of rules to delineate the responsibilities and accepted practices of individuals or businesses. Others went further to propose international standards. The Organization for Economic

---

14 Goldman, A. (2004) "Sweat, fear and resignation amid all the toys," *Los Angeles Times*, November 26, 2004.

Cooperation and Development (OECD), for example, proposed a Guideline for Multinational Enterprises in 1976. The International Labour Organization (ILO) acted similarly when it issued its Tripartite Declaration of Principles Concerning Multinational Enterprises and Social Policy in 1977.[15] In both cases, the objective was to define standards of corporate behavior and give monitors benchmarks when scrutinizing businesses.

Primarily, activist groups in developed countries were the major impetus driving the definition of standards, and the implementation and monitoring of corporate social responsibility programs. These civic groups were able to use their political power and organizational ability to target global companies that they perceived as not doing enough to comply with global voluntary standards. Such activists generally targeted global companies that had their headquarters in developed countries, but which produced products in developing countries. In a way, activist groups became the policing mechanism for a global code of conduct in key areas such as human rights, protection of the environment, and worker protection.

Interestingly, while the size and scope of activities of global companies gave them significant economic advantages, it also made them easier targets of activists groups. Large global companies had more products, more customers, more workers, more locations, and more investors. Hence, their image and reputation were more susceptible to negative ad campaigns from activist groups and the public press. The potential negative impacts of such campaigns on business drove many global companies, including those in the toy industry, to find a way of coming to terms with the new expectations.[16]

With the threat of legal sanctions and restrictive universal codes on the horizon, businesses began to evaluate their own corporate responsibilities and to develop policies appropriate to their industries and companies. They formulated codes of conduct and guiding principles of various sorts, and hired managers and trainers to implement them within their organizations. One company that was particularly proactive (and relevant to our purposes here) in developing effective guiding principles for its global operations was LS&CO (Levi Strauss & Co.).

LS&CO's Global Sourcing and Operating Guidelines (see Exhibit 6) were highly esteemed for their empathy, integrity, and lengthy provisions to protect subcontractor workers. These provisions—contained in a subset entitled Business Partner Terms of Engagement (TOE)—dealt with issues such as child labor, disciplinary practices, work hours, wages and benefits, freedom of association, discrimination, health and safety, and so on. The Guidelines themselves were derived from many discussions within LS&CO and not just in San Francisco where the company was headquartered. LS&CO rotated into its discussions representatives from all of its global operations. Despite such investment,

---

15 UNCTAD (1999) *The Social Responsibility of Transnational Corporation* (Geneva and New York: United Nations; www.unctad.org/en/docs/poiteiitm21.en.pdf).
16 Ibid.

implementation was not easy. In fact, when LS&CO implemented the guidelines in 1991, it found that about a third of its subcontractors were operating below the guidelines' standards. Rather than abandon the subcontractors, however, LS&CO worked with them, training them in the company's expectations and transferring to them the necessary expertise for subcontractors to reach performance standards. In time, LS&CO dropped about a sixth of its contractors on the grounds of non-compliance, but raised the performance and working standards of its remaining non-American subcontractors to levels higher than those required by local laws.

Mattel's Global Manufacturing Principles

Unlike LS&CO, Mattel's CSR initiatives began under less than favorable conditions. On December 17, 1996, NBC's *Dateline* program planted cameras secretly in one of Mattel's Indonesian plants. *Dateline* then used the footage of employees and their work conditions to accuse Mattel's contractors of hiring underage workers and making them work under poor conditions. The news broke at a time when the American public was sensitive and increasingly opposed to such practices. It also served to speed the development of a set of ethical manufacturing principles at Mattel.

At the time of the *Dateline* airing, Sean Fitzgerald, vice president (VP) for corporate responsibility at Mattel, had been working for two months with a task force to develop Mattel's Global Manufacturing Principles (GMP). The task force was comprised of participants from operations, manufacturing, marketing, legal affairs, government, and international operations, and all were of a rank of VP and above, with the exception of the legal representative. The tenets of the GMP were not specific at that point. In fact, there was only one principle at the time: that no one less than 18 years of age would work for Mattel. This principle set Mattel apart from other manufacturers since 14 years of age was the normal work age in most emerging countries.

The task force reviewed existing principles, especially those provided by the national association of toy manufacturers and large retailers such as Wal-Mart, Disney, and Target. When the task force thought its work was finished, Fitzgerald presented the principles to the CEO and executive committee of Mattel, who voted to adopt it. The 2000 version of the principles can be found in Exhibit 1.

After the executive committee adopted the GMP, Sean Fitzgerald lobbied members of the committee, requesting that they go further to promote the principles in a manner that would enhance Mattel's credibility with it customers, the public, and certain special interest groups. He argued that Mattel needed to bring in an objective expert to perform independent audits to monitor and track Mattel's progress in implementing the GMP. Eventually, the task members supported his ideas and Sean Fitzgerald went about contacting special interest, social issues in management academicians, and various activist groups for input. In his discussions, Prakash Sethi's name kept coming up. Fitzgerald contacted Sethi, a university professor whose interests are corporate social responsibility and corporate social accountability.

Nearly one year after the *Dateline* revelations (November 20, 1997), Mattel announced its intent to develop a code of conduct for its production facilities and contract manufacturers, as well as a global independent audit and monitoring system. A steering group called Mattel Independent Monitoring Council (MIMC) was formed and Mattel and Prakash Sethi formed two audit teams. One team was to be based in El Segundo and the other in Mattel's major office in Hong Kong. These groups, under the guidance of Prakash Sethi and MIMC, were to develop a comprehensive set of standards; each of which was associated with at least one principle of the GMP. Afterwards, the MIMC was to develop a comprehensive set of audit protocol and guidelines to be used for the verification of compliance of Mattel's plants to GMP.

Throughout—and not unlike LS&CO—Mattel used an open approach to corporate social responsibility discussions. It defined a set of principles, and created standards and audit protocols based on those principles. It then instituted an internal organizational unit to implement the practice worldwide. Additionally, Mattel hired Prakash Sethi and authorized him to conduct annual independent audits of a sample that the Mattel's GMP auditors cleared as being in compliance to the standards. When the process was complete, the independent auditors submitted a report of their findings and recommendations to Mattel, which posted them on the Internet.

Roughly two years later (2000), the GMP was expanded to include more human rights and worker rights issues—and product safety and quality principles were eliminated.

Vendors and the global manufacturing principles

Mattel began by implementing the GMP in its own plants, including those in China and, in 2000, extended the audits to its vendors. The premise of this approach was simple. Mattel had to get its own house in order before it could venture into other businesses with compliance requirements. Mattel also knew that auditing vendors for compliance to the GMP would uncover a number of problems unique to them.

For one, vendors found to be out of compliance would be required to invest more money in their facilities and employees to retain Mattel business. This would raise the vendors' cost of production and set them at a disadvantage against other vendors wanting to do business with companies that did not have CSR programs such as Mattel's. If, for example, a vendor committed 20% of its yearly output to Mattel, that meant that 80% of its business had to come from other sources. By increasing its overall costs of production through adhering to Mattel's GMP, vendors put the bulk of their business at a competitive disadvantage. Realizing this, some vendors simply refused to comply with the GMP guidelines, opting instead to do business with companies with fewer or no such requirements.

By as late as 2005, Mattel's independent monitoring of vendors was still a rarity. Only 9% of Standard & Poor's 500 companies had any monitoring procedure in place. Only 7% and 5% respectively conducted internal and external monitoring of supplier compliance with human, worker, and environmental protection issues.[17]

Ensuring product quality and safety compliance

In the midst of these vendor problems, Mattel chose to enforce its product safety and quality standards via a different mechanism—contracts. In China, the company used its subsidiary, Mattel Asia Pacific Sourcing (MAPS), to contract with 37 principal vendors (PVs), who were licensed to make Mattel toys. These were all Tier II factories. The contracts required that these vendors comply with Mattel's quality and safety procedures as well as the Global Manufacturing Principles. Principal vendors had to pass Mattel's production facilities review and its GMP audit.

The principal vendors also had to purchase paint from Mattel's list of certified paint vendors, of which eight were in China. If they used non-certified paint vendors, they had to test each batch of the paint to ensure compliance for lead composition. They also had to quarantine paint from non-certified paint vendors until a MAPS-approved lab approved the paint for use. The paint samples that were approved for use on Mattel products by the MAPS-approved lab were then assigned and affixed with batch and test numbers. Principal vendors also had to keep records to demonstrate their compliance with the process and they had to present these during periodic audits by MAPS inspectors.

Mattel required lead testing of paint at three points in its process after the completion of the initial batch of a production run, and three before completed toys were shipped to customers. However, a majority of Mattel's direct importers added an additional layer of product testing of their own by hiring independent labs or the MAPS lab to test products before they were shipped. In such cases, statistical sampling approaches were used.

Mattel also prescribed the process to be followed should defective paint be found. If a sample taken from a finished toys batch was found to be lead-compliant, all the toys associated with the batch were to be issued a certificate of

17 DeSimmone, P. (2004) "Persistent Violations Raise Questions about Monitoring," *Corporate Social Issues Reporter*, December 2004: 8-12.

compliance. Only batches with such certificates were to be shipped to buyers and retailers in the U.S. and Europe. Sometimes Mattel-approved labs issued certificates of compliance for products kept in storage until the time of shipment. If these toys remained within Mattel's production storage for more than a year, they had to be tested again in a process called product recertification.[18,19]

In striving to ensure quality control, Mattel qualified select principal vendors, paint vendors, and laboratories. It also set rigorous procedures to be used by certified entities. For example, it required that its partners retain all evidence that proved that they were in their compliance with the procedures and standards. These documents were reviewed during MAPS periodic and random audits. Once the certification of a vendor was complete, Mattel did not allow changes to manufacturing locations, materials, components, or material sources without approval from MAPS and a recertification. PVs were empowered to engage subcontractors that helped them complete toy production as needed. In such cases, the PVs were responsible for ensuring that subcontractors followed Mattel's guidelines including those for paint, specifically for instances in which subcontractors purchased paint from non-certified paint vendors.[20] Mattel's product safety standards and stipulations for paint were especially stringent because it was known to be a potential source though which lead could be transferred to children's toys.

Lead toxicity and children

Lead is one of the oldest known human poisons. It is a heavy, toxic malleable metal that occurs naturally. It has been (or is) used in the manufacture of glass and thermometers and even for the repair filling of human teeth by dentists. In 1970, scientific experiments conclusively proved that lead could cause acute poisoning in human beings as well as cause long-term adverse effect on human health.[21]

Lead poisoning has been found to be particularly dangerous for children. Research shows that, on average, children whose blood lead levels rose from 10 to 20 µg/dL due to lead poisoning lost two to three intelligence quotient (IQ)

18　Mattel's response to the August 22, 2007 Information Request from the Subcommittee on Commerce, Trade and Consumer Protection, September 5, 2007 (energycommerce.house. gov/CPSC%20lead/Responses/Mattel.090607.response.082207.pdf).

19　Testimony by R. Eckert before the Subcommittee on Commerce, Trade, and Consumer Protection of the Committee on Energy and Commerce, September 19, 2007 (archives. energycommerce.house.gov/cmte_mtgs/110-ctcp-hrg.091907.Eckert-testimony.pdf).

20　Ibid.

21　Markowitz, G., and D. Rosner (2000) "Cater to the Children: The Role of Lead Industry in a Public Health Tragedy 1900–1955," *American Journal of Public Health* 9.1: 36-46.

points.[22] Another study indicated that in a group of seven-year-old children who had been exposed to lead before they turned three years old, the IQ of the children continued to fall even after the blood lead levels (BLL) had declined.[23] Some research studies even link lead poisoning to children's behavioral disorders such as attention deficit disorders, reading disabilities, and increased social aggression.

Based on these findings, the U.S. Consumer Product Safety Commission (CPSC) in 1978 banned the manufacture of paint containing more than 0.06% lead by weight on interior and exterior residential surfaces, toys and furniture.[24]

In her testimony to U.S. Congress on the issue, Dana Best, an official of the American Academy of Pediatrics, stated that ingestion via the mouth was the common route of lead exposure for children. She also explained that, because children have significantly faster metabolisms, they breathe faster and digest proportionately more food and water than grown-ups. According to her testimony, children absorbed 5–50% of any lead that they were exposed to, compared to adults who absorb 10–15% of the lead that they ingested. Once lead enters the body, it remains there for years.[25]

Toys fail lead compliance tests[26]

On June 8, 2007, Intertek, a lab that performed pre-shipment lead testing for Auchan, a France-based importer, reported that a sample of Fisher-Price toys it tested had non-compliant paint on them. The toy sample was drawn from the product of toys assembled by Lee Der Industrial Company, one of Mattel's principal vendors in China. Knowing Mattel's connections to Lee Der, Intertek

---

22 Cranfield, R., C. Henderson, D. Cory-Slechta, C. Cox, T. Jusko and B. Lanphear (2003) "Intellectual Impairment in Children with Blood Lead Concentrations below 10 microgram per deciliter," *New England Journal of Medicine* 348.16: 1,517-26.

23 Chen, A., K. Dietrich, J. Ware, J. Radcliffe and W. Rogan (2005) "IQ and Blood Lead from 2 to 7 years of Age: Are the effects in older children the residual of high blood lead concentrations in 2 year olds?" *Environmental Health Perspective* 113.5: 597-601.

24 Ibid.

25 Protecting Children from Lead-Tainted Imports: testimony by Dana Best before the Energy and Commerce Subcommittee on Commerce, Trade and Consumer Protection, September 20, 2007 (archives.energycommerce.house.gov/cmte_mtgs/110-ctcp-hrg.092007.best-testimony.pdf).

26 Data in the next three sections were adapted from Mattel's Response to the August 22, 2007 Information Request from the Subcommittee on Commerce, Trade and Consumer Protection, September 5, 2007 (energycommerce.house.gov/CPSC%20lead/Responses/Mattel.090607.response.082207.pdf) and the Testimony by R. Eckert before the Subcommittee on Commerce, Trade and Consumer Protection of the Committee on Energy and Commerce, September 19, 2007 (archives.energycommerce.house.gov/cmte_mtgs/110-ctcp-hrg.091907.Eckert-testimony.pdf).

contacted Mattel's product integrity employees in Asia to stop shipment of toys abroad. It also contacted Lee Der Industrial, requesting that it immediately remedy the problem. Lee Der, a company that had worked with Mattel for 15 years, was instructed by Mattel's product integrity personnel to provide Intertek with another sample for testing after the error was corrected.

On June 28, 2007, Mattel's product integrity staff sent new samples from the Fisher-Price toys product batch that failed the lead test to a MAPS-approved laboratory in China for testing. On June 29 and July 3, Mattel's product integrity employees in China were notified of the results of Intertek's second and third lead test result on the new samples. Both samples passed the lead test.

On July 6, however, results from another MAPS-approved lab found non-conforming lead in a sample that had allegedly passed lead compliance testing. The lab also conducted lead tests on new samples drawn on July 5. It found that ten out of 23 samples from the Lee Der production sample contained paint with non-conforming levels of lead. Mattel's senior management stopped shipment of suspected Lee Der products on July 6 and extended the export freeze to all Lee Der products on July 17.

Mattel's product integrity personnel concluded that there was a persistent problem with Lee Der's production and informed Mattel's senior managers about the issue in correspondence between July 3 and July 12. Mattel's managers subsequently launched an investigation into the issue. The investigation established that the non-conforming lead levels were caused by the yellow pigment in paint used on portions of certain toys manufactured by Lee Der at a plant in Foshan City, China. The investigation also revealed that the undisclosed plant used paint from an uncertified paint vendor without testing it for lead compliance. This established the cause of the problem and enabled Mattel to define the scope of toys that might be affected, ascertain the dates of production, and estimate the number of lead-tainted toys that might have been shipped.

Overall, the initial investigation concluded that the lead-tainted problem potentially affected 83 different stock keeping units (SKUs) that were made by Lee Der between April 19, 2007—the date when the undisclosed Lee Der plant took delivery of the paint containing excessive lead content from its supplier—and July 6, 2007, when Mattel stopped taking delivery of Lee Der's products.

Lee Der's use of an unregistered facility to produce Mattel products was a violation of its manufacturing and procurement agreement with MAPS. Furthermore, the subcontractor's failure to test every batch of paint received from its paint supplier was also a violation of Mattel's standards. Mattel filed an initial report of the issue with the U.S. Consumer Product Safety Commission on July 20, 2007 and submitted a full report on July 26, indicating its desire to institute a fast-track recall of all Mattel products that could possibly be affected.

On July 30, 2007, just prior to the announcement of the date of the first recall, the paint used for a different toy, the Sarge car (see Exhibit 4), failed the lead compliance test during a recertification process. This resulted in a new investigation of Lee Der.

The next round of investigations revealed that the source of the lead-taint was the olive-green top of the Sarge car delivered to Lee Der by its subcontractor Early Light Industrial Company Ltd. However, Early Light in Hong Kong, which had been a Mattel suppler for 20 years, did not perform the job on its own. It subcontracted production to an undisclosed company—the Hon Li Da Plastic Cement Products Co. Ltd located in Shenzhen City, China. Early Light assembled the top component of the Sarge toy painted by Hon Li Da to the finished Sarge car part made in its manufacturing facility located in Pinghu, China. Early Light had failed to disclose to MAPS that Hon Li Da was its subcontractor, though it was required to do so by its agreement with MAPS.

The investigation, however, was unable to establish the actual genesis of the problem. It was not clear whether the Early Light plant failed to supply certified paint to Hon Li Da, or whether it supplied an insufficient quantity of such paint to it. The supply of inadequate paint might have forced the subcontractor to purchase paint. As high-quality, low-lead paint was more expensive than regular paint, the subcontractor may have attempted to buy cheap paint to save money. On August 6, 2007, Mattel concluded that the excess lead on the Sarge car was due to yellow pigment used by the undisclosed subcontractor, Hon Li Da, on the olive-green top. That same day, Mattel filed an initial report with the CPSC. On August 7, Mattel filed a full report with the CPSC asking for another fast-track toy recall.

As if that was not enough, between August 9 and 11, 2007, certain plastic Barbie accessories were shown to contain non-conforming levels of lead. Investigations revealed that the affected Barbie accessories were painted by one of or two affiliated subcontractors, Dong Lian Fa Metals Plastic Produce Factory, located in Huizhou City, China, and Yip Sing, based in Shenzhen City, China. Holder Plastic in Shenzhen, China, was the principal vendor that subcontracted the work to the two companies. Holder had also failed to identify its subcontractors to MAPS as it was obligated to do. In this case, Mattel's investigators found out that Holder did supply Dong Lian Fa and Yip Sing with approved paint; hence it was unclear why the subcontractors used paint that contained excessive levels of lead. Holder Plastic assembled the lead-tainted components into finished products manufactured in its plant.

Finally, on August 16, another lab test found non-conforming lead levels in the paint used on the Geo Trax vehicle's small yellow ladder and headlights. A subcontractor of Apex Manufacturing Co. Ltd, namely Boyi Plastic Products Factory, painted the SKUs with the lead-tainted ladders and headlights between July 31, 2006 and September 4, 2006. The subcontractor may have mixed non-compliant paint with the compliant paint that it received from Apex. Apex violated its agreement with MAPS by failing to identify its subcontractor, Boyi. Mattel estimated that the issue of non-compliant lead in paint potentially affected approximately 89,000 Geo Trax toys.

Non-conforming lead levels were also found and established in paint used on some 6-in-1 Big World Bongos Band between August 20 and August 27, 2007. Mattel's investigation showed that the affected 6-in-1 Big World Bongos Band were painted by a subcontractor, Wo Fong Packaging Co. Ltd, Dongguan City, China, for Shun On Toys Co. Ltd. in the same city. The vendor also violated its agreement with MAPS by failing to identify Wo Fong as a subcontractor. The primary vendor also failed to provide Wo Fong with certified paint for Mattel products. The reported non-compliant lead levels measured in the paint was ranged from 10,000 parts of lead (10%) per million to 110,000 parts per million (11%). According to applicable U.S. standards, the maximum levels of lead that was allowable in paint was 600 parts (0.06%) per million.

Rolling recalls begin

The lead-tainted toys issue resulted in a series of recalls. Mattel notified CPSC promptly of each of the events and submitted both initial and full reports, indicating a desire to execute a fast track recall.

Mattel announced formal recalls on August 2, August 14, and September 4. On August 1, 2007, Mattel decided to detain the distribution of all its finished products in Asia, including all toys made by Mattel-owned and -controlled plants. The company initiated an expanded lead testing for all the detained products. This exhaustive testing program resulted in the identification of additional toys with non-conforming levels of lead in their paint.

Mattel successfully executed each of its recalls, which affected 1.5 million sold toys.[27] The company used multiple channels including paper advertisements, media announcements, websites, and mass mailings to inform consumers and retailers about the recall and the products that were affected. Consumers were sent pre-paid envelopes to send in recalled products. The company issued vouchers equivalent to the price of the toys redeemable for other Mattel products. Mattel managers used television business program interviews with the CEO Robert Eckert and Thomas Debrowski to assure the public of Mattel's commitment to product safety and of the company's efforts to resolve the issue. There were no reported injuries to children due to the lead-tainted toys issue. Nevertheless, Mattel's stock price suffered (see Exhibit 2).

27 In 2007, Mattel recalled an additional 11.7 million toys that had magnets that could be swallowed by children. These products did not have the problem of excessive lead levels.

Finding the right way forward

After multiple TV interviews, several appearances before committees and sub-committees of the U.S. Congress, and several announcements on the radio and newspapers, Mattel completed its tainted-toy recall.

Debrowski now faced a decision about whether it made sense to reintroduce product safety and quality into the Global Manufacturing Principles program. If the product safety and quality issues were kept separate from the GMP, both issues might remain coherent and Mattel would have the freedom to design different monitoring procedures for each. The focus of the GMP was social responsibility; product safety and quality did not necessarily fit in that category.

Debrowski was also uncertain about having external auditors become responsible for auditing Mattel's product safety procedures. He also wondered about the risk of adding more components to the GMP as doing so would make plant audits longer and more expensive. Keeping both areas separate would enable vendors to focus on product safety and quality, even if they were not in full GMP compliance. The separation of both areas might also lead to the charge that Mattel did not consider product quality and safety as areas associated with its corporate responsibilities.

Furthermore, the separation of product safety and quality from GMP might disregard the fact that the two areas are interdependent and interrelated. The company might overlook interconnectedness of safety procedures to worker rights, workplace conditions, and human rights.

Debrowski wondered, "Should I recommend that product safety and quality be added back as a GMP audit component—or should I support the existing policy that exempts product safety and quality from the GMP audits?" He also wondered how Mattel might tighten its product safety and quality procedures to prevent a reoccurrence of the lead-tainted toys problem.

Exhibit 1 Global Manufacturing Principles

1. Management Systems

a. Facilities must have systems in place to address labor, social, environmental, health and safety issues.

2. Wages and Working Hours

a. Employees must be paid for all hours worked. Wages for regular and overtime work must be compensated at the legally mandated rates.

b. Wages must be paid in legal tender and at least monthly.

c. Working hours must be in compliance with country and Mattel requirements.

d. Regular and overtime working hours must be documented, verifiable and accurately reflect all hours worked by employees.

e. Overtime work must be voluntary.

f. Employees must be provided with rest days in compliance with country and Mattel requirements.

g. Payroll deductions must comply with applicable country and Mattel requirements.

3. Age Requirements

a. All employees must meet the minimum age for employment as specified by country and Mattel requirements.

4. Forced Labor

a. Employees must be employed of their own free will.

b. Forced or prison labor must not be used to manufacture, assemble or distribute any Mattel products.

5. Discrimination

a. The facility must have policies on hiring, promotion, employee rights and disciplinary practices that address discrimination.

6. Freedom of Expression and Association

a. The facility must recognize all employees' rights to choose to engage in, or refrain from, lawful union activity and lawful collective bargaining through representatives selected according to applicable law.

b. Management must create formal channels to encourage communications among all levels of management and employees on issues that impact their working and living conditions.

7. Living Conditions

a. Dormitories must be separated from production and warehouse buildings.

b. Dormitories and canteens must be safe, sanitary and meet the basic needs of employees.

8. Workplace Safety

a. The facility must have programs in place to address health and safety issues that exist in the workplace.

9. Health

a. First aid and medical treatment must be available to all employees.

b. Monitoring programs must be in place to ensure employees are not exposed to harmful working conditions.

10. Emergency Planning

a. The facility must have programs and systems in place for dealing with emergencies such as fires, spills and natural disasters.

b. Emergency exit doors must be kept unlocked at all times when the building is occupied. Emergency exits must be clearly marked and free of obstructions.

11. Environmental Protection

a. Facilities must have environmental programs in place to minimize their impact on the environment.

EXHIBIT 2 Stock market trend for Mattel's stock (2003–2007)

Source: MSN Money

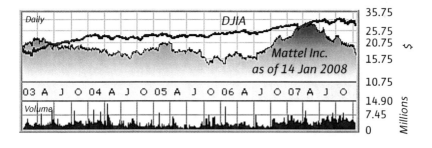

Exhibit 3 Annual corporate results for Mattel

Source: 2005 Annual Report of Mattel Inc.

Fiscal years	2003	2004	2005
Operating results in $ thousands, except per share data			
Gross sales	$5,379,523	$5,546,098	$5,623,553
Total domestic	3,203,814	3,209,862	3,159,569
International	2,175,709	2,336,236	2,463,984
Net sales*	4,960,100	5,102,786	5,179,016
Net income	537,632	572,723	417,019
Net income per common shares (diluted)	1.22	1.35	1.01
Provision for income taxes	203,222	123,531	235,030
Financial position (as of December 31) in $ thousands			
Total assets	$4,510,950	$4,756,492	$4,372,313
Long-term liabilities	826,983	643,509	807,395
Stockholders' equity	2,216,221	2,385,812	2,101,733
Corporate statistics (as of December 31)			
Number of employees	25,000	25,000	26,000

* Gross sales minus sales adjustments such as trade discounts and other allowances

Exhibit 4 Sarge car

Source: U.S. Consumer Product Safety Commission

EXHIBIT 5 Location of Mattel's factories

Source: Mattel

Where Do Mattel Toys Come From?

Half of Mattel's toys are made in facilities owned by Chinese
vendors. The other half are manufactured in Mattel-owned facilities
around the world, including China.

SHARE OF 2006
REVENUE BY DIVISION   **MANUFACTURING LOCATION(S)**
$5.65 billion total   Mattel-owned in **bold**

	FISHER-PRICE	
	Fisher-Price Baby Gear	**Tijuana, Mexico** and *Chinese vendors*
37%	DORA	Large items like Dora's Talking Kitchen in **Tijuana**, small items by *Chinese vendors*
	Little People	Large items like the Little People Animal Sounds Farm in **Tijuana** and small items by *Chinese vendors*
	Power Wheels	**Monterrey, Mexico**

	GIRLS BUSINESS	
29%	Barbie	11.5-inch standard dolls made in **Indonesia** and **China**, large Barbie toys like dollhouses in **Tijuana** and accessories like furniture by *Chinese vendors*
	Polly Pocket	*Chinese vendors*
	Disney Princess Dolls	**China** and **Thailand**

	BOYS AND ENTERTAINMENT BUSINESS	
27%	Hot Wheels	**Malaysia**
	Radica	**China**
	Matchbox	**Thailand**
	Pixar Cars	**Thailand** and *Chinese vendors*

7%	☆ American Girl	*Chinese vendors*

EXHIBIT 6 Levi Strauss & Co. global sourcing and operating guidelines

Source: www.levistrauss.com/Downloads/GSOG.pdf

Levi Strauss & Co.'s (LS&CO) commitment to responsible business practices—embodied in our Global Sourcing and Operating Guidelines—guides our decisions and behavior as a company everywhere we do business. Since becoming the first multinational to establish such guidelines in 1991, LS&CO has used them to help improve the lives of workers manufacturing our products, make responsible sourcing decisions and protect our commercial interests. They are a cornerstone of our sourcing strategy and of our business relationships with hundreds of contractors worldwide.

The Levi Strauss & Co. Global Sourcing and Operating Guidelines include two parts:

The Country Assessment Guidelines, which address large, external issues beyond the control of LS&CO's individual business partners. These help us assess the opportunities and risks of doing business in a particular country.

The Business Partner Terms of Engagement (TOE), which deal with issues that are substantially controllable by individual business partners. These TOE are an integral part of our business relationships. Our employees and our business partners understand that complying with our TOE is no less important than meeting our quality standards or delivery times.

Country Assessment Guidelines

The numerous countries where LS&CO has existing or future business interests present a variety of cultural, political, social and economic circumstances.

The Country Assessment Guidelines help us assess any issues that might present concern in light of the ethical principles we have set for ourselves. The Guidelines assist us in making practical and principled business decisions as we balance the potential risks and opportunities associated with conducting business in specific countries. Specifically, we assess the following:

- **Health and Safety Conditions**—must meet the expectations we have for employees and their families or our company representatives

- **Human Rights Environment**—must allow us to conduct business activities in a manner that is consistent with our Global Sourcing and Operating Guidelines and other company policies

- **Legal System**—must provide the necessary support to adequately protect our trademarks, investments or other commercial interests, or to implement the Global Sourcing and Operating Guidelines and other company policies

- **Political, Economic and Social Environment**—must protect the company's commercial interests and brand/corporate image. We do not conduct business in countries prohibited by U.S. laws

Terms of Engagement

Our TOE help us to select business partners who follow workplace standards and business practices that are consistent with LS&CO's values and policies. These requirements are applied to every contractor who manufactures or finishes products for LS&CO. Trained assessors closely monitor compliance among our manufacturing and finishing contractors in more than 50 countries. The TOE include:

- **Ethical Standards**—We will seek to identify and utilize business partners who aspire as individuals and in the conduct of all their businesses to a set of ethical standards not incompatible with our own

- **Legal Requirements**—We expect our business partners to be law abiding as individuals and to comply with legal requirements relevant to the conduct of all their businesses

- **Environmental Requirements**—We will only do business with partners who share our commitment to the environment and who conduct their business in a way that is consistent with LS&CO's Environmental Philosophy and Guiding Principles (See TOE Guidebook p. 68)

- **Community Involvement**—We will favor business partners who share our commitment to improving community conditions

- **Employment Standards**—We will only do business with partners who adhere to the following guidelines:

- **Child Labor**—Use of child labor is not permissible. Workers can be no less than 15 years of age and not younger than the compulsory age to be in school. We will not utilize partners who use child labor in any of their facilities. We support the development of legitimate workplace apprenticeship programs for the educational benefit of younger people

- **Prison Labor/Forced Labor**—We will not utilize prison or forced labor in contracting relationships in the manufacture and finishing of our products. We will not utilize or purchase materials from a business partner utilizing prison or forced labor

- **Disciplinary Practices**—We will not utilize business partners who use corporal or other forms of mental or physical coercion

- **Working Hours**—While permitting flexibility in scheduling, we will identify local legal limits on work hours and seek business partners who do not exceed them except for appropriately compensated overtime. While we favor partners who utilize less than sixty-hour work weeks, we will not use contractors who, on a regular basis, require in excess of a sixty-hour week. Employees should be allowed at least one day off in seven

- **Wages and Benefits**—We will only do business with partners who provide wages and benefits that comply with any applicable law and match the prevailing local manufacturing or finishing industry practices

- **Freedom of Association**—We respect workers' rights to form and join organizations of their choice and to bargain collectively. We expect our suppliers to respect the right to free association and the right to organize and bargain collectively without unlawful interference. Business partners should ensure that workers who make such decisions or participate in such organizations are not the object of discrimination or punitive disciplinary actions and that the representatives of such organizations have access to their members under conditions established either by local laws or mutual agreement between the employer and the worker organizations

- **Discrimination**—While we recognize and respect cultural differences, we believe that workers should be employed on the basis of their ability to do the job, rather than on the basis of personal characteristics or beliefs. We will favor business partners who share this value

- **Health and Safety**—We will only utilize business partners who provide workers with a safe and healthy work environment. Business partners who provide residential facilities for their workers must provide safe and healthy facilities

Evaluation and Compliance

All new and existing factories involved in the manufacturing or finishing of products for LS&CO are regularly evaluated to ensure compliance with our TOE. Our goal is to achieve positive results and effect change by working with our business partners to find long-term solutions that will benefit the individuals who make our products and will improve the quality of life in local communities. We work on-site with our contractors to develop strong alliances dedicated to responsible business practices and continuous improvement. If LS&CO determines that a contractor is not complying with our TOE, we require that the contractor implement a corrective action plan within a specified time period. If a contractor fails to meet the corrective action plan commitment, Levi Strauss & Co. will terminate the business relationship.

Discussion questions

1. Describe the following terms: *social contract, corporate social responsibility, corporate code of conduct.*

2. List the difficulties associated with manufacturing consumer products in emerging countries.

3. What factors make supplier monitoring in developing countries so complicated?

4. How can governments be both helpful and obstructive to global firms attempting to do business in a less developed country?

5. Is "constructive engagement" on the part of companies involved in China and elsewhere a viable strategy?

6. Compare the Levi Strauss & Co. and Mattel principles. Are Mattel's appropriate to the toy industry?

7. Was Mattel fair to vendors in insisting they comply with the Global Manufacturing Principles (GMP)?

8. Was Mattel's GMP to blame for the lead-tainted toy fiasco?

9. Should quality and safety be reintroduced to the GMP?

10. What should Thomas Debrowski recommend to Robert Eckert?

Teaching notes for this case are available from
Greenleaf Publishing. These are free of charge
and available only to teaching staff. They can be
requested by going to:
www.greenleaf-publishing.com/darkside_notes

4.3

Google, Inc.
Figuring out how to deal with China[1]

Anne T. Lawrence

In 2005, Google, Inc.'s top management team struggled to decide if the company should enter China—and, if so, how. Since 2000, the company had offered a Chinese-language version of its popular search engine, hosted on servers outside China. However, Chinese users found this service slow and unreliable, and Google was rapidly losing market share, particularly to the Chinese company Baidu. At the same time, the number of Internet users in China—and with them the potential for online advertising revenue—had been growing almost exponentially. Yet serious ethical questions remained unresolved. China operated the most far-reaching and sophisticated system of Internet censorship in the world. Any Internet company doing business there would have to filter content that the communist regime considered offensive. Moreover, the Chinese government had demanded that other U.S. Internet companies identify individuals who had used their email or blogs to criticize the authorities, and at least one dissident had been jailed as a result. Would it be possible for Google to enter China, while remaining true to its mission to make the world's information "universally accessible and useful" and to its informal corporate motto, "Don't Be Evil"?

---

1 Copyright © 2007 by the author. All rights reserved. This is an abridged version of a full-length case, *Google, Inc.: Figuring out how to deal with China*, licensed to Babson College and published by Harvard Business School Publishing. An earlier version of this case was presented at the 2007 annual meeting of the International Association for Business and Society. This case was the winner of the Dark Side Case Writing Competition sponsored by the Critical Management Studies Interest Group and the Management Education Division of the Academy of Management in 2007.

On July 15, 2005, Google's board of directors gathered for its regular meeting at the company's headquarters in Mountain View, California. On this occasion, CEO Eric Schmidt's presentation to directors was divided into three parts—"Highlights," "Making Slow Progress/Watch List," and "Lowlights/Serious Concerns." Schmidt had much positive news to report. Google, the world's premier provider of Internet search services, was producing strong advertising sales in the United States and Europe, generating innovative new products, and expanding its service in Ireland, India, and other countries. Schmidt had one major worry, however. Under the heading "Lowlights/Serious Concerns," the first item listed was "China."[2]

The question at hand was whether or not Google should directly enter the Chinese market for search engines. In 2000, the company had established a Chinese-language version of its popular search engine, hosted on servers outside China. When a searcher accessed google.com from inside the country, the company's servers would automatically deliver results in a Chinese translation.[3] This service left much to be desired, however; it was unreliable, and Chinese censors routinely removed search results. Google's senior policy counsel and a member of the company's core China team, Andrew McGlaughlin, described the problem in his blog:

> Google users in China today struggle with a service that, to be blunt, isn't very good. Google.com appears to be down around 10% of the time. Even when users can reach it, the website is slow, and sometimes produces results that when clicked on, stall out the user's browser. Our Google News service is never available; Google Images is accessible only half the time. At Google we work hard to create a great experience for our users, and the level of service we've been able to provide in China is not something we're proud of.[4]

The issue had recently become more urgent because Google had been losing market share, particularly to Baidu, a Chinese company. At the same time, the number of Internet users in China—and with it the potential for online advertising—had been growing almost exponentially. Google seemed to be missing a huge opportunity.

Yet serious ethical questions remained unresolved. China operated the most far-reaching and sophisticated system of Internet censorship in the world. Any

---

2   Google board meeting, Friday, July 15, 2005, confidential presentation slides, pp. 5-9. Google released these slides—with portions redacted pursuant to a stipulated protective order—in connection with a lawsuit filed by Microsoft Corporation alleging violation by Google, Inc., and Dr. Kai-Fu Lee, a former Microsoft executive, of Dr. Lee's non-compete agreement (Microsoft *v.* Lee, 05-2-23561-6, King County Superior Court, Seattle, WA).

3   Google's early efforts to provide service to the Chinese are described in: Clive Thompson (2006) "Google's China Problem (and China's Google Problem)," *New York Times Magazine,* April 23, 2006.

4   googleblog.blogspot.com/2006_01_01_googleblog_archive.html.

Internet company doing business there would have to filter content that the Communist regime considered offensive. Moreover, the Chinese government had demanded that other U.S. companies identify individuals who had used the Internet to criticize the authorities, and at least one dissident had been jailed as a result. Would it be possible for Google to enter China, while remaining true to its informal corporate motto, "Don't Be Evil"?

Google, Inc.[5]

Google defined itself as "a global technology leader focused on improving the ways people connect with information." In 2005, the company was the leading provider of Internet search services in the world. Its search engine offered a variety of specialized features, including the ability to search for images, videos, maps, news, products, and phone numbers. The company also provided free email, instant messaging and blogging services, and hosted all kinds of groups. One of the world's most recognized brands, the company's name had become a verb in many languages as people around the globe "googled" in search of information. In 2005, Google had more than 4,000 full-time employees and earned $1.5 billion on $6.1 billion in revenue; its market capitalization that year exceeded $80 billion.

Google was founded by Larry Page and Sergey Brin, who met in 1995 when both were enrolled in the doctoral program in computer science at Stanford. As part of a research project, Page developed a search engine algorithm he called PageRank. The problem that intrigued him was that leading search engines at the time, including Alta Vista and Yahoo!, ordered search results based on matches between words in a query and those on a website. This method produced results that were often poorly matched to the searcher's intent. Page's critical innovation was to rank search results based on the number and importance of backward links to a particular website, that is, how often it was cited by others. This enabled him to prioritize results based on likely relevance to the user. In 1997, Page and Brin offered their search service to the Stanford community under the domain name google.stanford.edu, where it attracted an enthusiastic following.

Page and Brin continued to work on the nascent search engine—which they named Google after *googol,* a mathematical term referring to the number 1 followed by 100 zeros—to improve its functionality. One idea was to "crawl" the Internet and download the entire contents of the Web in a cache where it could be readily retrieved in order to return super-fast results to searchers. Because the two graduate students had little cash, they bought cheap PCs from a local discount chain and wrote their own software to build a makeshift supercom-

5   Except as noted, this history of Google is largely drawn from: Vise, D.A., and M. Malseed (2005) *The Google Story* (New York: Random House).

puter. This necessity later turned into a competitive advantage as they were able to spread computing tasks over multiple computers, building redundancy into the system. Another idea was to add a "snippet" for each search result—several lines that highlighted the parts of a website relevant to the user's query. The two also developed the simple, clean design that became a hallmark of the Google site.

Page and Brin's original idea for commercializing Google was to license their technology to other Internet companies. However, the companies they approached were uninterested. At the time, Alta Vista, Yahoo!, America Online, and other portals believed their competitive advantage lay not in superior search, but rather in offering a range of attractive services such as email, shopping, news, and weather. Forced to move ahead independently, the two graduate students incorporated Google in September 1998 and raised initial capital from several angel investors. In 1999, the venture capital firms Kleiner Perkins and Sequoia Capital jointly invested $25 million, and John Doerr of Kleiner Perkins and Michael Moritz of Sequoia joined Google's board. In 2001, the company hired Eric Schmidt, CEO of Novell, to be its chief executive.

Google went public in an initial public offering in August 2004. Page and Brin, each of whom owned about 15% of the company, retained control through their ownership of Class B shares.

The business model

In 2005, Google's business model was based almost entirely on revenue from paid advertising. The company made money in two main ways:

- **AdWords**. Under this program, launched in 2000, text-based advertisements—called "sponsored links"—appeared on the right-hand side of the Google screen, separated from search results (which appeared on the left-hand side of the screen) by a vertical line. The ads were for products or services deemed relevant to words in the search query. For example, a search for "women's shoes" might produce an ad from zappos.com, an online retailer that billed itself as "the web's most popular shoe store." When AdWords first launched, advertisers paid based on number of times their ad was displayed. In 2002, Google began charging advertisers based on the actual number of times a user clicked on their ad. The price was set in an online electronic auction; advertisers—in effect—bid for click-throughs by Google searchers

- **AdSense**. In 2005, Google introduced AdSense. This program placed advertisements on the websites of other content providers, with the website operator and Google sharing resulting revenue. Participants in what the company called the "Google Network" ranged from major companies such as America Online to small businesses and even individuals who operated websites devoted to personal interests or hobbies

In the six months ending in June 30, 2005, 99% of Google's revenue came from advertising; 1% came from licensing fees and other revenue. Of the ad revenue, 53% came from AdWords and 47% came from AdSense.[6]

In 2005, the company's foreign advertising revenue was growing faster than its domestic advertising revenue. As of June 30, 2005, international (non-U.S.) revenue was up 143% over the prior year; U.S. revenues were up 74% during this period. Even so, advertising revenue relative to usage elsewhere continued to lag the United States. By mid-2005, more than half of Google's user traffic—but only 39% of its revenue—came from abroad.[7]

Mission and values

Google declared on its website that its mission was "to organize the world's information and make it universally accessible and useful." In their founders' letter to prospective investors, issued in advance of the initial public offering in 2004, Brin and Page further elaborated on Google's core values:

> Google is not a conventional company. We do not intend to become one. Throughout Google's evolution as a privately held company, we have managed Google differently. We have also emphasized an atmosphere of creativity and challenge, which has helped us provide unbiased, accurate and free access to information for those who rely on us around the world . . . Serving our end users is at the heart of what we do and remains our number one priority.[8]

Google's espoused commitment to its end users was reflected in its code of conduct. Declaring that the company had "always flourished by serving the interests of our users first and foremost," the code called for usefulness, honesty, and responsiveness in the company's dealings with customers. The code also addressed the issues of respect, avoidance of conflicts of interest, confidentiality, reporting procedures, protection of company assets, and legal compliance.

In 2001, a group of employees met to discuss the values of the company. An engineer at the gathering proposed the injunction "Don't Be Evil." This phrase stuck as an informal corporate motto. Later, when asked exactly what was meant

---

6 Google Inc., Form 10-Q, Quarterly Report for the Period ended June 30, 2005: 18.
7 Ibid.: 12,17,19.
8 Google Founders Letter, investor.google.com/ipo_letter.html.

by this, Schmidt commented, perhaps a bit ruefully, "Evil is whatever Sergey says is evil."[9]

In a 2004 interview with *Playboy* magazine, Google co-founders Brin and Page were questioned directly about the implications of the "Don't Be Evil" motto for the decision whether or not to enter China. The reporter David Sheff asked: "What would you do if you had to choose between compromising search results and being unavailable to millions of Chinese?" Brin had replied:

> These are difficult questions, difficult challenges. Sometimes the "Don't Be Evil" policy leads to many discussions about what exactly is evil. One thing we know is that people can make better decisions with better information.[10]

China—a major player

China, the nation that posed a "serious concern" for Google's board of directors and a potential challenge to the company's commitment to "do no evil" was one of the most economically dynamic countries in the world. With 1.3 billion people, it was also by far the most populous. In his book *China, Inc.*, Ted C. Fishman described the challenge posed by the rising Asian nation in the mid-2000s this way:

> China is everywhere these days. Powered by the world's most rapidly changing large economy, it is influencing our lives as consumers, employees, and citizens . . . No country has ever before made a better run at climbing every step of economic development all at once. No country plays the world economic game better than China. No other country shocks the global economic hierarchy like China . . . If any country is going to supplant the United States in the world marketplace, China is it.[11]

After World War II, the Chinese Communist Party under the leadership of Mao Zedong had established an autocratic, single-party state that imposed strict controls on China's society and economy. In the 1970s, Mao's successors had initiated a series of reforms that had gradually opened the nation to world trade. The U.S. Central Intelligence Agency (CIA) described these reforms:

---

9 Vise and Malseed, op. cit.: 211.
10 Sheff, D. (2004) "Playboy Interview: The Google Guys," *Playboy*, September 2004.
11 Fishman, T.C. (2005) *China Inc.: How the Rise of the Next Superpower Challenges America and the World* (New York: Scribner).

> China's economy during the last quarter century has changed from a
> centrally planned system that was largely closed to international trade
> to a more market-oriented economy that has a rapidly growing private
> sector and is a major player in the global economy. Reforms started
> in the late 1970s with the phasing out of collectivized agriculture, and
> expanded to include the gradual liberalization of prices, fiscal decen-
> tralization, increased autonomy for state enterprises, the foundation
> of a diversified banking system, the development of stock markets, the
> rapid growth of the non-state sector, and the opening to foreign trade
> and investment.[12]

As a result of these reforms, China's gross domestic product (GDP) grew ten-
fold over three decades. By 2005, China had become the second largest economy
in the world after the United States, as measured by purchasing power.

Despite its rapid integration into the world economy, China remained a single-party dictatorship. In April and May 1989—as communism was crumbling
throughout eastern and central Europe—students, intellectuals, and labor activists organized pro-democracy demonstrations across China. These culminated
in a mass protest in Tiananmen Square, a large plaza in the center of Beijing.
On the night of June 3 and the morning of June 4, the Chinese government
responded with a massive display of military force. Tanks over-ran the square
and the streets leading to it, and soldiers opened fire on protesters, killing as
many as 3,000 and injuring thousands more. The crackdown—known as the
June 4th incident or sometimes simply as "Six-Four"—effectively suppressed the
pro-democracy movement.

In 2005, the Chinese Communist Party faced on ongoing challenge: how to
maintain its tight control of all major institutions, while allowing the free flow of
money and information required in a market economy.

Internet access[13]

The Internet first became commercially available in China in 1995. In less than a
decade (see Figure 1), the number of Internet users in China soared from virtually
none to 103 million, according to government estimates. This number was second only to the United States (with 154 million active users[14]) and represented

---

12   CIA (2006) "China," in *The 2006 World Factbook* (Washington, DC: CIA; www.cia.gov, accessed
     October 27, 2006).

13   Data in this section, unless otherwise noted, are drawn from: China Internet Network Infor-
     mation Center (CNNIC) (2005) *16th Statistical Survey Report on the Internet Development in
     China* (Beijing: CNNIC; www.cnnic.cn/download/2005/2005072601.pdf, March 17, 2009).

14   U.S. data are for January 2006.

FIGURE 1 Internet usage and access in China, 1997–2005

Source: *16th Statistical Survey Report on Internet Development in China* (CNNIC, July 2005) and earlier semi-annual reports

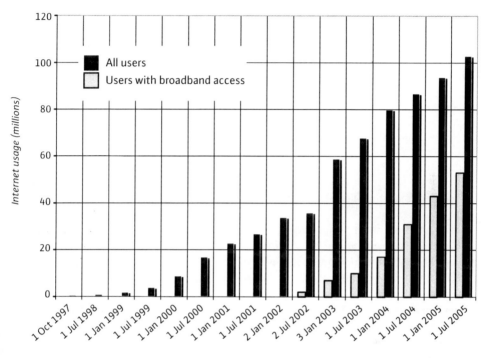

An Internet user is a Chinese citizen who uses the Internet at least one hour per week. Users in Hong Kong, Macao, and Taiwan are not included.

11% of all Internet users worldwide.[15] Charles Zhang, chairman and CEO of Sohu.com, a leading Chinese Internet portal, argued that government estimates were too low because they were based on polls conducted over telephone land lines. "Young people do not use fixed line phones," Zhang pointed out. "They all have mobile phones."[16] Other estimates put the number of Internet users in China in 2005 as high as 134 million.[17]

Approximately 46 million computers in the country were connected to the Web, and a rapidly growing portion of these had DSL or cable access; by 2005, as shown in Figure 1, more than half of all Web users had a high-speed connection. Sixty-nine per cent of users had access at home and 38% at work. A quarter of

15 Computer Industry Almanac Inc. (2006) "Worldwide Internet Users Top 1 Billion in 2005" (press release, January 4, 2006; www.c-i-a.com).

16 "China Surpasses U.S. in Internet Use," Forbes.com, April 3, 2006 (www.forbes.com).

17 "Net User Tally in China Nears 134 Million," *South China Morning Post*, February 4, 2005.

all users logged on at Internet cafés. Average time online was 14 hours a week; users went online, on average, four days out of the week.

Web access and usage were not evenly distributed across demographic groups or geographically. In 2005, 60% of Chinese Internet users were male and 40% female. Most were young, with the largest group (38% of all users) being 18–24 years old; seven in ten were 30 or younger. Internet users were a well-educated group: well over half had at least some college education. Judging from domain name registration, most Internet usage was concentrated in populous cities and coastal provinces. Twenty-one per cent of domain names registered under ".cn" were in Beijing, 15% in Guangdong province in booming southeast China and 10% in Shanghai.

Patterns of Internet usage

What were all these people doing online? In 2005, the most common use of the Internet in China was for entertainment. Thirty-eight per cent of users said this was their primary reason for going online.[18] Chinese Web surfers downloaded music, watched movies, and played online games. Email, instant messaging, online chat, and discussions were also very popular. Sina.com, a Chinese portal, reported that four million people used its forums every day. *New York Times* correspondent Clive Thompson offered the following vivid description of a typical Internet café in Beijing, which was populated mostly by teens:

> Everyone in the café looked to be settled in for a long evening of lightweight entertainment: young girls in pink and yellow Hello Kitty sweaters juggled multiple chat sessions, while upstairs a gang of young Chinese soldiers in olive-drab coats laughed as they crossed swords in the medieval fantasy game World of Warcraft. On one wall, next to a faded kung-fu movie poster, was a yellow sign that said, in Chinese characters, "Do not go to pornographic or illegal websites." The warning seemed almost beside the point; nobody here looked even remotely likely to be hunting for banned Tiananmen Square retrospectives.[19]

Others went online looking for news and information. Charles Zhang of Sohu. com explained:

> People log onto the Internet and Sohu.com because, in China, there is no Forbes, Reuters or *The Washington Post*. Print media was all state-controlled and official, and the Internet filled this void.[20]

18 *16th Statistical Survey Report on the Internet Development in China*, op. cit.
19 "Google's China Problem (and China's Google Problem)," op. cit.
20 "China Surpasses U.S. in Internet Use," op. cit.

Nearly as many users reported they went online primarily to get information—as said, they were seeking entertainment. When asked how they obtained information online, 58% said they used search engines and 36% said they used known websites. A majority of respondents to a 2005 survey by the Chinese Academy of Social Sciences agreed that, by using the Internet, people would have a better knowledge of politics and more opportunities to criticize government policies. In addition, a majority felt that government would be more aware of people's views and better able to serve citizens.

In contrast to patterns in the United States and Europe, shopping was not part of the online experience for most Chinese. Only 1 in 650 people in China had a credit card, and less than a quarter of Internet users had ever made an online purchase. Perhaps for this reason, search engines had not attracted many advertisers. In 2005, the annual revenue generated by search in China—for all companies combined—was just $140 million, according to Morgan Stanley's Hong Kong office.[21]

Internet censorship

Although by 2005 many Chinese were online, their access to information and freedom of expression were restricted by a sophisticated and comprehensive system of government censorship. The authorities enforced this system on three interconnected levels:

- Firewall devices at the border

- Government-mandated self-censorship by Internet service and content providers

- Self-discipline exercised by individual users

The Great Firewall of China

All information flowing in and out of China on the Internet had to traverse one of five main fiber-optic pipelines that connected the infrastructure of the Chinese Internet to the outside world. The Chinese government required the operators of these pipelines to install sophisticated router switches—many made by the U.S. company Cisco Systems—to block information flowing to or from specific

---

21   "Google Searches for a Home in China," *BusinessWeek Online*, June 27, 2006.

sites as it crossed the border.[22] These devices were widely known as the Great Firewall of China. As Jack Goldsmith and Tim Wu explained in their book, *Who Controls the Internet*:

> China has surrounded itself with the world's most sophisticated information barrier, a semi-permeable membrane that lets in what the government wants and blocks what it doesn't. In technical terms, it is a "firewall," rather similar to the security firewalls placed around corporations. Only this one is placed around a whole country.[23]

The government provided a blacklist of banned IP addresses and URLs featuring information and news about politically or culturally sensitive topics and required operators to block access to them. Users who attempted to access blocked sites would receive a non-specific error message such as "the page cannot be displayed."

Self-censorship by Internet service and content providers

Chinese government regulations prohibited use of the Internet "to harm national security; disclose state secrets; harm the interests of the State, of society, or of a group; or to take part in criminal activities."[24]

In order to obtain a business license, all providers of Internet services within China had to provide the government with customers' account numbers, phone numbers, and IP addresses. Under the terms of a required "Public Pledge of Self-Regulation and Professional Ethics," they also had to track what sites users visited and turn over information to the government if asked. Moreover, service providers had to set up an "editor responsibility system" to monitor content and to remove and report illegal postings on any sites they hosted.[25] These regulations applied not only to Chinese companies but also to foreign companies doing business there; Yahoo!, for example, had agreed to the Public Pledge in 2002. For their part, individual subscribers had to register with the local police bureau, register any websites they created, and to use their real names when emailing, blogging, or messaging.

---

22   In testimony on February 15, 2006 before the House of Representatives' Committee on International Relations, Subcommittee on Africa, Global Human Rights, and International Operations, and the Subcommittee on Asia and the Pacific, Mark Chandler, senior vice president and general counsel of Cisco Systems, responded to criticism of his company's actions in China: "Cisco does not customize, or develop specialized or unique filtering capabilities, in order to enable different regimes to block access to information. Cisco sells the same equipment in China as it sells worldwide."

23   Goldsmith, J., and T. Wu (2006) *Who Controls the Internet? Illusions of a Borderless World* (New York: Oxford University Press): 92.

24   OpenNet Initiative (2005) "Internet Filtering in China in 2004–2005: A Country Study" (posted June 14, 2005; www.opennetinitiative.net): 13.

25   "Internet Filtering in China in 2004–2005," op. cit.: 10.

The Chinese authorities required Internet cafés to install software to block websites with subversive or pornographic content and to keep records of the sites patrons visited for at least 60 days. Patrons had to present identification and register under their real names to use equipment at cafés.

Human rights activists reported that the Chinese government had launched an $800 million surveillance system known as Golden Shield to monitor civilian use of the Internet. The Security Ministry employed 35,000 Internet police whose jobs were "to monitor and censor websites and chat rooms in China," according to Harry Wu, publisher of the China Information Center.[26]

Individual self-discipline

Finally, the censorship regime depended on individual decisions not to engage in prohibited conduct or speech online. In some regions of the country, two cartoon police officers known as JingJing and ChaCha, appeared on the screen to remind users "to be conscious of safe and healthy use of the Internet, self-regulate their online behavior and maintain harmonious Internet order together." Fear was a powerful deterrent; individuals sought to avoid prosecution by staying away from sensitive content and not expressing views that could be construed as subversive.

Use of the Internet to repress dissent

The Chinese government did more than block access to content; it also used the Internet to collect information about dissidents and to prosecute them. The Electronic Frontier Foundation, a non-governmental organization (NGO) that described itself as "the leading and the oldest organization working to promote freedom online" noted the ominous potential of the Internet as a tool for identifying dissidents:

> [W]ithout careful planning, Internet routers can be turned into powerful wiretapping tools; web email servers can become a honeypot of stored communications plundered by state police to identify dissidents; and blogging services and search engines can turn from aids to free speech to easily-censorable memory holes.[27]

---

26 Testimony of Harry Wu, publisher, China Information Center, on February 15, 2006 before the House Committee on International Relations, Subcommittee on Africa, Global Human Rights, and International Operations, and the Subcommittee on Asia and the Pacific.

27 Open letter on February 15, 2006 from the Electronic Frontier Foundation (www.eff.org) to the House Committee on International Relations, Subcommittee on Africa, Global Human Rights, and International Operations, and the Subcommittee on Asia and the Pacific.

Two prominent incidents highlighted the Chinese authorities' capacity and willingness to use the Internet in this manner, as well as the cooperation of U.S.-based companies.

Shi Tao

In April 2005, journalist Shi Tao was sentenced to ten years in prison for disclosing "state secrets" overseas. Shi was head of the news division of *Contemporary Business News* in Hunan Province. A year earlier, Shi had been briefed on a Communist Party directive instructing the media how to respond to the upcoming 15th anniversary of the government crackdown on pro-democracy demonstrators in Tiananmen Square. That evening, Shi had used his personal Yahoo! email account to send a description of this directive to a New York website called Democracy Forum.[28]

Amnesty International subsequently reported, on the basis of a review of the court transcript, that Yahoo! had provided account-holder information that was used as evidence against Shi.[29] A Yahoo! senior executive testified in a Congressional hearing in 2006 that "the facts of the Shi Tao case are distressing to our company, our employees, and our leadership." He also noted, however, that Yahoo! was:

> . . . legally obligated to comply with the requirements of Chinese law enforcement . . . Ultimately, U.S. companies in China face a choice: comply with Chinese law, or leave.[30]

Zhao Jing

In 1998, Zhao—then working as a hotel receptionist—began writing essays for online discussion boards under the pseudonym Michael Anti. A prolific and popular blogger, Zhao soon developed a loyal following. The *New York Times* later hired Zhao as a writer in its Beijing bureau. In 2005, in response to a request from the Chinese government, Microsoft shut down Zhao's blog on MSN Spaces—not only in China, but everywhere. A Microsoft officer later stated, "Although we do

---

28 Human Rights in China, "Case Highlight: Shi Tao and Yahoo" (www.hrichina.org/public/highlight, March 16, 2009).

29 Amnesty International (2006) "Journalist Shi Tao Imprisoned by 10 Years for Sending an Email," in *Undermining Freedom of Expression in China: The Role of Yahoo!, Microsoft and Google* (London: Amnesty International; www.amnesty.org/en/library/info/POL30/026/2006): 15.

30 Testimony on February 15, 2006 of Michael Callahan, senior vice president and general counsel, Yahoo! Inc., before the House Committee on International Relations, Subcommittee on Africa, Global Human Rights, and International Operations, and the Subcommittee on Asia and the Pacific.

not think we could have changed the Chinese government's determination to block this particular site, we regret having to do so." He also noted that:

> It is a well-established principle of international jurisdiction that global Internet companies have to follow the law in the countries where they provide access to local citizens, even when those laws are different from those in their country of origin.[31]

Reporters Without Borders estimated in 2006 that 81 journalists and cyber-dissidents were imprisoned in China.[32]

Human rights activism

Intellectuals and activists around the world worked both to gauge the extent of Internet censorship in China and to circumvent it.

The OpenNet Initiative (ONI), a collaborative partnership involving research-ers at the University of Toronto, Harvard Law School, and the University of Cam-bridge, conducted a series of experiments in 2002 and 2005 to test the extent of Internet filtering in China. Using a network of trusted volunteers, ONI attempted to access various URLs and domains from multiple locations both inside and outside the Chinese firewall. The researchers also created test web logs on sev-eral popular Chinese ISPs and sent a series of test emails to and from Chinese accounts. The purpose was to reveal what content was filtered and what sites were blocked.

The study concluded that filtering of content was both extensive and grow-ing in sophistication. Tests showed that censors blocked information on a wide range of sensitive topics, including Falun Gong (a spiritual movement deemed subversive), Tibet independence, Taiwan independence, "human rights," "democracy," "anti-Communism," and the Tiananmen Square incident of June 4, 1989.

In 2005, compared with earlier tests in 2002, ONI found greater specificity in Internet censorship, as the regime had apparently moved to allow greater access to neutral content on topics such as Tibet and democracy, while blocking more politically sensitive treatment of them.[33]

---

31 Testimony of Jack Krumholtz, associate general counsel and managing director, Federal Government Affairs, Microsoft Corporation, on February 15, 2006 before the House Com-mittee on International Relations, Subcommittee on Africa, Global Human Rights, and Inter-national Operations, and the Subcommittee on Asia and the Pacific.

32 Testimony of Lucie Morillon, Reporters Without Borders, on February 15, 2006 before the House Committee on International Relations, Subcommittee on Africa, Global Human Rights, and International Operations, and the Subcommittee on Asia and the Pacific.

33 "Internet Filtering in China in 2004–2005: A Country Study," *op. cit.*

Activists both inside and outside China had worked hard to thwart the Chinese censors. Sometimes referred to as "hackivists," these groups and individuals had developed a number of increasingly sophisticated techniques for defeating the firewall. Many used proxy servers as intermediaries between Chinese users and blocked websites. For example, Human Rights in China, an international NGO, in 2003 began a program of establishing regularly changing proxy sites through which Chinese citizens could access an unfiltered Internet.

Technology that enabled users to anonymize their identities was also popular. In a project funded by the Open Society Institute, researchers at the University of Toronto developed software called Psiphon to allow users to send encrypted messages to a trusted computer in another country and receive encrypted information in return.[34] A company called Dynamic Internet Technologies sponsored a service called DynaWeb that allowed Chinese citizens to access the *Nine Commentaries on the Communist Party*, first published in the United States by *The Epoch Times*, and to renounce their party membership.[35] Global Internet Freedom Technology (GIFT), available from UltraReach Internet, was another such service.[36]

Radio Free Asia and Voice of America maintained websites in Mandarin, Cantonese, Uyghur, and Tibetan. The president of Radio Free Asia described its strategy for circulating content to individuals living under the censorship regime:

> [W]e are creating a widening network of human proxies, so informal that it has no visible shape but is very much alive. Message boards, emails, blogs, and instant messages pick up where the government has cut us off. Friends and family based in third countries post our articles on their own websites and then pass on the web address.[37]

Chinese Google.com

At the time Google was seriously considering direct entry into the China market, the company already had about five years of experience with the Chinese censorship regime.

In 2000, Google had launched a Chinese-language version of google.com, hosted in the United States, which could be accessed from abroad by Chinese users. By 2002, this service had captured about one-quarter of the Chinese mar-

34 psiphon.civisec.org.
35 www.dit-inc.us.
36 www.ultrareach.com.
37 Testimony of Libby Liu, president, Radio Free Asia, on February 15, 2006 before the House Committee on International Relations, Subcommittee on Africa, Global Human Rights, and International Operations, and the Subcommittee on Asia and the Pacific.

ket for online search. However, service was erratic as search queries attempted to traverse the firewall. The company experienced particular difficulties with its Google News China division. Users inside China who attempted to click on stories published by blocked news sources, such as CNN and the *New York Times,* received repeated error messages.

Then, in September 2004, the Chinese authorities abruptly shut down access to the entire google.com site. After about two weeks, service was restored. When the site came back online, the blocked news sources had been omitted. The company issued the following statement:

> On balance we believe that having a service with links that work and omits a fractional number is better than having a service that is not available at all. It was a difficult trade-off for us to make, but the one we felt ultimately served the best interests of our users located in China.[38]

But as Elliot Schrage, Google's vice president for global communications and public affairs, later explained, Google's troubles in China were hardly over.

> [We] soon discovered new problems. Many queries, especially politically sensitive queries, were not making it through to Google's servers. And access became often slow and unreliable, meaning that our service in China was not something we felt proud of. Even though we weren't doing any self-censorship, our results were being filtered anyway, and our service was being actively degraded on top of that. Indeed, at some times users were even being redirected to local Chinese search engines.[39]

Whatever compromises Google might have made in late 2004 to keep its service available in China, by early 2005 its market share, never dominant, was under increasing pressure. Google's toughest competition came from the rapidly growing Chinese firm Baidu, sometimes referred to as the "Chinese Google." The word *baidu,* meaning "100 times," was linked to an ancient poem about a man searching for his lover. In 2005, Baidu had around 400 employees, only 30 of whom had been with the company more than three years.[40]

Baidu had made very fast inroads among Chinese users; between 2003 and 2005 its share of the market for search had ballooned from 3% to 46%. During this period, Google's share of the market for search increased slightly from 24%

---

38 "China, Google News, and Source Inclusion" (googleblog.blogspot.com/2004/09/china-google-news-and-source-inclusion.html, March 17, 2009).

39 Testimony of Elliot Schrage, vice president, global communications and public affairs, Google, Inc., on February 15, 2006 before the House Committee on International Relations, Subcommittee on Africa, Global Human Rights, and International Operations, and the Subcommittee on Asia and the Pacific.

40 "Baidu's IPO and New Riches," *Comtex News Network*, June 21, 2005.

to 27%; Yahoo! (which had partnered with the Chinese firm Alibaba) and the Chinese portals Sina and Sohu had all seen significant erosion.

Some suspected that one of Baidu's competitive advantages was its close relationship with the Chinese government. Liu Bin, an analyst with BDA China, a research firm, commented:

> Baidu works with the government more closely than other search companies. They launch[ed] a more aggressive system to censor their key words. They started to censor their search service earlier and more extensively than others. That's why the government likes Baidu.[41]

'Figuring out how to deal with China'

Now, at the July 2005 board meeting, the issue of what to do about China was coming to a head. After the board had taken up various other agenda items, Sukhinder Singh Cassidy, Google's vice president for Asia, Pacific, and Latin American operations, took the floor to present her analysis of the China question.[42]

The Chinese market for search, Cassidy said, was highly competitive. The company's research showed that Google was losing market share. Its main Chinese rival, Baidu, had succeeded in attracting younger, better-educated users, many of them students. In part, this was because Baidu offered a full range of services, such as entertainment. In part, it was because Baidu's search quality was perceived as superior. The Chinese used Google mainly for searching sources *outside* China and used Baidu mainly for searching sources *inside* China, evidence showed.

The most popular Internet activities in China, Cassidy reported, were online chatting; downloading music, TV shows, and movies; and playing online games. Reading the news, searching for information, and sending and receiving email were also popular, although somewhat less so. Messaging, entertainment, news, and email were applications that Google did not offer in China, she pointed out.

Google's own research showed that the company was perceived in China as an international brand and technology leader, but "a little distant to average Chinese users." More than half of Internet users who knew about Google could not spell the name correctly, and more than half thought the company should have a Chinese name. By contrast, Baidu was perceived as being a Chinese brand with good technology, "friendly," "closer to average Chinese people's life," and as having entertainment products. In China, Cassidy noted:

41 "Google Searches for a Home in China," *BusinessWeek Online*, June 27, 2006.
42 The following summary of Cassidy's presentation is drawn from Google Board Meeting, Friday, July 15, 2005, confidential presentation slides with portions redacted, op. cit.: 72-109.

We are a premium brand, not considered a brand for mainstream users. People don't know much about us; there is a perception gap between who we are and how we are perceived in China.

In addition, Google was perceived as a "foreign company [that] is not in China."

On a slide titled "Key Learnings/Key Issues," Cassidy stated to the board: "[We] need to be there."

Discussion questions

1. From a *business* perspective, what are the arguments for and against entering the market for Internet search in China in 2005?

2. From an *ethical* perspective, what are the arguments for and against entering the market for Internet search in China in 2005?

3. If Google decides to enter China, how can it do so while mitigating ethically adverse impacts? Please formulate possible options and evaluate their strengths and weaknesses.

4. What do you think Google should do, and why?

Teaching notes for this case are available from Greenleaf Publishing. These are free of charge and available only to teaching staff. They can be requested by going to:
www.greenleaf-publishing.com/darkside_notes

4.4

Genocide in Rwanda
Leadership, ethics and organizational 'failure' in a post-colonial context

Brad S. Long, Jim Grant, Albert J. Mills,
Ellen Rudderham-Gaudet, and Amy Warren

In 1993, the United Nations appointed a small peacekeeping force—the United Nations Assistance Mission for Rwanda (UNAMIR)—to oversee a peace agreement between the Rwanda Government Forces (RGF) and a rebel force known as the Rwandese Patriotic Army (RPA). Two Canadian military officers—Lieutenant-General Roméo Dallaire and his deputy, Major Brent Beardsley—led the peace mission. The RGF and the RPA had signed a peace agreement to end a brutal civil war that had raged for two and a half years. The agreement was to come into effect later that year. Dallaire and his UN peacekeepers were to monitor the situation and attempt to prevent further bloodshed, which might jeopardize the peace agreement. However, it soon became apparent to Dallaire that forces sponsored by the Rwandan government were fostering ethnic disagreements to encourage mass murder. Dallaire notified UN headquarters, requesting extra resources to mount a pre-emptive action against those planning the mass murders.

Far from receiving assistance, Dallaire encountered bureaucratic, diplomatic, and leadership resistance. UN officials eventually ordered the withdrawal of all but 270 peacekeepers in the face of a genocide that "would prove to be the fastest, most efficient killing spree of the 20th century." Over the course of 100 days in 1994, approximately 800,000 Rwandans were killed in a genocidal campaign launched by Hutu extremists against Tutsi and politically moderate Hutu.

With the situation in Rwanda changing rapidly and hundreds of thousands of people being murdered, the UN seemed incapable of responding to Dallaire's numerous requests for assistance. Mired in excessive bureaucratic regulations and structures shaped by conflicting political interests, the UN had to undergo an elaborate series of international meetings, bargaining, and negotiation to provide any material support. The UN's political will was strongly influenced by Western nations who not only failed to halt the killing, but were involved in the period leading up to its commencement, with evidence showing not only negligence, but also complicity.

The case focuses on the organizational factors (i.e. United Nations, UN Security Council, UN Department of Peacekeeping Operations, UNAMIR) that played a role in "failing" to prevent genocide in Rwanda. In particular, it focuses on the interplay between the UNAMIR military leader, General Roméo Dallaire, the UN, and its member states—particularly the USA, Belgium, and France, as well as the Rwandan government.

The case works at several levels:

- It allows the instructor to draw on rich materials to engage the students in discussing the impact of organizational arrangements on such things as stress, decision-making, organizational politics, etc.

- It encourages students to consider the relationship between organizational arrangements (i.e. structures and processes) and the potentially devastating outcomes of decision-making

- By discussing the operation of an international organization such as the UN, the case contextualizes the notion of globalization and its relationship to organizations and their activities

Perhaps above all else, the case provides a stark discussion point for consideration of the relationship between ethics and organizational behaviour.

Introduction

The Rwandan genocide in 1994 resulted in the deaths of over 800,000 people. The killings occurred against a backdrop of politicking between key western members of the United Nations, whose peacekeeping role was described as at best ineffectual and at worst culpable. The role of the United Nations in the Rwandan genocide is the focus of this case.

The Republic of Rwanda is a small, landlocked, mountainous, heavily populated African nation without significant natural or geographical resources. A country of some 8.5 million people, it borders Uganda to its north, the Democratic Republic of the Congo to its north-northwest, Tanzania to its east-south-east, and Burundi to its south (see Figure 1). Kigali is the nation's capital.

FIGURE 1 The geographic location of Rwanda

Source: downloaded, with permission, from https://www.cia.gov/library/publications/the-world-factbook/geos/
RW.html

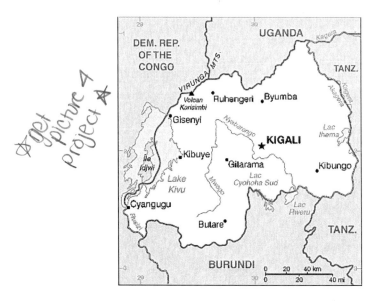

The people fall into two main groups—the Hutus, who form the majority of the population, and the Tutsis. Although both groups share a common Bantu culture, they have been engaged in a series of wars for much of the second half of the 20th century, including a fierce civil war that tore the country apart in the early part of the 1990s.

On August 4, 1993, the government of the Republic of Rwanda and the Rwandan Patriotic Army (RPA) signed a peace agreement in Arusha, Tanzania.[1] The Arusha Peace Agreement, as it became known, was designed to end the bitter civil war and open up the democratic political process in the country. It was also agreed that the United Nations would monitor the implementation of the peace agreement.

Two Canadian military officers, Lieutenant-General Roméo Dallaire and his deputy, Major Brent Beardsley, led the UN peacekeeping operation. Their mission was to monitor the situation and prevent further bloodshed which might jeopardize the peace agreement. It soon became apparent, however, that Rwandan government-sponsored forces were fostering ethnic disagreements to encourage mass murder. Nonetheless, from the very beginning Dallaire encountered bureaucratic, diplomatic, and leadership resistance to his various requests for resources and authority to take decisive action.

---

1 The text of the agreement can be downloaded from www.incore.ulst.ac.uk/services/cds/
agreements/pdf/rwan1.pdf.

Far from providing assistance, UN officials—under political pressure from national governments—ordered the withdrawal of all but 270 peacekeepers at a critical time. In the process, UN peacekeepers were unable to prevent the murder of ten Belgian peacekeepers and a genocidal campaign launched by Hutu extremists against the Tutsi and politically moderate Hutu that saw over 800,000 Rwandans killed over the course of 100 days in 1994.

Clearly the mission was a terrible failure, and Dallaire went on to blame his lack of leadership skills, arguing:

> When you're in command, you are in command. There's 800,000 gone, the mission turned into catastrophe, and you're in command. I feel I did not convince my superiors and the international community. I didn't have enough of the skills to be able to influence that portion of the problem.[2]

The Belgian government, who blamed him in part for the death of their ten paratroopers, also openly criticized him. Dallaire returned to Canada a broken man, feeling victimized, angry, and suicidal. Yet it is clear that, despite horrendous obstacles, his actions actually saved the lives of some 20,000 people who would otherwise have perished in the genocide.

So why was Dallaire unable to act effectively to prevent "the fastest, most efficient killing spree of the 20th century"?[3] To answer that question we need to examine the role of the United Nations and its member states.

Dallaire's problem simply stated: how to develop an effective peacekeeping force

On August 19, 1993, a small 18-member UN team arrived in the Rwandan capital, Kigali (see Figure 1), led by General Roméo Dallaire and Major Brent Beardsley. The role of Dallaire and his team was to assess the situation and make recommendations to the UN on the requirements needed for an effective peacekeeping force. With time being of the essence, Dallaire had 12 days to report his findings.

An initial part of Dallaire's assessment was to decide *if* the UN should commit to sending a full-fledged peacekeeping force to Rwanda, and he stressed to all who would listen that he was on a fact-finding mission. His assessment of the situation had to take into account a number of different considerations, including humanitarian, political, military and administrative factors. He was also on a tight schedule because the Arusha Peace Agreement had designated September

2 Quoted in Allen 2006.
3 Power 2002: 334.

10, 1993 as the day when a new transitional government would be established. The new transitional government was to consist of a coalition of all the various groups who were party to the Peace Agreement. Dallaire knew that the UN would be unable to send even a token force to Rwanda by September 10, but promised that, should a peacekeeping force be agreed to, he would do what he could to get it to Rwanda in record time. Although optimistic that a peacekeeping force would be dispatched in due course, Dallaire began to sense that his "fact-finding" objective was dampening expectations, and his own optimism was tempered by concern as he began his assessment.

Background to the Peace Agreement

In order to make any assessment, Dallaire needed to know something about the background to the Peace Agreement and he needed to know quickly. What he found out was disquieting and encouraged him to press for a large peacekeeping force with the power to intervene with force of arms if necessary.

Humanitarian concerns[4]

Chief among Dallaire's humanitarian concerns was the decades-old ethnic violence between the Hutus and the Tutsis. Not only was that violence in danger of erupting at any point, it had also created hundreds of thousands of refugees, mainly from the minority Tutsis who had over the years fled to neighbouring countries.

As Dallaire was to discover, much of the ethnic disagreements were rooted in an extended period of colonial dominance. The Belgians took over the territory following the defeat of Germany in World War I. The new colonial administration and a powerful group of Roman Catholic missionaries (called the White Fathers) were obsessed with notions of race and, based on little evidence, began the process of classifying the Hutus and Tutsis as distinct "races" of people. In effect, they reduced a number of highly complex issues of heredity, class, and social obligation to racial differences. The Tutsis were deemed to be "sub-Aryan" and of Christian ancestry, while the Hutus were treated as lowly Bantus. These classifications were exacerbated by administrative changes, complete with the issuance of racial identification cards that ensured Tutsis were privileged over Hutus. Tutsis played important roles in the developing "native administration" and even in the priesthood.[5]

Following World War II, as people throughout the colonial world struggled for independence, Rwandan liberation forces were deeply divided along eth-

---

4   Much of this section is based on Mthembu-Salter 2002.
5   Until the post-World War II era, only Tutsis were allowed to become priests.

nic lines. The Union nationale rwandaise (UNAR) was formed and led by Tutsi monarchists determined to retain their political privileges in a post-colonial state. The Mouvement démocratique républicain (MDR), on the other hand, was formed by a self-proclaimed Hutu leader, Gregorie Kayibanda, with the aim of fostering social revolution, first against Tutsi rule and then the colonial administration. The ensuing struggles resulted in pogroms against the Tutsis, with over 300,000 fleeing to Uganda and Burundi. Arguably, the MDR's focus on the Tutsis coincided with Belgian interests in prolonging colonial rule: certainly they did not intervene to prevent the widespread violence against the Tutsis. In 1962, however, Belgium finally granted independence to Rwanda and Kayibanda became the country's president.

Several times over the next few years, Tutsi refugees attempted to invade Rwanda. This led to further repression of those Tutsis still living in the country. In 1973, Juvénal Habyarimana staged a coup. Kayibanda was removed, the national assembly was closed down, and the MDR was banned. Habyarimana ruled as a dictator for the next two decades. In 1981, he formed his only political party, the Mouvement républicain nationale pour la démocratie et le développement (MRND), whose hand-picked delegates presided over a restored, but sham, national assembly.

Meanwhile, in the late 1980s, Tutsi refugees organized themselves into a guerilla army called the Rwandese Patriotic Front (RPF). In 1990 they invaded Rwanda and, by 1991, were in control of two northern provinces until their advance was blocked by French troops who were deployed to defend Habyarimana. The French also put pressure on Habyarimana to establish multi-party elections. In 1992 he formed a new multi-party government and began peace talks with the RPF, which led to the Arusha Peace Agreement.

The problem of how to deal with the massive repatriation of potentially hundreds of thousands of people while avoiding a renewal of violence crossed Dallaire's mind as he paid attention to his other concerns.

Political concerns

Political problems confronted Dallaire as soon as he set foot on Rwandan soil. As he delved into the background to the Peace Agreement, it was hard to know how committed each side was. He was quickly reassured by his meeting with the Rwandan foreign minister, Anastase Gasana, a member of the MDR, who was very much in support of the Arusha accords. Yet the reaction from the Rwandan Ambassador to the UN, Jean-Damascène Bizimana, was disquieting. Bizimana seemed less than thrilled by the Peace Agreement. Dallaire was also concerned that the Rwandan government had made no attempt to arrange a meeting between him and the president. As Dallaire pondered this, he felt it was an ominous sign. However, he had cause for optimism once more as he met with the leadership of the RPF, who strongly supported the Peace Agreement. Optimism turned to disquiet as the RPF leaders raised concerns about the fact that some of the country's 600,000 displaced people had begun to return to their homes in the designated demilitarized zone. When Dallaire suggested that this was to be expected and that the UN should attempt to make the area safe for their return, he was met with resistance. The RPF leaders expressed the concern that the situation could compromise the RPF's security, but Dallaire began to wonder that day whether it may have also had something to do with the resettlement ambitions of displaced Tutsis currently living in Uganda. Finally, when Dallaire met with Juvénal Habyarimana he was worried that the president had yet to publicly embrace the UN mission; nonetheless, it appeared at face value that he was committed to begin the peace process.

Dallaire could see that the various humanitarian problems were going to be difficult to deal with in the face of both entrenched and emerging political ambitions. These political factors were surely containable, but they would make the problem that much harder—especially given the administrative problems the country faced as it prepared for a new, multi-party, multi-ethnic state.

Administrative concerns

Given the background to the war, almost two decades of dictatorial rule and the immense problems facing the country, Dallaire was concerned about the lack of a supportive administrative system. He needed to create a sense of structure to deal with a number of factors, including the repatriation of refugees, the reintegration of people into the life of the country, the establishment of a new interim government, a planned demobilization of troops, and an associated distribution of pensions and retraining for the demobilized soldiers. He also needed an administrative structure to help with the establishment of a democratic parliamentary system, complete with a new police force and armed services. Much of the latter depended on the will of Juvénal Habyarimana, a former dictator, who still retained control of the national army and much of the police forces (the Gendarmerie).

On this front Dallaire hoped to gain some administrative assistance from the UN, but he would have to rely on a military presence to contain any potential social breakdown that could result from the restructuring of the government and armed forces. To that end, he decided that if the UN determined to send a mission he would situate it south of the demilitarized zone, in the sector controlled by the existing Rwandan Government Forces (RGF).

Military concerns

For Dallaire, the military situation was highly problematic. In addition to the RGF and the military wing of the RPF—the Rwandese Patriotic Army (RPA)—any UN peacekeeping force would have to contend with the 6,000-strong Gendarmerie, the 1,500-strong Presidential Guard, and various militia groups estimated to consist of between 15,000 and 30,000 members.

When Dallaire first visited the leaders of the RPF and the RPA, he did what he could to assess their military strength. From what he could see, the army was well led, well trained, and highly motivated. Although he had some concerns about the military threat posed by the RPF's combat-proven and battle-ready army, he had a different order of concern about the undisciplined character of the RGF. Unlike the RPF, the RGF leadership was far from committed to the peace process and some openly spoke of their hatred of the RPF. Dallaire was troubled not only by the lack of discipline among the RGF, but also by a double standard in the treatment of their soldiers. He found that the main army consisted of poorly trained and ill-equipped soldiers who lacked discipline and whose morale was low. Dallaire worried that these troops could pose a threat to law and order as the country moved to implement the terms of the Peace Agreement.

The elite units of the RGF posed a threat of a different kind, particularly the Presidential Guard that Major Brent Beardsley observed, which consisted of highly trained but aggressive and arrogant officers and men. Dallaire knew that it would be difficult to handle this unit (and others like it) in a handover of power that would lead to many of them losing their elite status through either reintegration back into civilian life or being rolled into the new integrated army. Then there were the various militia, including:

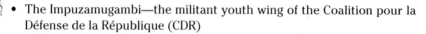

- The Interahamwe—a militant youth wing of the MRND who dressed in fatigues and carried machetes

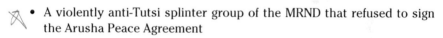

- The Impuzamugambi—the militant youth wing of the Coalition pour la Défense de la République (CDR)

- A violently anti-Tutsi splinter group of the MRND that refused to sign the Arusha Peace Agreement

As he weighed his various concerns, Dallaire was torn between recommending a classic "chapter-six" *peacekeeping* operation, whereby the UN would send a small peacekeeping force to monitor and oversee the peace process, or a "chapter-seven" peace *enforcement* mission, whereby the UN would send a coalition of armed military forces to invade the country and impose peace on the warring groups. He had ruled out recommending diplomatic pressure alone to contain the problem.

Dallaire makes his decision

Dallaire knew that a chapter-seven recommendation would not be acceptable to UN headquarters. It was rarely used. It was first used in Korea in the early 1950s, and then in the Gulf War in 1991. More recently it had been used in Somalia in 1992, but the death of several US and Pakistani soldiers had made UN member states more cautious to take future action of this kind.

Although Dallaire believed that a classic peacekeeping (chapter-six) mission could be successful, he had two major concerns:

1. It had to be implemented almost immediately

2. UN troops should be authorized to use whatever force was necessary, including deadly force, to prevent crimes against humanity

It was this modified chapter-six recommendation that Dallaire sent on to the UN. In it he set out four options for troop deployment.

- Option 1 was based on estimates from previous UN assessments and called for 8,000 UN troops

- Option 2 called for 5,500 troops and was based on Dallaire's best esti-mate of what he would "ideally" need to manage the situation

- Option 3, which Dallaire dubbed a "reasonable viable option," called for 2,500 troops but it would involve considerable risks

- Option 4 called for 500–1,000 troops and was based on estimates by the US, France, and Russia

Feeling this last option could not work, Dallaire only included it to deal with the concerns of interested foreign governments and to lay out the dangers involved in such a course of action.

The UN responds

The United Nations, established in 1945, is one of the world's best-known and largest organizations, with 191 member states and an annual budget in excess of $2.5 billion. Peacekeeping operations at the UN come under the jurisdiction of the Department of Peacekeeping Operations (DPKO), which in 1993 (until 1996) was run by the Under-Secretary-General for Peacekeeping Operations, Kofi Annan. Annan was assisted by Iqbal Riza (Assistant Secretary-General), and Maurice Baril (head of the military division).

When Roméo Dallaire first visited the UN building in New York he was surprised to find that, in contrast to the grandeur of the general assembly chambers, the offices of the DPKO were by far the drabbest and most cramped offices. This was in keeping with its relatively low political status at the UN. It was clearly, or so it seemed to Dallaire, well below the Department of Political Affairs (DPA), which on many occasions interfered in the work of peacekeeping missions without consulting the DPKO's political staff.

He was made aware of the political manoeuvring at the UN when it was strongly suggested that, to gain Security Council approval, he needed to recommend a mission to Rwanda that was small and inexpensive. This weighed strongly on his mind as he balanced his options at the end of his technical mission on September 5, and it was why, despite his own preference for a larger force, he spent some time developing an option that only called for 2,500 troops.

Despite the urgency of the situation and Dallaire's concern to move quickly, he was forcefully reminded that it could take at least three months or more for an agreement to deploy any troops. Dallaire was asked to prepare a report with a recommendation for the immediate deployment of a small force. Thus, before the process was put in motion, Dallaire's choices were already limited to options 3 or 4.

Dallaire's report was then passed on to the DPKO leadership before being sent forward as a formal report to the UN Secretary-General, Boutros Boutros-Ghali. Once it reached this stage the report would then be passed on to the Security Council. If successful, the recommendation would then go to a vote to be ratified. As expected, the process began very slowly and gave every impression of being set to take considerable time to reach resolution. Only the dramatic intervention of the leadership of the RPF, who flew to New York to lobby the UN, broke the impasse and sped up the process. On October 5, the Security Council approved the United Nations Assistance Mission for Rwanda (UNAMIR) mandate and agreed to deploy, in phases, a total of 2,600 troops. Roméo Dallaire was duly appointed force commander.

Dallaire returns to Rwanda

Anxious to get under way, Dallaire returned to Rwanda on October 22 and began the process of monitoring the fragile peace. Over the next 12 weeks, he would encounter a number of challenges—both on the ground and with UN bureaucracy. It would take every ounce of Dallaire's leadership skills to deal with the overwhelming problems that were facing him. His efforts to patrol the demilitarized zone (an area 120 km long and 20 km wide) were severely hampered by a number of problems, including a severe lack of resources, political in-fighting between departments, and a lack of cooperation on the part of the political head of the mission, Jacques-Roger Booh-Booh, the Special Representative of the UN Secretary-General. The presence of the UN's Belgian peacekeeping troops was also problematic because these soldiers were negatively associated with the previous colonial rule. As Dallaire struggled with these bureaucratic issues, he was faced with growing tension and a series of unsolved killings. In addition, the country's main radio station, RTLM, stirred up racial hatred against the Tutsis and orchestrated a campaign against the presence of Belgian peacekeeping troops.

Problem areas and bureaucratic responses

Dallaire's problems multiplied as soon as he returned to Rwanda. The day he left New York there was a *coup d'état* in neighbouring Burundi that threatened the fragile peace in Rwanda and eventually saw some 300,000 refugees flooding into the country. When Dallaire appealed to the UN for extra troops to deal with the situation, he was turned down because he had not included the request in his original report in September.

The resource issues included:

- An initial lack of blue berets and other UN regalia that took weeks to arrive

- An acute shortage of food and lodgings for his troops

- A mishmash of unserviced vehicles

- Poorly armed, officer-heavy troops

- A general lack of equipment, including pens and paper

A request for the latter was turned down for budgetary reasons. Part of the problem with the food shortage was that, when a country donated troops to a peacekeeping mission, they are, under UN rules, supposed to bring enough rations to be self-sufficient for two months. Bangladesh, which supplied a large contingent of troops to Rwanda, didn't follow this rule and it was left to Dallaire to cope with the problem. He dealt with the issue by sharing supplies, including those for himself and his fellow officers. In the face of shortages among his men, Dallaire was shocked to find that the head of the mission (Booh-Booh) expected him to commandeer a large house, fancy car, and a range of perks. Dallaire decided to live as modestly as possible. He returned his Mercedes staff car and rented a small house that he shared with two other officers and a driver. He was determined to send a firm signal to his troops and the people of Rwanda that he was there on humanitarian grounds and would not jeopardize the mission by being seen to live high above everyone else.

With most countries reluctant to supply troops, it was left to Bangladesh, Tunisia, and Belgium to supply them. The Bangladeshi troops were grossly under-armed and led by an over-abundance of officers. The Belgians, on the other hand, were well armed, but as former colonizers they were a problem for the mission and Dallaire would have to do what he could to dampen tensions against their presence. This was not helped by the fact that RTLM was stirring up local feeling against the Belgian troops, or that the Belgian troops themselves acted aggressively to the local population and used racist language to describe how they had previously dealt with Africans in Somalia. Dallaire attempted to deal with the radio station by appealing to the United States to jam the transmissions; the US refused.

Washington, still reeling from a humiliating retreat in Somalia, could see nothing to be gained from another intervention in Africa. With estimates of $8,500 per flight-hour, the exercise was also seen as too costly. President Clinton would later apologize for US inaction, saying that they just didn't know the extent of the killings. Thwarted by the US government, Dallaire could nonetheless deal directly with the Belgian troops, telling them that he would not tolerate "racist statements, colonialist attitudes, unnecessary aggression, or other abuses of power."[6] However, Dallaire was unable to overcome ingrained racist attitudes that were embedded in the official operating rules of the Belgian army. Told that they had to sleep in tents to be close to the airport they were sent to protect, the Belgians refused, citing a regulation that stated that Belgian soldiers should live in buildings and not under canvas because it was important that they "maintain a correct presence in front of the Africans."[7] As a result Dallaire agreed to allow the Belgian troops to be spread out across the city in various buildings. Little did he know that it was a decision that would come back to haunt him.

Making UNAMIR's presence known

With few resources, Dallaire faced a monumental problem of ensuring that UNAMIR's presence was known throughout Rwanda. He decided to deal with the problem by arranging for a flag-raising ceremony. Dallaire had always been interested in what he called "the showcase occasions put on to influence and impress people and bring home the symbolism of events."[8] Dallaire felt that holding a flag-raising ceremony in the demilitarization zone would not only signal the UN's presence, but also serve to stress the urgency of the peace process. To that end, he chose a mountaintop that had been the site of fierce struggle but was subsequently rendered neutral territory. At the symbolic ceremony, the troops of the Organization of African Unity (OAU) handed over control of the zone to Dallaire and his UNAMIR troops.

Big problems and petty politics

When Dallaire first returned to Rwanda, he was effectively in charge of both the political and military operation until someone could be found to serve as head of the mission. On November 22, exactly one month after Dallaire's return, Jacques-Roger Booh-Booh arrived in Rwanda to take over the political aspects

6 Dallaire 2003: 113.
7 Dallaire 2003: 121.
8 Dallaire 2003: 103.

of the mission and to act as its overall head. Dallaire's hopes that this would signal the beginning of greater political pressures to deal with the many problems at hand were soon dashed by Booh-Booh's work ethic and political approach. In the face of a massive human tragedy, Booh-Booh and his staff adopted diplomatic office hours, working from nine in the morning to five at night, with a long lunch break. There were also tensions over differential treatment of civilian office staff and the military, with the local chief administration officer, Per O. Hallqvist, assigning more resources to the civilians on the basis that soldiers are only there for the short term and thus should make do, while the office staff were there for the long haul and should be taken care of. Dallaire's attempts to have Hallqvist overruled were rejected by the DPKO, who argued that Hallqvist was acting within his UN authority.

A week before Booh-Booh arrived in Rwanda, there had been a series of killings within the demilitarized zone. Dallaire's investigations had not been able to find the perpetrators, but in the process he uncovered weapons caches. The knowledge of these caches gave Dallaire several sleepless nights as he deliberated what he should do about them. Finally he recommended to Booh-Booh that he be allowed to search and seize the weapons caches. A horrified Booh-Booh refused the request, saying that the action was likely to damage the peace process as the UN forces would be seen as taking action only against the government side (who were the likely owners of the caches). Dallaire accepted the decision but very reluctantly. It was another decision that was to haunt him later.

At the end of December, Dallaire and Beardsley drafted a required three-month report to the DPKO. Although optimistic in what had and could be achieved, the report stressed an urgent need for logistical support and the deployment of phase two troops ahead of schedule. It was then given to Booh-Booh to include in his overall report, but, as Dallaire was only to find out much later, his report was watered down to reassure the Security Council that slow but steady progress was being made. As a result, Dallaire did not get the extra assistance required.

A warning letter

Perhaps the first signs of an impending genocide came on December 3 when Dallaire received a letter from a group of senior RGF and Gendarmerie officers who warned that elements close to the president were out to undermine the peace process by massacring Tutsis. Not sure how to react to the letter, Dallaire established his own unofficial two-person intelligence unit to investigate the claims. It was through these investigations that the weapons caches came to light.

In the New Year, on January 10, a top-level military trainer with the MRND approached the UNAMIR and asked for a secret meeting, stating that he had important information on the intentions of Hutu extremists in the MRND party. He informed Luc Marchal, one of Dallaire's deputies, that the MRND had established a number of highly efficient death squads—organized through the Interahamwe—to murder massive numbers of Tutsis. Part of the plan was also to murder ten Belgian soldiers because the extremist Hutu leaders believed that Belgium would have no stomach for taking further casualties and would withdraw their troops from Rwanda. This was to prove prophetic.

Dallaire did not take time to think about his next step this time. He made the decision to mount a search-and-seize operation within 36 hours, and he took the unprecedented step of going over Booh-Booh's head by making his request directly to DPKO (see Appendix). Dallaire slept that night excited that UNAMIR would finally take the initiative by showing the warring parties that the UN was prepared to enforce the peace process where necessary.

The next day Dallaire was unprepared for the reply from UN headquarters. He was told that not only was he not to use deterrent operations such as he proposed, but that he was to strictly remain within the limits of a chapter-six mandate. Furthermore, he was required to hand over the information from the informant to President Habyarimana. Worst still, Dallaire gained the distinct impression that DPKO now saw him as a loose cannon rather than a determined force commander.

Pressure mounts to end the mission

Tensions mounted over the first three months of 1994, and the establishment of an interim government—one of the key aspects of the peace process—had not progressed. Yet when Dallaire flew to New York on March 29 to press for increased assistance, he was surprised to find that the UN was thinking of withdrawing from Rwanda. In particular, the United States was strongly pressing the Security Council to end the UNAMIR mission and the Rwandan representative who, as of January 1, 1994 had a seat on the 15-member Security Council, was supporting them. Only the urging of the French and the Belgians, fearful that they would have to deal with the situation alone, ensured that the mission would continue for at least 60 more days.

On April 6 the Security Council passed Resolution 909, which extended the UNAMIR mandate for six weeks, after which it would likely be withdrawn. Remarkably, to Dallaire's total surprise, the mission's budget was also cut. But that day of April 6 was to be overshadowed by a more immediate and critical incident.

April 6: the Peace Agreement explodes and the genocide is unleashed

At the beginning of April there had been some hope that the peace process would move forward, with President Habyarimana flying off to Dar es Salaam to discuss the process. On the evening of April 6, the plane carrying Habyarimana and members of his armed forces was shot down over Kigali and all were killed. Hutu extremists used this as the signal to launch genocide against Tutsis and politically moderate Hutus.

The entire administrative mechanism governing Rwanda was used to deliver a meticulously planned extermination of Tutsis, and all Hutus were implored and equipped to do their share. The presence of UN peacekeepers was used as a rallying point for the genocide as evidence of continued Western interference, and the peacekeepers became a convenient target upon which blame for the death of the president could be laid. In the first 24 hours, ten Belgian peacekeepers had been killed.

The UN retreat

The death of peacekeepers so early into this conflict was an ominous sign for members of the UN Security Council, who were still scarred by the recent loss of life in Somalia in what was supposed to be a simple humanitarian mission. In particular, Somalia marked a dramatic turning point in the US administration's perspective toward peacekeeping operations as they watched television images of dead American soldiers being dragged through the streets of Mogadishu.

From this disaster emerged Presidential Decision Directive No. 25 (PDD-25), in which President Clinton outlined limitations on future US involvement with the UN unless strict conditions were met. Primary among these was that future participation in peace operations would be limited to those cases that directly advanced US interests. Belgium, as had been predicted by Hutu extremists earlier on, was insistent on an immediate withdrawal of its forces from Rwanda, but did not want to be seen as acting independently. It found an ally in the United States, who moved for a withdrawal of all peacekeepers.[9]

On April 21, a meeting of the Security Council was convened and Resolution 912 was passed, which reduced the number of UN troops to a token force of 270 peacekeepers. In an unintended ironic turn of phrase, US Secretary of State Madeleine Albright described the reduced force as enough "to show the will of the international community."[10]

---

9   Melvern 2000: 163.
10   Quoted in Allen 2006.

Dallaire, who had been surprised many times by the inefficiencies, caution, and politics of the UN, was not prepared for the withdrawal of most of his troops in the face of rampant killings. He had "expected the ex-colonial white countries to stick it out even if they took casualties."[11] Later he would summarize the situation thus:

> Ultimately, led by the United States, France, and the United Kingdom, [the UN Security Council] aided and abetted genocide in Rwanda. No amount of its cash and aid will ever wash its hands of Rwandan blood.[12]

A question of genocide

One of the things that allowed the Security Council to withdraw most of its troops was the characterization of the bloodshed as civil war or, worse, "tribal war." The US Ambassador to Rwanda, for example, waited almost a month into the genocide before declaring a "state of disaster," but then minimized the problem by characterizing it as "tribal killings."[13] Eventually, under some pressure to respond to the scale of the killings, the US State Department spoke of "acts of genocide." When asked how many "acts of genocide" it took to make "genocide," a spokesperson for the US State Department responded: "That's just not a question that I'm in a position to answer."[14]

Dallaire made constant attempts to get the UN to characterize the killings as genocide, knowing that this would require it to act more decisively. Defined as "a criminal act, with the intention of destroying an ethnic, national, or religious group,"[15] the UN—under its 1948 Convention on the Prevention and Punishment of the Crime of Genocide—has an obligation to respond where genocide is acknowledged to be occurring. Article VIII of this treaty states:

> Any Contracting Party may call upon the competent organs of the United Nations to take such action under the Charter of the United Nations as they consider appropriate for the prevention and suppression of acts of genocide . . .[16]

---

11 Quoted in Power 2002: 367.
12 Dallaire 2003: 323.
13 Allen 2006.
14 Quoted in Power 2002: 364.
15 Destexhe 1995: 5.
16 Convention on the Prevention and Punishment of the Crime of Genocide (www.unhchr.ch/html/menu3/b/p_genoci.htm).

Not only does the word "genocide," first coined to describe Hitler's designs for the extermination of Jews, carry a legal obligation, it further has been imbued with moral judgement.

By defining events as "tribal killings," "civil war," or even "acts of genocide," the UN was able to defer taking more decisive action. As Dallaire and his remaining troops did what they could to protect people, the distinction between a civil war and genocide became critical in the events in Rwanda in 1994. Had the attacks on Tutsis been labelled as genocide, it would have triggered the machinery of the United Nations to take firm and decisive action to prevent it. However, the UN was slow to act and has since been criticized for the time it took it to actually label the events in Rwanda as genocide, waiting until June 28, 1994 to make the initial declaration and until July for a panel of experts within the UN to confirm it was indeed genocide. The UN was finally satisfied that the events that were going on in Rwanda met the criteria established under the 1948 Convention, by which time 800,000 people had already been murdered. As some commentators have noted:

> For an event that was so widely covered by the media, the genocide in Rwanda largely remains misunderstood by the international community.[17]

As international awareness of the genocide grew, the member states of the UN could no longer simply ignore the situation in Rwanda. UN Resolution 919, authorized well into the genocide, sought to establish an expanded UNAMIR II humanitarian mission to help protect the population. The chair of the Security Council, however, admitted that the expansion was a fiction, as the resolution had been gutted by the US which was intent on successfully brokering a ceasefire before peacekeeping troops were committed. Even then, the continued characterization of the conflict in Rwanda as a civil war between two feuding parties, and not genocide, contributed to the weakness of the Security Council. Moreover, the fact that the US worked actively and effectively against an effective UNAMIR was one of the most significant failures, far exceeding the failings of the UN itself.

The aftermath: globalization, leadership, organizational failure, and post-colonial values

The tragic events in Rwanda in 1994 could easily be seen as something well beyond the reach of organizational analysis, well beyond the apparently mundane analysis of organizational processes and structures. Yet the genocide itself

---

17 Berry and Berry 1999: 4.

was well organized, relying on structured militia, government, and police forces. The fact that genocide was able to progress and at such a rapid pace was also due to a failure of organization, in particular the United Nations, which is one of the largest institutions in the world. Thus, the ingredients of this case are very much about organizational analysis and deal with key issues such as leadership, ethics, organizational structure and culture, and globalization.

General Roméo Dallaire has since blamed himself and his lack of leadership skills for failing to convince the UN and its DPKO of the severity of the situation, but he has harsh words for the UN itself. He contends that the UN's process of peacekeeping is deeply flawed, arguing that:

> Even if he had received the political and humanitarian training the job demanded, the UN's rules would have robbed him of the ability to use his military skills.[18]

The troops under his operational command:

> . . . were ultimately under the command of their nations, so . . . if a national capital feels that a [rescue] mission is unwarranted, or too risky, or something, the soldiers can turn around and say, "No, I can't do it."[19]

He recommends that the UN should undergo a renaissance that is:

> . . . not limited to the Secretariate, its administration, and bureaucrats, but must encompass the member nations, who need to rethink their roles and recommit to a renewal of purpose. Otherwise the hope that we will ever truly enter an age of humanity will die as the UN continues to decline into irrelevance.[20]

Dallaire saves his harshest words for key member states of the United Nations. He claims that, while countries argued over the characterization of the killings, "they knew how many people were dying,"[21] adding that no matter what word was used the action was racist. Commenting on the difference between the enormous efforts that the UN put into Yugoslavia compared with Rwanda, Dallaire felt that:

> Africans don't count; Yugoslavians do. More people were killed, injured, internally displaced, and refugeed in 100 days in Rwanda than in the whole eight to nine years of the Yugoslavia campaign.[22]

---

18 Allen 2006.
19 Ibid.
20 Dallaire 2003: 520.
21 Allen 2006.
22 Quoted in Allen 2006.

Yet, while peacekeeping troops remain in the former Yugoslavia, they are "off the radar" in Rwanda.[23] And, finally, Dallaire asks:

> Why didn't the world react to scenes where women were held as shields so nobody could shoot back while the militia shot into the crowd? Where . . . boys were drugged up and turned into child soldiers, slaughtering families? . . . Where girls and women were systematically raped before they were killed? Babies ripped out of their stomachs? . . . Why didn't the world come?[24]

His answer:

> Because there was no self-interest . . . No oil. They didn't come because some humans are [considered] less human than others.[25]

Glossary[26]

Kofi Annan: As the Under-Secretary-General for Peacekeeping Operations, oversaw the UN's Department of Peacekeeping Operations from 1993 to 1996.

Arusha Peace Agreement: Signed in Arusha, Tanzania, it agreed to end the civil war between the Rwandan Government Forces (RGF) and the Rwandese Patriotic Army (RPA).

Maurice Baril: Head of the military division of the DPKO during the Rwanda genocide.

Major Brent Beardsley: Roméo Dallaire's military assistant.

Jean-Damascène Bizimana: The Rwandan Ambassador to the UN at the time of the peace accord. Later, the Rwandan representative on the UN Security Council.

Jacques-Roger Booh-Booh: In charge of the UNAMIR mission from November 1993 to May 1994.

Boutros Boutros-Ghali: Secretary-General of the UN from 1992 to 1997.

Chapter-seven: Refers to Chapter 7 of the United Nations Charter, which lays out a course of peacekeeping activities.

Chapter-six: Refers to Chapter 6 of the United Nations Charter, which lays out a course of peacekeeping activities.

CDR (Coalition pour la défense de la république): A violently anti-Tutsi splinter group of the MRND that refused to sign the Arusha Peace Agreement.

Lieutenant-General Roméo Dallaire: Commander of the United Nations peace mission UNAMIR.

---

23 Allen 2006.
24 Ibid.
25 Ibid.
26 Many of these definitions and descriptions are based on the glossary in Dallaire 2003: 523-44.

DPA: United Nations Department of Political Affairs.

DPKO: United Nations Department of Peacekeeping Operations.

Anastase Gasana: A leading member of the MRND who served as the Rwandan foreign minister at the time of the peace accord.

Gendarmerie: A para-military police force of the Rwandan government.

Major General Juvénal Habyarimana: The President of Rwanda and head of the ruling MRND party; the main signatory to the agreement for the RGF.

Per O. Hallqvist: The Chief Administration Officer in Rwanda until February 1994.

Impuzamugambi: The militant youth wing of the CDR.

Interahamwe: The militant youth wing of the MRND.

MDR (Mouvement démocratique républicain): The main opposition party to the MRND and which was a part of the Rwandan coalition government that signed the peace agreement.

MRND (Mouvement républicain pour la démocratie et le développement): Led the peace talks on behalf of the Rwandan government.

OAU: The Organization of African Unity.

Presidential Guard: Habyarimana's personal guard.

Iqbal Riza: Assistant Secretary-General of peacekeeping at the DPKO during the Rwanda genocide.

RTLM (Radio Télévision Libre des Mille Collines): The main radio station that stirred up hatred against the Tutsis.

RGF (Rwandan Government Forces): The armed forces of Rwanda.

RPA (Rwandese Patriotic Army): The military wing of the RPF.

RPF (Rwandese Patriotic Front): Led the talks on behalf of the Tutsi-dominated rebel forces.

UN (United Nations): One of the main international witnesses to the peace agreement and agreed to monitor the peace process.

UNAMIR (United Nations Assistance Mission for Rwanda): Established by UN Security Council Resolution 872, October 5, 1993, as a response for assistance in the implementation of the Arusha Peace Agreement.

Appendix: Timeline

1992

3 December. UN Resolution 794 authorizes a chapter-seven mission in Somalia, which allowed an invasion force to use "all means necessary" to create a secure environment for the delivery of humanitarian aid: 37,000 troops from 20 countries are committed to the mission.

9 December. UN troops led by US forces come ashore, without opposition, on the shores of Mogadishu.

1993

4 August. Arusha Peace Agreement signed.

19 August. Dallaire and his UN team arrive in Rwanda to undertake an assessment.

5 September. Dallaire takes his recommendation to the UN offices in New York.

10 September. Deadline for the establishment of a transitional government.

3 October. Eighteen US soldiers killed and 84 wounded in an ambush in Mogadishu as part of the UN chapter-seven mission in Somalia.

5 October. The UN Security Council approves the UNAMIR mandate and appoints Dallaire as force commander.

22 October. Dallaire returns to Rwanda.

26 October. Belgian army reconnaissance group arrives in Rwanda.

18 November. A series of killings occur in the demilitarized zone.

19 November. Seventy-five members of the Belgian contingent arrive in Rwanda.

22 November. Jacques-Roger Booh-Booh arrives to take over as head of the UN mission.

3 December. A group of senior RGF and Gendarmerie officers warn of impending massacre of Tutsis.

4 December. Last of the Belgians arrive, including Colonel Luc Marchal.

15 December. Bangladeshi contingent arrives in Rwanda. French paratroop battalion leaves Rwanda.

1994

10 January. Informant warns of death squads and plans to assassinate ten Belgian soldiers.

11 January. Dallaire sends coded message to DPKO requesting support for search-and-seizure action.

12 January. DPKO refuses Dallaire's request.

9 February. Contingent of Ghanaian troops arrive in Rwanda.

6 April. Security Council passes Resolution 909 to extend the UNAMIR mandate by six weeks. Juvénal Habyarimana is killed when his plane is shot down.

References

Allen, T.J. "The General and the Genocide" (www.amnestyusa.org/amnestynow/general_and_genocide.html, January 31, 2006).

Berry, J.A., and C.P. Berry (1999) *Genocide in Rwanda: A Collective Memory* (Washington, DC: Howard University Press.)

Dallaire, R. (2003) *Shake Hands with the Devil* (Toronto: Vintage Canada).

Destexhe, A. (1995) *Rwanda and Genocide in the Twentieth Century* (New York: New York University Press).

Melvern, L. (2000). *A People Betrayed: The Role of the West in Rwanda's Genocide* (New York: Zed Books).

Mthembu-Salter, G. (2002) "Rwanda" (selfdetermine.irc-online.org/conflicts/rwanda_body.html, January 31, 2006).

Power, S. (2002) *A Problem from Hell: America and the Age of Genocide* (New York: Basic Books).

Discussion questions

1. Who was responsible for the genocide in Rwanda?

2. Discuss the moral obligation of external governments and international organizations to become involved in the prevention of genocide, and the arguments for and against an earlier intervention in Rwanda.

3. Identify the major stakeholders of UNAMIR's goals and activities. Discuss the stakeholders' varying and conflicting interests and how the lack of interest influenced the course of events leading to the genocide.

4. Describe the main features of the organizational design of UNAMIR in Rwanda. Be sure to consider the issues of the division of labour, standardization, hierarchy, degree of centralization and formalization, the form of departmentalization, and whether the mission has a mechanistic or organic structure, as well as UNAMIR's relationship to the UN.

5. Roméo Dallaire was very committed and motivated as the force commander of UNAMIR and adamantly fought to keep the peacekeeping mission going in Rwanda, despite its failure to prevent genocide. Assess Dallaire's leadership capabilities using concepts such as power, contingency theory, motivation, leadership traits, and ability to manage change.

6. Compare and contrast a mainstream organizational approach (e.g. contingency theory) with post-colonial theory in explaining the inaction by the UN to stop the genocide.

7. What can be learned from the Rwandan genocide that can help stop such a tragedy from happening again?

Teaching notes for this case are available from Greenleaf Publishing. These are free of charge and available only to teaching staff. They can be requested by going to:
www.greenleaf–publishing.com/darkside_notes

About the contributors

Matt Bladowski, BBA, MBA, is the president of Gratifiedent, a business consulting company for dentists. He is also active in the UWO Schulich School of Dentistry where he lectures to students on business. Prior to this he managed market research and strategic management activities for Royal Group Technologies, a major building product manufacturer.

Jill A. Brown (PhD, University of Georgia) is assistant professor of management in the College of Business and Economics at Lehigh University, Bethlehem, Pennsylvania. Her work has been published in *Journal of Management Studies, Oxford Handbook of Corporate Social Responsibility* (OUP, 2008), and elsewhere. She has taught business ethics and strategic management, among other courses, and has been actively involved in the International Association of Business & Society as well as the Academy of Management.

Ann K. Buchholtz (PhD, New York University) is associate professor of management in the Terry College of Business at the University of Georgia. Her work has been published in *Academy of Management Journal, The Academy of Management Review, Business & Society, Business Ethics Quarterly*, and elsewhere. She is division chair-elect of the Social Issues in Management division of the Academy of Management and serves as inaugural chair of the Academy's ethics adjudication committee.

Martin Calkins is assistant professor in the College of Management at the University of Massachusetts, Boston. He earned a PhD in management from the University of Virginia, Master of Divinity and Master of Theology degrees from the Weston School of Theology, and a Master of International Management from the American Graduate School of International Management. His academic interests include the roles of casuistry and virtue ethics in moral reasoning, the limits of cognition in moral deliberation, the concept of justice in secular and Muslim societies, and the ethical aspects of contemporary business issues such as China's and India's adoption of the automobile.

Adenekan (Nick) Dedeke, PhD, is currently a Visiting Professor of Information Systems and Operations Management in the Information, Operations & Analysis Group, College of Business Administration, Northeastern University, Boston. He teaches management information systems and operations management, and has been a member of the Decision Sciences Institute, IEEE and Association for Computing Machinery (ACM) for over three years. His work has been published in *Managing Service Quality, International Journal of Industrial and Systems Engineering,* IEEE's *Computer, Journal of Cases on Information Technology,* and similar journals. He has also published two books.

Sherry Finney is an assistant professor in the Department of Organizational Management at Cape Breton University (CBU), Nova Scotia, Canada. She holds a Bachelor of Business Administration from CBU, a Master of Business Administration from Saint Mary's University and a PhD from the University of Warwick, UK. Her research interests include internal marketing for change management, tourism marketing, and case writing/case teaching methodology. She has received international awards for her case writing and has published her cases in several leading textbooks. Some of her research has appeared in *Business Process Management Journal* and *Journal of Education for Business.*

Mary Godwyn, PhD, is an assistant professor of sociology in the History and Society Department at Babson College (Babson Park, Massachusetts). She has published in journals such as *Symbolic Interaction, Current Perspectives in Social Theory,* and *Journal of Small Business and Entrepreneurship.* She teaches introductory and advanced courses in sociology, women's studies, and gender studies. She has lectured at Harvard University and has taught at Brandeis University and Lasell College, where she was also director of the Donahue Institute for Public Values.

Jim Grant, PhD (ABD), is a professor of human resource management and industrial relations in the Manning School of Business Administration at Acadia University in Wolfville, Nova Scotia, Canada. He has published several articles in journals such as *Management & Organizational History, Sex Roles,* and *Labor Law Journal.* He has taught organizational behavior, human resource management, and labour relations for several years, as well as maintaining membership of several scholarly associations including the Academy of Management, the Administrative Sciences Association of Canada, and the Labor & Employee Relations Association.

Ralph Hamann is senior researcher at the University of Cape Town (UCT) Environmental Evaluation Unit, co-director of the UCT Cape Urban Observatory, and extraordinary associate professor at the Sustainability Institute at Stellenbosch University, South Africa. He is on the editorial boards of *Environment: Science and Policy for Sustainable Development* and of *Development Southern Africa.* Recent publications include *The Business of Sustainable Development: Human Rights, Partnerships and Alternative Business Models* (UNU Press, 2008).

Anita Howard is a PhD candidate and instructor in the Department of Organizational Behavior at Weatherhead School of Management, Case Western Reserve University, Cleveland, Ohio. Her current research interests are intentional change and executive coaching, emotional and social intelligence, leadership and professional development, and positive psychology. She holds a BA in Sociology from Boston University and did graduate work as a Merit Fellow in social psychology at Harvard University. Anita also completed postgraduate training in family systems therapy at the Kantor Family Institute in Cambridge, Massachusetts.

Anne T. Lawrence is Professor of Organization and Management at San Jose State University. She holds a PhD from the University of California, Berkeley, and completed a two-year postdoctoral fellowship at Stanford University. Professor Lawrence is the lead author of *Business and Society: Stakeholders, Ethics, Public Policy* (Irwin/McGraw-Hill, 12th edn, 2008). Her articles and cases on issues of corporate social and environmental responsibility have appeared in many journals, textbooks, and anthologies.

Monique Le Chêne is an ethnologist and lives in Chambéry, France.

Benoit Leleux (MSc, MEd, MBA, PhD) is the Stephan Schmidheiny Professor of Entrepreneurship and Finance at IMD in Lausanne, Switzerland, where he is director of the MBA program. He was previously Visiting Professor of Entrepreneurship at INSEAD and Director of the 3i VentureLab and Associate Professor and Zubillaga Chair in Finance and Entrepreneurship at Babson College, Wellesley, Massachusetts, from 1994 to 1999. He obtained his PhD at INSEAD, specializing in corporate finance and venture capital. His research papers have appeared in *Strategic Management Journal* and *Journal of Business Venturing*. He is the author of *From Microfinance to Small Business Finance* and *Nurturing Science-Based Startups: An International Case Perspective* (Springer Verlag, 2007).

Brad S. Long (MBA, CMA, PhD candidate) is an assistant professor of management in the Gerald Schwartz School of Business at St. Francis Xavier University, Antigonish, Canada. Brad has published (or has been accepted for publication) in *Journal of Business Ethics*, *Canadian Journal of Administrative Sciences*, *Critical Perspectives on International Business*, and *Journal of Individual Employment Rights*. Brad teaches courses on leadership, business ethics, human resource management, and organizational behavior, and is pursuing a program of research into spirituality in the workplace.

Dr. **Rosemary A. McGowan** is the program co-ordinator for the leadership programme at Laurier Brantford, Ontario, Canada. She holds a PhD (Schulich School of Business, York University), an MBA (Gold Medalist Graduate, School of Business and Economics, Wilfrid Laurier University), and an MA (University of Waterloo). She teaches courses in leadership, organizational studies, strategy, project management, and business communication skills. Her case "John Hamilton's Work and Eldercare Dilemma. Break the Silence? Sustain the Silence?" won a national Best Case Award. She has served as an academic reviewer for journals such as *Culture & Society* and *Case Research Journal*, and conferences organized by bodies such as the Administrative Sciences Association of Canada and the Academy of Management.

Elizabeth McLeod is a PhD candidate in business administration at Saint Mary's University in Halifax, Nova Scotia, Canada. Her dissertation research is in the area of information privacy and she has won previous national recognition including best paper (student) with Brad Long at the 2006 Administrative Sciences Association of Canada (ASAC) Conference. Her MBA thesis was focused on e-business security and privacy practices. She has previously published *Realizing Where We Have Been: Critical Reflections on Making History and the ASB (Atlantic Schools of Business)* with Anthony Yue, Gabrielle Durepos, and Albert Mills. Elizabeth is currently employed in a staff position at Saint Mary's University where she has worked for the previous 18 years.

Albert J. Mills, PhD, is a professor of management and director of the Sobey PhD (Management) program at Saint Mary's University (Nova Scotia, Canada). He is the author, co-author, and co-editor of over 20 books, including *Sex, Strategy and the Stratosphere* (Routledge, 2006), *Understanding Organizational Change* (Routledge, 2008), and the *Sage Encyclopedia of Case Study Research* (Sage, 2009). He is the former president of the Administrative Sciences Association of Canada and serves on the editorial boards of seven scholarly journals; he is the critical management studies editor of *Canadian Journal of Administrative Sciences*, and the associate editor of *Gender, Work and Organization* and *Qualitative Research in Organizations and Management*. A former winner, finalist, and organizer of the Academy of Management (AoM) Darkside Case Competition, he currently serves as the co-chair of the Critical Management Studies Division of the AoM.

Jean Helms Mills, PhD, is a professor of management in the Sobey School of Business at Saint Mary's University in Halifax, Canada. She has published her work in *Culture and Organization, Gender Work and Organization, Management and Organization History, Organizational Research Methods*, and the *Journal of Management History*. Jean is a past associate editor of *Culture and Organization* and is currently an associate editor for *Gender Work & Organization*. She is co-divisional chair for critical management studies at the Academy of Management and a two-time finalist in the Darkside Case Competition.

Caroline O'Connell, BPR, MBA, LLB, has worked as a criminal defense lawyer and taught management and marketing at St. Francis Xavier University in Antigonish, Nova Scotia, Canada. Her doctoral studies at Saint Mary's University in Halifax, Nova Scotia, included work in organizational crisis and management communication during crisis. She has presented papers at conferences in North America and Europe. A paper arising out of the Westray tragedy that provided the basis of the case in this volume was published in the *Canadian Journal of Communication*. She now lives in Dublin, Ohio.

Latha Poonamallee is an assistant professor in organizational behavior at the School of Business & Economics in Michigan Technological University, Houghton, USA. She received her doctorate from the Department of Organizational Behavior at Case Western Reserve University, Cleveland, Ohio. Her research lies in the area of leadership, partnerships, and processes of radical social change toward building sustainable communities. She has been a member of the Critical Management Studies Division of the Academy of Management from 2003.

Emmanuel Raufflet (PhD McGill) is an associate professor in management at HEC Montréal. He has co-edited *Responsabilité sociale de l'entreprise: enjeux de gestion et cas pédagogiques* (2008) as well as two other books. His work has been published in the *Journal of Business Ethics, Journal of Corporate Citizenship, Management International*, and *International Studies in Management and Organization*. He has won several case awards including the Emerson Award for Best Case in Business Ethics (2005 and 2007) and the Best Workshop Case Award (Bronze) (2008) at NACRA (North American Case Research Association).

Ellen Rudderham-Gaudet is a PhD candidate at the Sobey School of Business, Saint Mary's University, Halifax, Nova Scotia, Canada. Ellen is currently completing her thesis involving over five years of research on members of Rotary International. She is a mother/teacher/facilitator/coach/consultant with a strong preference to advise, research, and learn in ways that make the dark sides of organization/life a bit brighter!

Dr. **Francine Schlosser**, building upon 15 years in business experience in auditing, logistics, and business development, received her PhD from the University of Waterloo in 2004 and is now an associate professor in management at the Odette School of Business, University of Windsor, Ontario, Canada. Her articles have been accepted for publication in academic journals including the *Journal of Organizational Behavior, Journal of Strategic Marketing, Journal of Business Research*, and *Journal of Managerial Psychology*. Dr. Schlosser is also faculty mentor for CBAR— a student outreach center providing market research and business plan development.

Dr. **Paul Michael Swiercz** is a professor and former chairman of the Department of Management at The George Washington University (GWU) in Washington, DC. Dr. Swiercz has published more than 35 refereed research articles; his case studies on Home Depot and Delta Airlines have appeared in six best-selling strategy textbooks. His case study "Food Lion vs. the UFCW: Time for a Change?" was selected for the Best Case Award by the 2002 Academy of Management. Dr. Swiercz has served as editor of the journal *Human Resource Planning* and is director of the Strategic HRM Partnership Project at GWU.

Amy M. Warren (BComm co-op, MER) and PhD candidate is a professor with the Faculty of Business at Memorial University in Newfoundland and Labrador, Canada. Most recently she has conducted research on the topic of the abolishment of mandatory retirement in Canada. Over the past five years, she has taught courses on human resource management and labour relations.